The explosive story of one cop's war on Britain's most notorious drugs gangs

Pete Ashton

Monday Books

A CIP catalogue record for this title is available
from the British Library

ISBN: 978-1-906308-54-4

Typeset by Andrew Searle
Printed and bound by
CPI Group (UK) Ltd, Croydon, CR0 4YY

www.mondaybooks.com
http://mondaybooks.wordpress.com/
info@mondaybooks.com

Dedication

To Carmel and my boys, Sean, Matthew and
Daniel, my close family and friends, and all
the brave lads and lasses who climb above
the parapet to give the bad people of this
world a swift kick in the balls.

Contents

Not handcuffed to some wanker
Who doesn't know me
And doesn't know our lives are made
From all the efforts of the masses,
And all the people who deserve a better fate

Paul Weller, *Back in the Fire*

Author's note

I've tried to be as open as possible about police undercover techniques and equipment without aiding criminals.

A number of names and descriptions – particularly those of fellow police officers, especially undercovers, informants and witnesses – have been changed, for obvious reasons. Some of the criminal names are also aliases. Many of the people I have turned over still don't know my involvement as a police officer; revealing myself might endanger others.

A number of venues – pubs, mainly – which were used by dealers for the supply of drugs are named. It is not suggested that the owners or staff operating those premises at the times in question had any knowledge of the drug trade taking place on or around their property. It is in the nature of these criminals that they often operate below the radar of the average Joe. (Of course, where they were aware, the staff and owners had often alerted the police in the first place, and helped us greatly.) Where these premises are still open today, no connection should be made to any criminality exposed during the course of my undercover work and their current operation.

Not all drug dealers are bad people, though many are. Most drug users are not.

Pete Ashton, September 2013

Preface

IT WAS A COLD, grey November Monday morning, and I was rattling northwards on the train out of King's Cross when my mobile rang.

I was nursing the mother of all hangovers, having spent the weekend getting smashed in London with some of my mates from the Army and the Metropolitan Police, and honouring the war dead at the annual Remembrance Sunday service in Whitehall.

My head was pounding, and I didn't want to talk to anyone.

I looked at the screen: it said 'Jazz'.

Jazz was my handler.

Groaning, I pressed the green button and held the phone to my ear.

'Pete?'

'Yep.'

'You alright, mate?'

'Nope.'

'Right… Anyway, Operation Stealth want you for a quick job. Heroin and crack… You'll be in and out in four weeks. You up for it?'

I paused. I was 42 years old, and I was getting a bit long in the tooth for drugs-buying. I'd been at it for a decade, now, and I'd spent the last 48 hours telling anyone who'd listen that I was kicking it into touch.

'Pete? You still there mate?'

But there's always one more job, isn't there?

'Yep, I'm still here. Yeah, I suppose I'm up for it. When?'

'They want to start tomorrow.'

'No problems.'

I hung up and looked at Slug, who was sitting opposite me. He was smirking and shaking his head. I groaned again, and looked out of the grimy window at the damp Leicestershire countryside racing by.

Op Stealth. There's a blast from the past. Stealth was Nottinghamshire Police's version of the Met's Operation Trident, a specialist unit set up to combat the explosion of Yardie gun crime in the city. That – and the growing propensity of the homegrown scum to carry weapons – had led to the city being nicknamed 'Shottingham'. A bad joke, perhaps, but it was one which had the ring of truth to it: a significant number of people had been blown away in gang feuds, or hit in the crossfire, and shots had been even fired at police officers.

The mayhem would rage for some years – maybe it has never really gone away – and would include four killings which shocked the whole country: those of the schoolgirl Danielle Beccan, of the city jeweller Marion Bates, and the mother and stepfather of one of those involved in another gangland murder.

When Jazz made his call to me, Stealth had only been running for a matter of months. Eventually, the team would nick hundreds of people, and recover an armoury of firearms, stolen motors and counterfeit cash, enough drugs and real money to pay off half the national debt, but already the results were coming in.

The impetus for the call was the execution a few days earlier of a 33-year-old mother-of-three called Terrisia Jacobs. Mrs Jacobs had been shot dead at 2.30am outside Nottingham's Drum nightclub, in a classic gangland hit which was like something out of *The Sopranos*: a hooded man had calmly walked up behind her, put a gun against her head in front of dozens of witnesses, and brazenly pulled the trigger. Shot at point-blank range, she was dead before she hit the floor and lay there, her blood and brains sprayed all over the pavement and the club wall.

Not a nice way to go, but don't feel too sorry for her: she was a nasty crack dealer, and a player in the city's drugs scene.

The Detective Superintendent leading the enquiry called a press conference at which he described the shooting as a 'tragic loss of life'. He was making the usual appeal for witnesses, but there was no shortage of those. The place had been crawling with clubbers at the time, and at least 40 of them saw it happen, but – for some reason – people who wanted to chat about it were thin on the ground.

Despite this, the local Old Bill were sure they knew who was behind the job. Unfortunately, knowing it and proving it to the satisfaction of a jury are different things, so they were taking the Al Capone approach. Capone was busted for tax evasion rather than his more colourful crimes; likewise, if they couldn't get the Jacobs killers for the murder, maybe they could nail them and their network for their crack and heroin dealing?

Which was where I came in.

Chapter 1:

The Roots of a Fighting Man

I WAS BORN IN PRESTON, LANCASHIRE, in 1962, one of six sons brought up in a terraced house in the heart of the town's docks.

Although Preston is a dozen or so miles from the Irish Sea, the River Ribble was dredged and widened to allow ocean-going container ships and tankers to pass through. In the 1960s, pretty much every man-jack in town worked on the river, among them my dad and his brothers, Occasionally my old man would come home from work with a bunch of green bananas that he'd smuggled out in his bag, and my earliest memories are of the dock strikes, and long-haired blokes in donkey jackets flicking tabs and waiting for a scuffle.

Dockers' wives saw very little of their husbands – they were either out grafting or on the piss – so my mum did all the work. She was strict with us lads, but then she had to be. She came from a hard family, who solved their problems with fists, and sometimes this meant life was a bit surreal. I remember standing naked in the Belfast sink in our kitchen, being scrubbed down by my mum, with Tom Jones belting out *What's New, Pussycat?* on the radio, and my Uncle Brian hiding upstairs from the Scouse gangsters who were hunting him down with guns.

Modern-day Preston has massive unemployment, child poverty is rampant, and drugs are rife. Young lads look up to the dealers – they're the ones with the cash, the cars and the girls. Back in my childhood, drugs were unheard of, and your social life revolved around the pubs and the working men's clubs. The fellas we looked up to were the drinkers and fighters, and my extended family had plenty of both. We were encouraged to fight from an early age. It was the way things were – not just for the kids, but for the whole town. I remember a couple of transvestite dockers who would get together once a week in the tap room of a local boozer, drinking pints of bitter and smoking fags while dressed to kill in fishnet stockings, high heels and wigs, with stubble poking through their foundation. They must have had the piss taken out of them, but if you did it once you wouldn't do it twice, because they were proper hard bastards.

I went to school under sufferance, and didn't place a whole lot of importance on it. The teachers were more violent than the dockers. One particularly colourful character, a technical drawing teacher, was the spitting image of Bill Oddie from *The Goodies* – which he clearly loved, because he'd quote from the show at every opportunity. This guy had a plimsoll wrapped in black tape that he called 'Super Wellie', and he would use it at every available opportunity, bringing it down onto the upturned hands of children with as much force as he could muster. I overstepped the mark one day and he got me in a stranglehold and squeezed until I started to pass out, much to the amusement of my mates. These days she'd probably end up seeing the inside of a prison cell, on a wing full of sex offenders and bent police officers; back then he was just someone you didn't want to upset.

There was also a wizened old woman with a hunchback and a blue rinse who I still have nightmares about. She'd work her way round the classroom like a demented granny, wielding a massive, hardback book while she checked your homework. Anyone who produced substandard work was simply smashed over the head with it. Sometimes the old bat's feet left the floor with the effort. I remember one day when she ripped up the pages of crap I had written into little pieces, and placed them carefully on top of my head. Then she let out a blood-curdling screech of 'CONFETTI!' and smashed the book down on my head with all her might, before moving onto her next victim.

In the early 1970s, I followed my brothers into the local scout group. I quickly discovered that bullies existed there, too. I remember one night being forced to bend over while the scoutmaster hit me across the backside with a cricket bat because I was having trouble catching a tennis ball in a game. I ran straight home to tell my mum and dad. I was hoping my dad might go down and sort this bloke out.

Instead, he said in a very matter of fact way, 'Well, lad, if you can't take that type of discipline like a man then you'll have trouble lasting in any organisation.'

Around the same time, I was hanging round with a bunch of kids from a local children's home, who were also members of the Preston Marine Cadets. I was intrigued by the stories they told me; they seemed to have a lot more action and fun than the scouts, and there was no evidence of them getting whacked on the arse by a nonce with a cricket bat for dropping a fucking tennis ball. What's more, they had a cracking blue uniform, so I decided to give it a go.

The cadets shared their location with a unit of sea cadets and a girls' nautical training corps at 277 TS Galloway. We met on a Friday and Monday nights and often spent weekends away at camp. The Marine Cadets was run by two ex-Marines, Lt Jock McLeod and Sgt Jim Bland, and they had a real aura about them. They were a pair of scary hard bastards, but they never once laid a finger on any of the cadets. For the first time, I found people outside my family who I could really respect and look up to. I'm grateful for the example they set me.

In September 1978, their influence led me into the Army when I joined the Junior Leaders Regiment Royal Artillery in Nuneaton, Warwickshire. The place was designed to turn out future senior NCOs for The Royal Regiment of Artillery. I sailed through 12 months of weapons training, gunnery, drill and adventure training without busting a gut – finally having found something I was good at – and passed off the square as an adult gunner at the end of it. After a short period of leave, I joined 16 Regiment Royal Artillery, posted at Kirton Lindsey in North Lincolnshire.

* * *

I SETTLED EASILY into Army life, and spent the following eight years in one miserable Cold War posting after another, often drunk and rolling around in the gutter with other squaddies or the odd civilian.

My weapon of no-choice was the Rapier anti-aircraft missile. Soldiers have always complained that their equipment is crap – I dare say Roman legionaries moaned about the gladius – but the Rapier really *was* useless. Your chances of using it to shoot down enemy aircraft were next to nil, though, by comparison with today's Army, we were fortunate; aside from one minor piece of bad manners by the Argentineans, we never had to use any of it in anger.

In 1981, we were posted to Dortmund in West Germany and enthusiastically assumed our role of waiting to provide air defence against the Red Menace if it ever poured over the borders from Russia. For 'waiting to provide air defence' read 'sweeping gun parks, pushing Land Rovers round the barracks to save on fuel, practising call-out procedures for the Third World War, and taking part in drunken brawls with the rest of the garrison.'

Dortmund had four gunner regiments within a few miles of each other, and we shared a camp with 26 Regiment Royal Artillery. This was a bit like asking Rangers and Celtic fans to share a minibus. 16 Regiment recruited mainly from around the Glasgow area, with a smattering of northern English lads like myself, and 26 were from Essex. We kicked the living daylights out of the mat every opportunity.

Dortmund city centre back then was a nasty, violent place. Groups of immigrant Turks and squaddies defended their territory with extreme aggression. 16's patch was a boozer called the Hansa Becher, a typical squaddie haunt with cheap beer and local girls who were too ugly to work in the nearby red light area. The clientele were almost exclusively single gunners from 16, and so we nicknamed ourselves the Hansa Commandos. There was a lot of rivalry between us and pretty much everyone else, and every now and then someone would go a bit over the top. The Army would then encourage us to drink in camp for a while, rather than go down town and besmirch the name of our country and get ourselves arrested.

Each battery had a room in its barrack block converted into a bar which sold subsidised beer. One night our bar was broken into and a stash of Kit Kats was stolen, presumably by a group of squaddies returning from a night on the lash. The following night I was in the NAAFI bar with a lad called Andy Bishop, who was a bit of a rogue. We were due a kit inspection in the morning so we each bought ten Kit Kats, being careful to ask the NAAFI manageress for a receipt (to save ourselves from being accused if we were caught with the chocs). Next morning, I hid the Kit Kats in the webbing of a couple of new lads in my troop and stashed the receipt in my combat jacket pocket. We paraded outside the battery block with our kit in front of us, and the Sergeant Major began his inspection with a troop Sergeant called Gus. Gus was a giant of bloke who played rugby for the British Army and was one of the strongest men I have ever come across; he was also in charge of the battery bar, and he was after the blood of the Kit Kat nickers.

'Show me your washing and shaving kit from your left-hand kidney pouch!' growled the Sergeant Major, in broad Glaswegian.

The entire troop reached for their webbing, unfastened their pouches and produced their washing and shaving equipment... Except for the young lad standing next to me, who produced a handful of Kit Kats. He stood there, mouth open, holding the offending items in his shaking hands, and protesting his innocence.

Gus, towering above him, grabbed him by the front of his combat jacket. Just then, there was a muffled cry from the front, as another young recruit found his ammunition pouch was stuffed with Kit Kats, too. Gus went ballistic.

Eventually, the two lads convinced him of their innocence, but the knowledge that someone was clearly taking the piss, as well as the Kit Kats, was too much for Gus to bear. One afternoon... Bingo! He called in to see his mate, the Battery Quartermaster, and found Andy Bishop, who worked in the stores, sitting behind his desk scoffing a Kit Kat, with a pile of others at his elbow.

Gus glared at him and demanded to know where they had come from. Bishop stopped nibbling, looked Gus in the eye, and said, 'Ashton gave them to me.'

Gus let out a fearsome roar and ran from the stores. I was sweeping up leaves from underneath the Land Rovers when I saw Gus running towards me, screaming like a banshee. Discretion being the better part of valour, I dropped the brush and ran for my life. I still see Gus at regimental reunions, and he remains convinced that I nicked the Kit Kats. Gus, I didn't do it!

* * *

WE STILL WENT out into the city from time to time. One day I was on the lash with the Hansa Commandos and we found our way to a local boozer called the Power Pub. It was a disco bar and a neutral drinking haunt with mixed clientele from any regiment, and even some locals. There was never normally any trouble in there, but within half an hour some of our lads were embroiled in a punch-up with a group of Germans. This spilled out onto the street before it was stopped by a group of junior NCOs from 16 who were having a quiet drink in the pub with their German girlfriends, and most of the Hansa Commandos left. For some unfathomable reason, I stayed on.

A short time later, I was thrown out of the pub, and punched the pub window in frustration. To my horror, a crack appeared down the centre of it. A group of German bouncers then chased me down the street and up on to some flat roofs, yelling at me to *kommen hier*, *schnell*. It all ended with the musing my head as a dancefloor and throwing me through a garage roof, twice, before handing me over to the police. The following Monday morning I was marched out in front of the RSM to be told that the damage I'd caused came to £800. I only took home £200 a month.

I didn't have a clue how I was going to repay it, short of signing on for the full 22 years. As luck would have it, shortly afterwards we were deployed to San Carlos Water in the Falkland Islands. The war had just ended and we had missed the whole thing, but no-one knew if the Argies might have another pop. We were one of three air defence regiments rotating through four-month tours just in case. This involved sitting in trenches, overlooking the bay, freezing our nuts off, and dying of boredom. The one advantage was that there was nothing to spend your money on, so I was able to save up the £800.

We flew from Germany, via Dakar in West Africa, and onwards to Ascension Island, a big pile of volcanic ash plonked right in the middle of the Atlantic Ocean just south of the Equator. From there, we transferred to a cruise ship, the Cunard *Countess*, for a 10-day voyage south towards the Falklands. Sadly, she had been commissioned as a troopship, so there was no tennis court or cocktail bar. Life on board was inevitably taken up with weapons training, fitness drill, honing our first aid skills, and endlessly practising aircraft recognition – the latter being something I feel our American allies should take a bit more seriously, given their penchant for 'friendly fire' incidents. Many of the aircraft types used by the Argies were classed as friendly in our role in Europe, but hostile in the South Atlantic.

Happily, the swimming pool hadn't been decommissioned, and so we spent our afternoons lounging around the pool. It was during one of these lazy sessions that I first noticed a group of suntanned and well-manicured blokes who clearly weren't with us. As it turned out, they were waiters from the ship, and I quickly realised that they were flirting with any of the squaddies who would give them the time of day. Being a sheltered sort of lad, the only openly gay people I'd seen at that point were Larry Grayson and Kenneth Williams, and I found the whole thing slightly scary.

Evenings saw us pouring copious amounts of beer down our necks and playing bingo, hosted by the RSM. It was quite funny watching some of the toughest men in the battery sweating and biting their nails over a line or a full house. It all helped the time pass, but not very quickly, and it seemed like an eternity before we arrived in San Carlos and were airlifted, section by section, to our site – relieving our colleagues from 14 Battery who had been posted there immediately before us.

Our site was on a hill at the end of Bomb Alley and, as the helicopter lifted and whizzed away out of sight, I turned to survey the grey scene that would be home to me and six other lads for the next four months. It was a big, mice-infested hole in the ground, covered in Harrier stripping and camouflage. Only a nearby Rapier missile launcher and tracker shelter, protected by a bit of a bunker built against the (very) off chance that we might be attacked, showed we were in the right place.

There were 11 other virtually identical sites scattered around San Carlos Water, all designed to pretend that the Army was providing air defence cover for the dozen or so ships that were anchored in the bay, in blissful ignorance of how crap Rapier really was.

The Battery HQ was based in a Portakabin camp called Kelly's Gardens, which was near to San Carlos settlement and was also inhabited by our infantry cover – initially, a company of Gurkhas who patrolled the hills every night. Those guys were horribly efficient and professional, and we would never have known they were there, in stark contrast to their replacements, the Royal Irish Rangers. The Paddies bumbled in halfway through the tour, and every night we would hear them stumbling about and cursing in the dark – they were so bad that they actually disturbed our sleep. One particular night, they wrongly thought they had seen some movement around our position, so they fired a flare which lit up the night sky and helpfully silhouetted our section. We shouted fully justified abuse at them, to which they responded with their own volley of obscenities. Thank God, the Argies never came into contact with them as they couldn't have hoped for a better morale boost.

* * *

ANY SOLDIER WHO says he looks forward to war is either lying, or seriously lacking in imagination, or mad, and I spent most of my waking moments praying that hostilities didn't break out again. We were all armed with our personal weapons, along with a general purpose machine gun and, oddly, an 84 mm Carl Gustav anti-tank rifle, but I didn't honestly hold out much hope of our fighting off an Argie charge. For starters, we only had four belts of ammunition for the Gimpy, so if we were attacked we would have run out of ammo in around 45 seconds – always assuming that the man firing it survived that long. As for the Charlie G, we were more likely to see the London Philharmonic Orchestra coming over the hill than an enemy tank. But it was covered in dust and had never been zeroed, so in the million-to-one event that we'd needed it to take out a rogue T55 (or a string section), the projectile would probably have sunk one of our own boats instead. It's fair to say that we weren't exactly armed to the teeth.

Gus was the sergeant in charge of our section, which was good and bad at the same time. He was a top sergeant, and he could get us organised when he needed to. Ultimately, that might save our bacon. On the other hand, a tiny part of him was still inwardly fuming about the Kit Kat affair, and I knew I was unlikely to get away with much pissing around. And, compared to some of the other unit leaders, he was very strict with our ammo. We wouldn't fire our weapons unless we were zeroing them in on one of the extremely rare range days.

After a couple of weeks, one of our number, a lad known as Biter, was moved to another section to replace a sergeant who had gone home on compassionate leave. Shortly after his arrival, Biter was in their living area eating his lunch when a burst of machine gun fire erupted outside. Being used to the quiet life with us, Biter instinctively screamed for the section to stand to, grabbed his webbing, rifle and steel helmet and ran outside... to be greeted by a gunner from the section blatting away at a flock of upland geese that were flying overhead. Gus would never have stood for that.

I had my own moments of panic, too. One day I was sitting in the tracker bunker with the radio headset on, daydreaming and writing a letter home, when a call came across the airwaves. *'Hello Charlie-Charlie Alpha, this is Two-air raid warning red, battle stations, weapons free on all fixed-wing aircraft – three times Mirages approaching at 100 miles.'*

Shit! I stared at the radio set. My eyes opened wider still when the tracking kit alarmed onto an unknown aircraft which was approaching at speed. I fumbled with the controls and looked through the eyepiece of the tracker, sweat running down my forehead, and immediately locked onto one of our own Chinooks, which was dashing back to the safety of San Carlos Water. The ships anchored out in the bay were gunning their engines and firing chaff to confuse any incoming Exocets. *Shit shit shit!*

I was dimly aware of the rest of my section, all charging around like blue-arsed flies, running to foxholes with their weapons or trying to find the helmets they had last seen weeks ago.

I was trying to remember the words to the *Our Father*, when a flight of Phantoms from Port Stanley intercepted the incoming Mirages, and that was enough to send the Argies back home. Shortly afterwards, we got the clear signal, the battery was stood down, and I went off to change my underpants.

A few nights later I was on sentry duty with our bombardier in charge, Geordie G, while the rest of the section slept. Geordie was a great lad, feared and respected in equal measure. He showed extreme loyalty to his mates and was always a reassuring influence to have around – in his mad bastard sort of way. The Rapier wasn't working, as usual, and with the minutes passing at a snail's pace we decided to head off and make a brew. We still had to listen to the radio, of course, so we clipped a remote handset on some wire and reeled it out behind us as we walked the 50 yards or so to the living area, enabling us to listen to and transmit on the radio while we were brewing up. We placed the handset onto a makeshift table and set about boiling some water. As I prepared the tea, we were both startled by the sound of the handset sliding off the table and landing on the floor. Somebody, or something, had obviously tripped over the cable outside – and given that we were the only people awake from the section that was a bit worrying.

'What the fuck was that?' I said.

Geordie bent down to pick up his sub-machine gun. He cocked it in a business-like way, picked up a torch, checked that it was working, and then handed them both to me. 'You'd better go and find out,' he said.

I took the weapon and the torch, gulped, and made my way outside, knees knocking, in search of an infiltrator. I crept around, spinning round at intervals whenever I heard a crack or a rustle. After 10 minutes of nothing, I returned to report back, and found Geordie snoring. It perfectly summed up the adrenalin-fuelled and death-defying nature of life in the Army.

Sleep was very important to us, to be fair, and Geordie was a keen exponent. The first night I was on duty with him I noticed that he had brought his sleeping bag into the bunker as well as his webbing and personal weapon. I said nothing, until an hour or so after our shift started when he unzipped the bag and climbed into it.

'Night, Pete,' he said, cheerfully. 'You want to get your head down.'

Being the junior on this jaunt, I was a bit uncomfortable. 'Aren't we supposed to be on sentry duty?' I said.

Geordie leant forward. 'Listen son,' he said. 'If the Argy special forces decide to attack us during the night, they're going to kill us. It'll be much easier on us if we're asleep when it happens.'

I couldn't really argue with that, and whenever I was on stag with Geordie I had to go through the charade of pretending that I was tired the next day. Our routine involved the night shift gunner making breakfast for the rest of the section before waking them. I used to stand over the petrol cooker, rubbing sleep from my eyes and doing comedy yawns as I made Gus his sausage sandwich. After breakfast, I'd wander off and pretend to sleep for six hours.

* * *

AFTER WHAT SEEMED like years, we reached the end of the tour and were transferred by helicopter to a troopship and then on to Port Stanley to pick up the rest of the battery. We were allowed into Stanley one day, and after a respectably brief and cultural walk around the capital we all met up at the legendary Globe Hotel to get shit-faced. We were all humble enough to admit that, compared to the lads who had preceded us and recaptured the islands, we hadn't done a great deal. But, that said, we *had* given up four months of our lives (including my 21st birthday) to do our bit in keeping the islands British, so we rather naively expected a warm reception from the islanders.

We got nothing of the sort – quite the opposite, in fact. Basil Fawlty could have learnt a bit from the miserable bastards.

We hadn't had the opportunity to drink much alcohol during those interminable four months, so we were soon drowning in the stuff, and loud and raucous sing-songs quickly broke out, much to the annoyance of the locals behind the bar – a particularly sullen bunch, all bearded, and dressed in Parkas and woolly hats, and all getting plenty of abuse.

They threatened to stop serving us, but changed their minds as a riot threatened; I suspect they were half-wishing those civilised Argentineans were still around.

When it finally came time to leave, we decided to take a little souvenir from the place. I opened the top of my combat trousers and Geordie G handed me the poker – thankfully cold – that was on the hearth. I limped out into Stanley singing *Flower of Scotland* at the top of my voice with all the rest of the lads, but as we staggered towards the landing craft to take us back to the ship MV *Keren* it was announced that we were going to be searched before boarding, just in case we had picked up anything illegal. Bollocks. I breathed a regretful sigh and dropped the poker into Port Stanley harbour. As it turned out, the kit search never actually materialised, much to the relief of one Lance Bombardier. When we had arrived back in Dortmund and were unpacking our kit, Andy Bishop approached this lad and asked to look in his sleeping bag. Bishop un-wrapped the sleeping bag and retrieved a Colt .45 automatic which he'd planted there... He then calmly tucked the shooter down the front of his trousers and walked away.

Bishop was a bit of an oddball. One night I was boozing with him in the battery bar when I jokingly suggested we mugged the barman as he took the night's takings down to the guardroom at closing time. Bishop made no comment but looked thoughtfully in the direction of Shakey MacBeth, the barman. Shakey was a very friendly and popular bloke, and nobody would ever have wished him any harm. Shortly before closing time, I felt a tap on my shoulder and Bishop motioned for me to follow him. We went to his room where he produced two balaclavas and two small metal bed-ends which people used as clubs from time to time. Somewhat non-plussed, I asked him what was happening.

'We need to lie in wait for Shakey,' he said.

I looked at him. 'I was joking, you daft bastard!'

Bishop just shrugged his shoulders, hid the balaclavas and bed-ends, and the subject was never mentioned again.

Back in Germany, we quickly slipped back into the old routine of pushing wagons around, kit inspections and insane boozing. And fighting. I soon became the latest bed warmer for a Hansa Becher girl, and one Sunday afternoon we were walking hand-in-hand through the city centre when a large group of American sailors caught my eye. They were strolling towards the red light district, being very loud and quite annoying, but I thought nothing much of it and we wandered on our way. A couple of hours later, I persuaded Heidi to pop into the Hansa Becher for a slurp or two, and as we turned the corner towards the boozer we witnessed a scene of impressive carnage. The Yanks were brawling with the Hansa Commandos, and it was all hands to the pump: in a pleasing display of post-war European solidarity, even the German barman was fighting alongside our lads.

I was about to join the fray when the German civvie police screeched up alongside a Rover or two of MPs, and the combatants scattered. Later I asked the lads what had caused the fight. 'The Yanks came in the pub,' said one of them. 'It was all going fine, until one of the tossers asked Kev if he wanted to hear a joke.'

The joke was, 'What's got 100 arms, 50 legs and no heads? *HMS Sheffield*.'

Kev promptly slotted him straight between the eyes, and bedlam erupted in a re-enactment of a scene from *The Quiet Man*.

Exciting as it was, at times, all good things come to an end, and the time arrived when I had to leave 16 Regiment. The move was partly accelerated when the regiment was kicked out of Dortmund in the mid-80s after a soldier stole a petrol tanker from a local field regiment, before crashing it into a taxi rank and killing a couple of Germans.

In 1984, I was posted to the Royal Artillery Parachute Team based in Woolwich. I spent the next two years jumping out of perfectly good aircraft into showgrounds and football stadiums around the country. While it was entirely different to my time with 16, it was good fun and we had plenty of laughs. But it was not without its risks. I remember parachuting into the Norfolk Tattoo one cloudy day. We jumped from about 5,000 feet, which gave us about 20 seconds of freefall, with smoke canisters for visual effect. Two groups of three were jumping, the idea being that we would all link up in mid-air before splitting apart to deploy the chutes.

It should have been an easy and straightforward display. After about 10 seconds, you reach terminal velocity of 110 mph; you then 'wash off' your speed as you approach formation by pushing your arms forward. It was all going smoothly until a Zimbabwean lad, relatively new on the team, flew in to link up with me and my oppo. He failed to wash off his speed, and smashed straight into us and knocked us for six. The three of us scattered across the sky. The other two lads quickly regained stability and deployed their parachutes, but the idiot had hit me with such force that I was semi-conscious. To make matters worse, he'd also ripped my right arm out of its socket – and given that you open your main parachute with your right arm I was in a lot of trouble.

I plummeted towards the ground, tumbling out of control and gaining speed. I remember seeing green grass and grey sky intermittently flashing past like a deadly kaleidoscope. As my right arm flapped in the wind, I regained enough of my senses to open my reserve parachute with my left hand. I deployed it just in time, and saved my life. But it was not without cost. In those days, the reserve chute was just a very basic, circular canopy, designed to open instantly and get you down just about alive. As soon as I pulled it I stopped immediately – from 110mph to about 10mph in a matter of a second or so. This knackered the whole of the right-hand side of my body – I wasn't right for months afterwards.

I floated, out of control, to earth and ended up in a heap in a ploughed potato field about half a mile away from where I should have landed. I just about remember a bloke cycling up to me as I sat in dazed agony in the field. 'Well done, mate,' he said. 'That was a brilliant display. The best I've ever seen, by a country mile!'

I guess the moral of that story is: if you have a stupid African in your team, never parachute on a cloudy day in Norfolk.

On one of my last sorties with the team, I dropped into the Rhine Army Centre at Bad Lippspringe in West Germany and was blown off course (bad steering, to be honest). My parachute collapsed over a forest and I fell through the trees, fracturing a vertebrae. On the upside, this does mean that I can honestly claim to have been injured parachuting into Germany during the war – no need to mention that it was the Cold War.

I'd had a terrific grounding in the Army, and I'd made a lot of mates in 16. But by the end of my shift with the parachute team I knew it was time for a change. I decided to put in my papers and follow my two older brothers into the police.

Chapter 2:

Thin Blue Line

I WENT BACK TO my parents' house in Preston for a year while I went through the selection process.

In those days, they were still recruiting white male heterosexuals with gay abandon, and eventually I got accepted and landed a job with the Metropolitan Police. In the period between leaving the Army and joining the Old Bill, I worked intermittently as a labourer and nightclub bouncer. I rarely missed an opportunity to roll around in the gutter with anyone who wanted to take me on, and began getting a bit of a reputation. I was actually becoming a pain in the arse, particularly for my very good mate Ray, who watched me trying to fight the world and his wife, and frequently dug me out or cleared up the mess.

When I wasn't working, I usually found myself in a boozer, and it was there that I met my wife. It was the August of 1987, shortly after I'd left the mob, and I went to a local club with a mate, intent on having a skinful and seeing where the evening took us. As we skulked around the bar, we saw a lass we'd been at school with called Donna. She was with a pretty little dark-haired girl who took my eye. When she opened her mouth it turned out she was a Scouser. Despite this, I decided to ask her out, and it was one of the better decisions I've made. Carmel and I are still together 25 years later, and I love her to bits. She has always been a reassuring voice of good reason in my 'jump in at the deep end' approach to life, and she has stood by me in some difficult times.

We headed down to the Big Smoke together so that I could complete my training at Hendon, and I got my first post at West Ham. Before joining the Met, I'd considered myself to be a reasonably well-travelled, streetwise guy, but nothing prepared me for the melting pot of humanity that is the East End. Life moved at 110mph, in a violent, dog-eat-dog frenzy. There had been some legendary gangsters spawned there over the past half a century, and the area had a culture all of its own, but it had lost the steely sense of community that had been prevalent in the 1950s and 1960s. Then, the diamond geezers really had looked after their own. Now, pensioners who'd been top dogs 30 years earlier often lived behind locked doors in high-rise flats, too terrified to venture onto streets full of new gangs from alien cultures. All too often, they got cut off and died, cold and alone, only to be found curled up on their kitchen floor when the smell got too much for their neighbours.

I cut my teeth in the late 1980s and early 1990s in places like Stratford, Forest Gate, and Manor Park, areas populated by a heady mix of West Indian and Asian groups, with the odd dash of Irish and the remaining original East Enders thrown in.

The East Enders had a distinct mentality. There was a pub near West Ham's ground that had a bouncer who was rumoured to be an IRA man. Known as Blackhands, he wasn't an imposing sort of character to look at – in fact, he looked a lot like Buddy Holly. But he could handle himself rather better than Buddy. One night, a disturbance kicked off in the boozer and a local kid was kicked out by Blackhands and sent on his way with a dismissive cuff round the ear. The little prat, clearly annoyed by his humiliation, threatened to come back with some mates to sort the bouncer out.

The following Sunday evening, the pub was full of local families enjoying a quiet drink when suddenly the doors flew open and in walked the bounced kid, backed up by a few of his pals. Give him credit, he was true to his word – if a little stupid. The youngsters squared up to Blackhands and offered him outside for a round of fisticuffs. Their first mistake was in entering the pub in the first place: this had cut off their escape route. And things suddenly took a turn for the worse when the pub doors were locked and a group of customers overpowered the young lads and then held them down on the dance floor while Blackhands appeared from behind the bar carrying a pool cue. He adjusted his glasses and then coldly and systematically beat the lads, one at a time, around their heads with the pool cue until they were unconscious, like a scene from some mafia movie. If it hadn't been for someone phoning the police, I'm pretty sure one or more of them would have been killed. When I turned up with my colleagues, the lads were still unconscious on the floor in pools of blood, while multi-generational families were just sitting around them, drinking their ale and port-and-lemons without batting an eyelid.

As we moved around the pub in an attempt to find out what had happened, we were met by the heralded East End wall of silence. Young, old, male, female... not one of the buggers had seen anything.

* * *

DURING THAT PERIOD, the police's relationship with some sections of the public became slightly frayed. Being used as strike-busters from time to time didn't help. During the ambulance strikes of the late 1980s, I was called up to man a police ambulance, and, armed with the six-week medical assistant 3rd class course I'd done in the Army a decade earlier, and which I had forgotten in its entirety, I set out to heal the sick and lame.

In the first week, we were called to a shooting outside a pub in Canning Town, where a lad in his early 20s had been shot in the back as he was walking into the boozer. When we arrived on the scene we did a quick examination that revealed a tiny entry wound in the small of his back but no exit wound. It looked to me like it was a small calibre round, probably a .22, so I stuck a field dressing over the point of entry to stem the small trickle of blood. But the lad started complaining that he couldn't feel his legs. So we carefully placed him onto a stretcher and took him to Newham General Hospital. We successfully handed him over to the hospital staff and then stood around the reception having a chinwag with the local police officers. Then I noticed a group of heavies in their forties hanging around and muttering. One of the local coppers explained that the gunshot victim was part of a local crime family. The gangsters refused to talk to the police and insisted that they could sort this little problem out themselves.

Exactly one week later, a car pulled up outside Accident and Emergency at Newham Hospital and a bullet-riddled body toppled out onto the forecourt. Problem solved, it seems.

We came across our fair share of odd situations during our time on the ambulance. There was a Scottish bloke living in the East End who, on having been diagnosed with a terminal illness, decided to end it all after a heavy night on the piss. He returned to his bedsit in Manor Park and plunged a carving knife into his stomach in a drunken and unsuccessful attempt at hara-kiri. He slipped off into unconsciousness, but woke up the following morning and saw the handle sticking out of his ample gut. His Dutch courage had long since worn off so, instead of finding a bigger knife to have another go, he gingerly reached for his telephone and dialled 999.

I suppose he expected the city's finest paramedics to rush to his aid, and he was understandably crestfallen when I walked into his flat with my mate, Big Eric. He was even less impressed when we stood around scratching our heads discussing whether or not to pull the knife out. We opted, much to his relief, for the ring bandage option and a speedy evacuation to hospital. He was then subjected to our lengthy Chuckle Brothers impression, as we placed him on a stretcher and said, 'To me… To you' all the way down the stairs.

The following week we were called to a report of a collapsed male. The flat was on the 14th floor, and we were met by a bloke who said his brother was 'ill in bed'. We followed him into the bedroom, where we found that diagnosis to be something of an understatement. The poor bastard was as stiff as a board. Eric and I looked at the guy standing in front of us with his pleading eyes and the woman leaning over the bed in desperate hope. We took one look at each other in bewilderment and uselessness. Finally, Eric whispered, 'You're the medic, mate… It's your call.'

Eventually, I decided to take the guy to hospital and let the doctors break the bad news – after all, only doctors can pronounce life extinct. But before that, for some unfathomable reason I decided to try to resuscitate him – or at least, pretend to. The woman clutched her rosary beads and looked on as I gave this plainly dead man the kiss of life and then pushed up and down on his chest a few times, while Big Eric covered his eyes. Having made my best efforts to resuscitate, the next problem was that the stiff was a big bloke and wouldn't fit on a stretcher. So we had to carry him, in his underpants and vest, down the 14 flights of stairs, to our van.

We recruited a bemused neighbour to open doors for us, as I held the corpse under his armpits and Eric held him under the knees.

'Are you sure he's actually alive?' asked the neighbour, doubtfully.

'Shhh!'

Grunting under the weight, our hands slippery with sweat, I ended up hanging on to the chap by his wrists while Eric gripped his ankles, and by the time we'd reached the bottom we looked like we were giving him the bumps. It was an ignominious end to a no-doubt proud man's life, but the farce plummeted further when we reached the street. It was busy with pedestrians: surely we couldn't drag a dead body from the flats? We resorted to hiding behind a hedge until things quietened down. When our chance arrived, we staggered out from behind the bush and threw the guy in the back of the Sherpa. On arrival at Accident and Emergency, the crash team were waiting outside (we had called in almost an hour ago). They weren't particularly impressed.

The following day we were sent to a report of a collapsed bloke who had fallen off a ladder while doing a spot of DIY. On our arrival we were met by a scene of total hysteria. The chap was lying on the floor while a neighbour and a family member were desperately performing the kiss of life and chest compressions. Big Eric and I took over and worked on the poor bloke while the neighbour tried to comfort the family. A short time later, an Army ambulance turned up and we placed the man in the back. A medic and I worked on him while a driver from the Women's Royal Army Corps drove us slowly through the dinnertime rush hour traffic towards Newham Hospital. I couldn't understand why we were taking so long, and between blowing into the bloke's mouth I asked the driver why she was waiting for the traffic lights to change despite having blue lights flashing and sirens blaring.

'I can't break the law, but I can ask other drivers to give me the right of way by using the sirens,' was her incredible reply.

This was East London, for goodness' sake. *No-one* obeyed the traffic lights.

Half an hour later we pulled into A&E and were met by the same reception team who had dealt with my previous day's delivery. It was just my bloody luck that today's patient had pegged out while we crept through the traffic. I got a few more strange looks as I handed over another dead body, and knocked off work early to have a few stiff drinks.

All this had made me think that maybe I wasn't cut out to be a substitute ambulance driver, and, unsurprisingly, the decision-makers agreed. I was posted to help man the station van that drove around the section picking up any prisoners and their arresting officers. Much more my cup of tea.

* * *

MAGGIE THATCHER WILL be remembered for many things – the riots in Brixton and elsewhere, the Miners' Strike and the Wapping trouble being right up there. But the defining moment of her long premiership came on 31st March 1990, with the most iconic show of public disobedience in many a long year. For all Maggie's faults, she did like a joke, but not everyone saw the funny side of the Poll Tax, and some of them decided to make a point about it in Trafalgar Square.

I was sent as part of a foot unit from West Ham Police Station to wait outside Downing Street. I thought this would be a bit of a giggle, but it soon turned serious. We watched over 200,000 unwashed protestors march past, banging drums and shouting, wave upon wave of them carrying black flags. They were only separated from us by some flimsy crash barriers, and it made the hair stand up on the back of my neck.

As the day wore on, the whiff of trouble got stronger. Some of the idiots began proudly showing us the carrier bags full of half bricks and bottles which would be heading our way. The protestors were getting more fractious, and I can't deny that the tension was rising on our side as well. It inevitably kicked off when a police inspector became pissed off with a demonstrator in a wheelchair who was refusing to move on. He called the carriers up to arrest the obstructing protestor.

The sight of the much-hated Territorial Support Group, or 'Thatcher's Storm Troopers' as my dad liked to call them, was the trigger that the troublemakers in the crowd (and police) were waiting for. A wall of missiles and crush barriers flew at our lines, and that persuaded our section inspector to retreat behind the Cenotaph where he remained for the rest of the day.

What I saw next influenced my career for the next few years. As we uniformed bobbies wondered what to do next, the TSG mob hurled themselves into the crowd like whirling dervishes. They were joined by the mounted branch which made repeated charges, forcing the protestors back with their long batons. Standing on reserve outside Downing Street, I watched this pitched battle unfold with considerable awe. I had never seen anything like it in my life, even in the Army. It was fucking awesome.

At one point, the crowd rushed towards a police line further down the road, and the line unfathomably broke and the cops were chased towards Nelson's Column. As I watched, one young copper stopped, turned round, drew the 18-inch wooden truncheon from his pocket, and began a solo charge back at the oncoming rioters. Bizarrely, this caused them to stop, turn on their heels and run back in the direction they had come – right into the welcoming hands of the TSG. Oh how we laughed.

From around 4pm, reports of events become confused and contradictory. It seems that the mounted police (who had earlier attempted to clear Whitehall) charged out of a side street, straight into the packed crowds in Trafalgar Square. Whether intentional or not, this was interpreted by many in the crowd as an unwarranted provocation, and further fuelled their anger. At about 4.30pm, four TSG riot vans drove directly into the crowd outside the South African Embassy, attempting to force their way through to the entrance to

Whitehall where police were re-grouping. The crowd attacked these vans with wooden staves, scaffolding poles and other items to hand in an attempt to slow them down. The rioting escalated.

The scaffolding adjacent to South Africa House was scaled, and Portakabins built into it were set ablaze. As clouds of smoke billowed over the capital, the Tube system came to a standstill and nearby stations were closed. We managed to contain the trouble in the Square until early evening, when some armchair general decided it would be a decent idea to let the anarchists loose into theatreland.

Shops were looted, cars were torched and restaurants were attacked while terrified diners cowered inside. While all this was happening, my unit was still being held back in reserve near Downing Street. Our inspector had emerged from behind the Cenotaph and was sat the front of the coach puffing on his pipe and ignoring the audible boredom behind him. Finally, at about 7pm, we were called up to a church at St Martins-in-the-Field to clear a sit-down protest from the steps. They were mostly Greenham Common-type women who, while being quite abusive, weren't in the slightest bit violent. But with a heady cocktail of tedium, anger and testosterone fizzing around inside us, their passive-aggressive brand of foul-mouthed offence got short shrift – much to the annoyance of some bystanders, who also got a whack. From today's perspective, this may sound harsh, but *Ashes to Ashes* wasn't far wrong, and there were plenty of real live Gene Hunts knocking about. And, don't forget, the area was in a state of anarchy. Normal policing methods had collapsed.

Anyway, it was all undeniably therapeutic, and all I could think was, *I want to join the TSG.*

Chapter 3:

Thatcher's Storm Troopers

IN 1991, I JOINED the Territorial Support Group. I was in a unit which covered Bethnal Green, Barking and Dagenham, Hackney and Stoke Newington. On certain days, we were Central London Reserve, which meant that we could be called anywhere at very short notice.

Our unit consisted of 21 constables, three sergeants, and one inspector, and the team was split up into three public order carriers. The unit I joined was full of ex-Special Patrol Group officers. The SPG, disbanded in 1987, had been a bunch of hard, cynical bastards – the Dirty Dozen of the Met – and some of my new colleagues had not long been re-instated after lengthy suspensions following the Wapping dispute. Our work comprised front-line riot policing, surveillance, firearms duties, and generally being called in as the sledgehammer when normal policing was unable to crack the tougher nuts.

Our bread and butter work was anti-robbery patrols around Hackney and Stoke Newington. Sir Paul Condon, then police commissioner, caused outrage by suggesting that the majority of robbery suspects in London were black. This was not brilliant PR but, to be fair to Condon, my experience – certainly at that time – backed this up. A lot of second-generation Jamaicans with serious crack cocaine habits caused serious trouble, and we didn't mess about. We would routinely turn up mob-handed and have gangs of suspected street robbers spread-eagled in lines against the wall while we searched them. Inevitably, you end up stopping a lot of innocent kids and we were undeniably hated by the wider mass of young black youths. There was nothing positive or warm about the relationship.

There was also a popular theory that mixed groups of black and white youths were up to no good – hence our mantra of *Black and white–stop on sight*. I'm not sure what Sir William Macpherson would have made of that. But his suggestion that the Met was 'institutionally racist' – made in the aftermath of the infamous murder of Stephen Lawrence – was largely irrelevant to the TSG. Sure, we locked up plenty of black lads. But we also waded in against the extreme right-wing of the NF or the BNP, or left wing counter-demonstrators from groups like Red Action. Race, in my experience, was an irrelevance. I just wanted to nick scumbags. I couldn't care less what colour their skin was.

Sometimes we were well-prepared, but at other times we were taken by surprise. I remember one Saturday morning early in 1992 on Central London Reserve, when we were called to an urgent assistance shout from the British Transport Police at Waterloo Station. A right-wing skinhead band called Blood and Honour were playing a gig that day, and their concerts were planned like military operations to stop left-wing anti-fascist groups attacking them. You had to have right-wing connections to attend, and would be directed to the secret venue via a number of marshalling points.

On the day in question, one of these marshalling points was Waterloo. During the morning, a lone BTP officer patrolling the station became aware of two groups of skinheads gathering on either side of the station, exchanging pleasantries. (It is a popular misconception that all skinheads are Nazis in 12-hole Doc Martens. There are lots of authentic, ska-loving lefty skins, too – plus, of course, plenty of apolitical types like me.)

Within minutes, a group of BTP officers had formed up and made a single cordon in an attempt to clear the two factions, with little success. Carnage ensued, and the BTP bobbies were caught in the middle. They requested urgent assistance from the Met and we obligingly screeched up onto the concourse and launched ourselves into the riot. Another unit of TSG was also nearby, so about 60 riot-trained officers were on scene within a couple of minutes and able to rescue the BTP and push both groups to opposite sides of the station.

For the next few hours, we stood in fill riot gear between the two factions, as they were reinforced from all over London. We performed numerous baton charges while small groups from left and right probed our lines, looking for weak spots. A constant shower of missiles rained down on us from either side.

With skinheads in both groups, it was difficult to identify who was after whom, and it was hard to keep them separated. They were very committed, and the prospect of being arrested or batoned didn't seem to bother them much. We spent the day wading into pitched battles, cracking a few skulls and breaking up the punch-ups, only for them to regroup and start again in smaller groups on both sides of our lines.

By the evening, the Nazis had moved onto Essex for their concert, and we had managed to contain the leftists on the south bank of the Thames and eventually disperse them from there into the West End.

A lot of the extreme right-wingers were basically little more than glue-sniffing criminals, and we knew them well. A few months earlier, we'd been called to Kilburn in North London, a predominantly Irish area. A Bloody Sunday protest march was in progress, and the parade was worming its way through the streets towards Parliament, where they intended to hand over a petition demanding another enquiry into the incident. Blocking their path were about a hundred members of the British National Party, the National Front, Chelsea's Headhunters hooligan gang, and the newly-formed Combat 18. They were intent on ambushing the march, and the TSG was deployed to keep an eye on them. Since all was relatively calm when we arrived, I approached a couple of them who I recognised for a chat.

'How come you lads aren't down at West Ham for the match?' I said.

'This ain't a time for football, mate,' said one of them. 'These IRA bastards are planting bombs all over London and here's you lot letting their fucking supporters march through the fucking city. It makes me disgusted to be British.'

Shortly afterwards, a number of coaches rolled up and an unsporting chief inspector earnestly announced to the extreme right that they were all under arrest to prevent a breach of the peace.

'If you behave yourselves,' he said, 'you can board these coaches without being handcuffed and will be taken to a local public house in time to see the football results.'

The self-appointed guardians of the nation's honour dispersed onto the buses without complaint, and were happily driven away after making their token gesture. Which was kind of disappointing to a good number of the TSG.

Whether or not you agreed with the politics of these guys, I suppose they had a reasonable argument, IRA-wise. This was a time, remember, when Provo bombs or recognised coded bomb threats regularly brought the capital to a standstill.

One Saturday morning (everything seemed to happen on a Saturday, which led me to think that criminals and terrorists must have nine-to-five jobs during the week), we were on area reserve and doing a bit of training when we were called out to the City of London.

A pair of traffic wardens had been prowling their beat when they saw a large tipper truck park up near to Bishopsgate tube. Two masked men jumped out and drove off in a vehicle that had been following them. The City of London's control room suspected it was a 'spectacular' – a giant bomb – and called in the troops.

We were positioned at the second (outer) cordon, about half a mile away, and were told to await developments while local units evacuated the rabbit warren of streets and offices.

We'd been sitting in our carrier for some time, and were getting increasingly bored, when one of the lads in the back said, 'This is a load of bollocks. Nothing's going to happen.'

BANG!

A freelance photographer working for the *News of the World* had taken advantage of the earlier confusion and managed to hide in the bank directly opposite the tipper truck, hoping to get shots of the explosion. I guess he hoped they'd be his once-in-a-lifetime scoop. He got his scoop, alright – the one they used to body-bag what was left of him when the 2,000lb bomb exploded 20 yards away from the window he was peering out of.

An unsuspecting traffic cop who hadn't been listening to his radio had somehow driven down one of the side streets and come across an abandoned van with the doors swinging open. He got out of his patrol car and was walking towards the vehicle just as the bomb exploded. The shock waves were channelled down the tight maze of streets in his direction, and the force picked him up and threw him back 10 yards, depositing him on his arse in a state of some considerable shock. Even half a mile away, our carrier was rocked on its springs and a door handle landed on our bonnet. My immediate expectation was of a secondary device which would send us all to our maker: it was a known tactic for terrorists to place follow-up bombs in areas where the security services would be gathered. Thank God, there was no second bang.

We were ordered to go to the London Wall to assist with casualties. We drove there through a blizzard of office paper floating down from the sky – the explosion had caused hundreds of millions of pounds-worth of damage to the centre of London's financial district, and had wrecked offices and banks. When we arrived at the Wall, we saw a number of victims sitting silently on the pavement, cut to shreds by flying glass. Most were foreign tourists visiting the city. We did our best to try and assist the paramedics by offering comfort and first aid to the poor sods, and then had to save a group of Japanese tourists from a lynching. They had gathered round and were calmly taking photographs of the injured, and a bunch of locals were confronting them.

The rest of the day was spent guarding the cordon. Two things really stick in my mind. The first is the superstars from the Salvation Army who raided a blown-out Marks and Spencer's and pinched all the sandwiches from the wrecked fridges to help feed us. The second was the fleet of double-glazing vans that suddenly appeared and began leaving business cards at all the damaged premises. It's an ill wind that blows nobody any good, especially in an entrepreneurial city like London.

***

EVEN BOMBS HAVE their lighter side. Late one Saturday night, we were called to a tube station where a suspect package had been called in by a member of the public who had then vanished. Our three carriers pulled up and we all split up into pairs and began searching the area. I was working my way along the street with my partner Kev when he stopped and looked in a bin that was directly outside a mini cab office. At the bottom of the bin was a black box.

'Here, Pete,' he said. 'What do you think of this?'

I peered into the bin. Then I looked at him, and he looked at me.' Well,' I said. 'It's either a bomb, or it isn't. It's fifty-fifty, I suppose.'

In reality, the odds were far greater that it *wasn't* a bomb, so I bent down confidently, picked the object up, and turned it over. To my monumental shock, I discovered that it was metal and that there were wires sticking out of it, along with a dial.

'Fucking hell!' I yelled, and dropped it back into the bin. We both legged it back to our inspector to report what we had seen. I took a mighty and justified bollocking for touching the package before we evacuated the area and cordoned the tube station off until the bomb squad arrived.

A couple of hours later the bomb disposal man wandered in and asked to be briefed by the officer who found the package. Rather embarrassed, I explained what I'd seen and how I'd handled the situation, and predictably got another bollocking. He then walked out to the bin and returned a short time later, throwing the 'bomb' up and down in the air and catching it as he walked.

It turned out to be a shower unit, placed in the bin by a rival mini cab firm who had then made an anonymous phone call to the police, knowing it would shut their rivals down for the night.

I got a lot of stick from the rest of the team, and it was made significantly worse a few days later when we attended a briefing at New Scotland Yard on 'the Operational Methods of Dealing with Suspect Packages'.

The lecture hall was packed with TSG and firearms officers from all over London, and the guy giving the lecture turned out to be the same bomb disposal officer who had attended the mini cab office that night. And right at the beginning of the lecture he pressed a button and this message flashed up on the overhead projector:

'NEVER TOUCH A SUSPECT PACKAGE!'

Loud cheers went up from my unit, and someone called out, 'Have you got that, Ashton?'

I hung my head in shame.

***

ALONG WITH THE bombs and shower heads, we also had the new policy of 'Care in the Community' to deal with. This consisted of closing down hospital psychiatric units and asking paranoid schizophrenics to live in communities with insufficient care and support. To my mind, this was unfair on the patients, the innocent people who were terrorised by those patients who failed to take their medication, and the police who then had to turn up and deal with them.

One afternoon we were called to Dagenham, where a chap was running up and down the street armed with two carving knives. We arrived, kitted up in full riot gear, just as the poor guy had barricaded himself into his house. He had also turned all his lights off, so the place was in total darkness. Armed response vehicles had been called and had set up a cordon, but we were tasked with breaking in and disarming him.

My section formed a serial of six officers, consisting of two groups of three with long shields; the other two carriers formed separate shield serials. We went around the back of the house to enter via the kitchen. As we arrived at the back yard an armed officer moved to let us in, and we used a sledge-hammer to open the kitchen door. It was pitch black inside, so we used a powerful Dragon light to help us see. As we began pulling down the kitchen barricade, the guy came running through the house, armed with a sickle, and launched himself at our shields. The guys at the front door, hearing this, smashed the door off its hinges, which caused the bloke to turn and run back that way.

We then had to walk through the tiny kitchen in single file. To my enormous joy, I was the first in and, as I tip-toed through our man reappeared from nowhere and attacked me with the sickle. I did all I could to keep him at bay by jabbing my shield at his head. I was holding my own until an idiot of a sergeant who was outside ordered the Dragon light to be switched off and moved round the side of the building; that plunged the kitchen into total darkness and caused the schizo to go absolutely ballistic. He could see me silhouetted against the street lights, but I couldn't see a fucking thing as he pulled the top of my shield down and began hacking at my protective helmet. All I could do was to whirl my shield around in an effort to put him on his arse. The lads behind me grabbed hold of my belt and began pulling me towards the kitchen door and we all ended up in a heap in the back yard while the bloke waved his sickle and screamed abuse at us from the doorway. As we struggled to get to our feet, the armed response lads came to our rescue and ran at the bloke screaming, 'Armed police... Stand still!'

The poor bastard shrieked and ran back inside. We composed ourselves and followed him. By now, the guy had turned his attention to the lads at the front of the house. In an attempt to confuse him, we then began banging our shields on the floor so that he would return to us, allowing the lads on the front inside. We carried on with this drill until we managed to contain him in his living room. Our long shields had been formed up to block the living room door and he was pacing up and down attacking the shields from time to time. The lad was clearly very distressed, and sobbing and babbling.

One of our bobbies tried to talk to him and calm him down. We were in a safer position now, and all we wanted him to do was put his weapon on the floor and sit down so that we could help him without hurting him. But after an hour we were getting nowhere fast. The bloke was getting more distressed and had started hacking at his wrists with a carving knife. A shout went up and we ran screaming into the room, to force him onto the floor with the combined weight of our shields and bodies.

The back-up team moved in and handcuffed him, and he was then led from the house and taken to the local secure hospital while we returned to our base for a heated debrief. The situation had ended as happily as could be expected for all concerned, even after I had told the sergeant who had ordered the Dragon light to be moved exactly what I thought of him, which was that he was a prick.

Incidents like that didn't always end happily. A week or so later, we were called out to a housing estate near Tottenham where a pair of local detectives had been attacked by a desperate guy with a knife. The attacker was a prisoner who'd been showing the cops around an area where he had committed burglaries, which he needed to do to feed his massive crack habit. His *modus operandi* was to climb onto ledges that ran around the blocks of flats and jump in through open windows in the early hours of the morning to steal jewellery. The victims thought they were safe leaving their windows open as they were a hundred feet up in the air. He would then swallow the jewellery so that they couldn't be found if he was stopped by the police.

He was being a good lad and had coughed to loads of burglaries, so the two coppers felt they owed him a favour when he asked if he could just pop home and see his nipper before going off to prison. Once at his home, he asked if they could take the handcuffs off so that he could give his kid a hug, but as soon as they released him he legged it into the kitchen and picked up a knife. He then slashed one of the officers in the face before escaping and running off into the estate. The officers gave chase and followed him to a flat on the 10th floor of a nearby tower block, where they waited outside, safe in the knowledge that he couldn't go anywhere.

Soon afterwards, we turned up in our carriers and jumped out, ready for action in full riot gear. As we were being briefed, somebody shouted to us that a man had climbed out onto a window ledge 10 floors up. We all looked up, just in time to see him slip and fall through the air, arms and legs windmilling as he plummeted, screaming, onto the concourse 20 yards away from where we stood. He didn't make a pretty sight. When the local police arrived he was still alive but unconscious; he died later in hospital on the operating table, coughing up jewellery.

* * *

THERE WERE A FEW characters on the TSG, none more than a lad called 'Bucket' Barton. He was an ex-Para and a top lad, as long as you bore in mind that he was a bit eccentric. On one occasion I was partnered up with him during an England and Germany football match, and we were posted to the Waterloo station area to stop rival football hooligans clashing.

We were turning over every likely hooligan we found, when I noticed that Bucket was taking laces out of a German supporter's shoes while he was searching him.

'What you doing that for, Bucket?' I said.

'To slow the bastard down when we're chasing him later,' he said.

The next time England entertained Germany we went to a briefing where we were asked if anyone spoke German. I'd done my three years in Germany, so with ill-judged enthusiasm I volunteered to act as the police interpreter for the day. If the powers-that-be had taken note of the looks of amusement and disbelief on the faces of my colleagues they might have conducted a little test on my expertise; I could order beer, sausage and chips, advise you to go straight ahead at the next junction, and tell you that I loved you. And that was it.

Instead, they issued me with a loudhailer and put me on a police carrier with spotters from the football intelligence unit. We dutifully raced around the capital with sirens blaring to every fight involving German fans as I yelled through the loudhailer, 'Schnell macken, Boxhead!' ('Move quick, German person!' – with 'Boxhead' being squaddie-speak based on the shape of their WW2 helmets.)

I was quickly relieved of my megaphone, and told to concentrate on doing what TSG yobs do best, without the comic-book German.

Bucket was soon promoted and posted to a gentler pastime as a custody sergeant in a fairly busy East End nick. Our unit was in this area for a few weeks conducting high visibility patrols, and one evening we got into a confrontation with a group of Rastafarian drug dealers, resulting in one of them being nicked for threatening behaviour.

When we brought the bloke into the custody area we were pleasantly surprised to see Bucket sitting behind the desk. The Rasta man was kicking off a bit, spitting and swearing.

'Calm down please, sir,' said Bucket. 'There's no need for this. Name and date of birth please?'

By way of reply, the Rasta spat on the floor in front of the custody desk.

Bucket shifted in his chair, and politely repeated the request; once again, the prisoner spat on the floor.

Bucket looked at him, long and hard. Then he said, calmly, 'I'm afraid that if you do that again, sir, I will be forced to mop the floor with your dreadlocks.'

Video cameras were not then common in custody areas.

The Rasta, obviously not knowing Bucket as well as we did, hawked and spat another lump of mucus onto the floor in front of the desk.

To a man, we winced and cringed.

Bucket calmly smoothed down his hair, stood up, walked around the desk, got hold of the guy by his legs and turned him upside down. Then, true to his word, he mopped the floor with his head.

I'd be lying if I said this sort of thing didn't happen, and I know some people will be muttering to themselves about police brutality or racism. It was nothing to do with racism – if this kid had been a white hippy he'd have got exactly the same treatment. And as for brutality... The East End was a rough, tough place, teetering on the edge of complete lawlessness. Given half a chance, dealers like this guy would have run amok, and we were the only people standing between him and his ilk and the ordinary folk. You can only have one top gang on the streets, and it has to be the police; if you're going to be the boss, you can't take a step back, you have to bend others to your will. Believe me, if we didn't, nice, law-abiding people were going to suffer, badly.

As another example, I remember walking round the corner to the TSG base one day from the gym – the first two hours of every shift were spent on fitness and strength work. I happened to be carrying a thick roll of Laura Ashley wallpaper that Carmel had asked me to pick up from the centre of town.

I was about to cross the street when I saw this bloke arguing with his girlfriend; as I watched, he grappled with her and they fell onto the bonnet of Bucket Barton's VW Polo.

'Oi,' I said. 'Can you get off my mate's car, please?'

The lad stood up and looked at me. 'Fuck off,' he said.

What can you do? If I let that go, he thinks he can roll all over people's cars, tell the Old Bill to fuck off, and nothing will happen. Next thing you know, someone's *really* getting hurt.

I headbutted him straight in the face – that way, it's impossible to say who butted who – and he went down like a sack of shit, with blood pouring out of his nose. In the police, certainly in those days, there was an old saying that if you laid hands, or your forehead, on someone, you'd better nick them. You don't want them showing up at the front counter a few hours later making all sorts of allegations – you need to get your retaliation in first. So I nicked him for assault-police, under Section Whatever of the Ways and Means Act.

That was some time in the late summer of 1992, and it was only one of many little incidents that made me think it was time to get out of the festering shithole that was London.

In the September of that year, Carmel gave birth to our first son, Sean, and that wonderful, if sobering event, sealed the deal. It was time to leave the capital, its criminals, and its lunatic coppers behind.

Chapter 4:

Hot Fuzz

WHAT CAN I SAY about Derbyshire? It's a beautiful part of the country, but when I transferred to the county the force was still suffering from decades of under-funding. The miners' strike of the 1980s was still festering and engendering a lot of bitterness – in fact, it's *still* festering – and, to make matters worse, the constabulary had recently failed to win its certificate of competence.

So I wasn't that impressed with what I found.

If this sounds like I thought I was a big noise, up from the Smoke, and I was going to sort everything out, it isn't like that. A lot of transferees from the Met to the shires certainly fall into that trap, but I don't think I did. I'm happy to admit that I made plenty of mistakes of my own in Derbyshire, and I believe that most of the individual cops were good people. They were ill-equipped to combat the growing heroin problem that was beginning to grip the more deprived parts of the county, but this is no slight on their inherent quality. It was just inevitable. In London, the Met was policing nearly 10 million people, and the city was rife with first division gangsters, firearms, and drugs. At that point, these things were only just becoming known outside the big cities.

More worryingly, the force allowed its officers to police the very same small, tight-knit communities in which they had grown up, which left them open to misplaced loyalties and corruption. Outsiders, especially from the Met, were looked on with a mixture of mistrust and suspicion by the home-grown officers.

I was initially posted to Chesterfield. This is a pokey little market town just south of Sheffield, surrounded by small mining villages, and it had, following the pit closures, a real unemployment problem that has never gone away. The town has a violent, rowdy nightlife, and the local population like to think they're as tough as nails – until they get a bit of their own medicine, when they turn into a bunch of whining bastards.

On my arrival at Chesterfield, I was posted to the town centre unit and left alone to police my area how I saw fit – which worked fairly well, for a short time. The main problems on my beat were drug dealers and football hooligans. I attacked them with equal enthusiasm, and a naïve belief that I would be backed by my bosses.

Both groups were joined at the hip and I took them on from every direction. My time on the TSG had given me a good working knowledge of drugs and the law relating to misuse, and I loved to get amongst it. I was a great believer in the powers of stop-and-search, something many of the local officers seemed scared to employ, mainly because they had never really been shown how to. Whenever I came across our local pushers I had my hands in their pockets, and drug seizures in the area reached an all-time high.

They retaliated by making lots of complaints and allegations that I'd planted stuff on them or roughed them up. I batted them all off, but before long I was transferred to another nick. That was an important lesson about the difference between policing in London and in the sticks. What works in the capital doesn't necessarily work elsewhere. Not least because you were always bumping into the people you'd nicked.

In the Met, if I ever did a drugs warrant I'd make sure to spice things up a little by pissing in the dealer's kettle, or on his toothbrush. I wasn't averse to giving people a few digs, either – though only if they needed it. You'd then nick them for assaulting you, and when they protested that they hadn't touched you you'd ask your mate in the carrier to smack you in the face to provide you with the evidence. I'd had my nose broken a few times, so all I had to do was slap it, blow hard and blood would come pouring out.

In London, I could have lived half a mile from where I worked and the chance of me being spotted out and about in my civvies off-duty was minimal. I was just one of half a million people in that particular square mile. In Chesterfield, I lived three miles from the nick and within a week everyone knew me, and what I was about. Before long, some of the local drug dealers found out my address and threatened to attack the house. Carmel was six months pregnant with our second son, Matthew, at the time, and we thought it wise to get a panic alarm installed. It might have been a sleepy hollow, but it was stressful enough.

One Sunday night, my dad rang. 'I've just had a phone call,' he said. 'Some feller asking if I'm the father of PC Ashton. When I said I was, the bloke told me to tell my bastard son to get off his back or he was going to come across to Preston and torch my fucking house.'

This particular fool was a local football hooligan and drug dealer who had been spraying graffiti about me around Chesterfield. He was also a police informant, as it turned out, and a junkie – eventually he ended up shooting up more smack than he was selling, and took to breaking into houses and stealing and selling his family's stuff to fund his habit.

As I say, it was a shaky time for me, particularly with Carmel being heavily pregnant, but I wasn't fighting on my own. Another copper – I'll call him Trevor, though he has since died – was also targeting the hooligans and dealers, and had been taking stick from a group of lads, the most outspoken of whom was the same guy who had called my dad.

One evening, Trevor came round to my house. 'That big gobshite,' he said. 'I want to sort him out, once and for all. Will you help?'

'Yeah, of course,' I said. 'What have you got in mind?'

'I want to get hold of him,' said Trevor, 'take him up onto the moors, kill him, and bury him in a grave covered in lime.'

I blinked and coughed. 'Are you serious?'

'Yeah. What do you think?'

'Well, I'm not saying I don't like the plan. In theory, it's a great plan. I just think there's a few flaws in it.'

He looked disappointed. 'What do you mean, flaws?'

'Well, Trevor, when you come up with a plan you have to look at all the ifs, buts and maybes,' I waffled. 'I think there are a few ifs, buts and maybes left in this one.'

To my relief, Trevor said he'd get back to me with a better plan. As it turned out he didn't need one: the arsehole who had been hassling us overdosed not long afterwards.

* * *

AFTER A WHILE, things settled down a bit. I was posted to Chapel-en-le-Frith in the Peak District, where I kept my head down for a while, chasing sheep off the A6 and generally dying of boredom.

It was a pretty gentle sort of place, so when Matthew was born I had plenty of time to go on the piss for two weeks to celebrate. When I eventually went back to work on a Sunday morning, I expected the usual domestic call and stranded cat – but I was surprised. At 10am, I was sent to a flat in nearby Whaley Bridge where a lad had collapsed. He was an ex-junkie who had moved up to Derbyshire to escape his heroin addiction. He'd had one or two relapses, but he had generally done well for himself and had met a local lass with whom he rented a flat. The day before they'd got engaged, and gone out for a meal with the girl's parents. Unfortunately, the lad drank too much, and when a dealer offered him a £10 bag of smack for old time's sake, he succumbed. During the night he injected the heroin and died of an overdose on his bathroom floor. It was genuinely tragic.

His poor fiancée got up the following morning and found him, stiff as a board. Probably trying to protect him, she disposed of his works and pretended she was mystified by the cause of death, though it was pretty clear. I did what I could as the girl's parents tried to console her, and the doctor formally pronounced life extinct. Half an hour or so later, undertakers arrived. I was immediately amused: the dead lad was 15 stone, at least, and the two undertakers were in their 60s and would have weighed about ten stone, dripping wet. I always had a strict rule that I wouldn't ask undertakers to arrest criminals as long as they didn't ask me to touch dead bodies. But I couldn't watch them struggle to lift him, and volunteered to help. They immediately chose the top half of the body, and I found out why when I picked the kid up by his knees and got a blast of dead man's guff, right in my face. I dropped him, went outside and emptied two weeks of Stella Artois.

A few days later, I got a call from the operations room at Buxton. The sergeant explained that the dead body was being taken back down south the next day, and that the fiancée wanted to view the body to say her goodbyes.

'I'll give the coroner's officer a bell to arrange a viewing, shall I?' I said.

After he had stopped laughing, the skipper managed to tell me there were no coroner's officers in the Peak district. 'It's down to you to sort out, lad,' he chuckled. 'Just sign for a key and let yourself into the mortuary.'

Brilliant.

Within an hour I was in the mortuary. I turned the alarm off and stood in front of a row of fridges. Not being a fan of corpses, I forced myself to open them one at a time, so I could unzip the body bags and check the occupants' faces in search of my man. When I found him, I took the body out of the fridge and carefully placed it on a trolley. Then I wheeled it into the chapel of rest and stood back to inspect my work. Leaving his head sticking out of the body bag didn't strike the right note, so I went off in search of a sheet. I eventually found a blue curtain and covered the bag, leaving the head showing. Following the procedural instructions that I had picked up on my arrival, I then pressed the play button on the tape recorder and organ music began playing. I showed the girlfriend and her mother into the chapel so that they could say their goodbyes.

I couldn't hang around for too long so I left it a decent 10 minutes and then crept back into the chapel, coughed, in my best impersonation of an undertaker, and escorted them into the car park leaving the body inside.

After saying my goodbyes to the grieving couple I returned to the chapel, and began manoeuvring the trolley out. But I was stopped by a real undertaker who looked surprised to see me. 'Have you booked the chapel in advance?' he asked. 'Only we have a widow waiting to see her deceased husband. You'll have to wheel him in there and wait.'

He nodded to one of the side rooms. I sighed and reversed into the dark, small room with my late companion while they brought the lady in. At which point, I felt something feathery touch the back of my leg. It made me shiver. Turning to see what it was, I looked down at an open coffin containing a dead old woman lying in state, with a lily in her hands. They would have heard my scream in Manchester.

* * *

IT SEEMED AS THOUGH Derbyshire police couldn't quite decide where I was best placed. Everywhere they had tried so far was so removed from how I'd learned my coppering in London that my methods had jarred. After a year in the countryside, I was eventually released back into an area where there were real criminals – Alfreton, just south of Chesterfield.

Like Chesterfield, Alfreton is made up of a number of small villages that have never recovered from pit closures. There was mass unemployment in the area and high drug abuse, which added up to a high crime rate. But I was over the moon to get back amongst it. I didn't have a particularly subtle attitude to drugs back then. This would eventually change quite radically, but at the time they were druggy shitheads and I was The Enforcer. I spent as much of my working day as possible harassing them.

The beat that I was assigned to covered a small town called South Normanton which is just near junction 28 of the M1. There was quite a bad smack problem in the area at the time, and two of the main culprits were a father and son team called the Battersbys.

Battersby senior was a scrap metal dealer and a keen fan of cock-fighting, as well as being an informant for a local detective who was keen to protect him. Battersby junior was a nasty little bastard who was never to be found without his trusted Stanley knife. Between them, they controlled the drugs scene in South Normanton, and ran a little army of smackheads who would run around smashing the windows of anyone who crossed them.

The Battersbys' main enforcer was a male stripper called Silverman, who bullied his way around the area high on coke-induced paranoia. His stage name was 'The Vixen', much to our amusement; he wondered why we found it so funny, and eventually we pointed out to him that a vixen was a female fox. It was hardly a suitable name for a gangster of his repute.

I first came across The Vixen early one Sunday morning when I stopped a car that was four-up on the A38. We pulled the car over to the side of the road and checked it out on the police national computer, the PNC. An information marker flashed on the vehicle showing that it was connected to the Battersbys. So I wandered up to the driver's door and spoke to him, while my partner chatted with the other occupants. The driver was a big, stocky lad with shoulder-length hair, and he took quite an aggressive tone when I tried to speak to him.

Eventually, I said, 'Step out of the car, please.'

As he got out, I noticed that he was extremely tense. My warning bells were ringing, so I surreptitiously unclipped my CS canister and prepared it for use.

'There's a strong smell of cannabis smoke in this vehicle,' I said, 'so I'm going to search you.'

As I said that, he pushed me to one side and began rummaging for something in his trouser pocket. Assuming he was reaching for a weapon, I aimed the CS at his face and fired a two-second burst straight up his nose.

CS 'gas' is actually the agent mixed with a kind of glue, and it travels as a liquid jet so it's extremely accurate. My target fell to the ground and lay there, coughing and vomiting on the side of the road. I quickly handcuffed and searched him. I didn't find a thing, but my partner told me that as he had fallen he had thrown a package down the side of the embankment. We called a dog handler up, and a quick area search of the embankment revealed a one-ounce bag of amphetamine sulphate. That was a result. One gangster nicked for possession with intent to supply.

We carefully – but not *that* carefully – placed the guy in the back of our patrol car and drove him to the cells. Every couple of minutes he sneezed and sent a cloud of snot and tear gas into the car.

Eventually, it got so bad that I turned round to him. 'If you don't stop that,' I said, 'I'm going to stick your head out of the window and wind it up to your chin.'

He stopped.

And so began a stormy relationship between me and The Vixen. After this first brief encounter, I harassed him on every possible occasion; in turn, he complained about me to any copper who would listen.

As I said, Battersby senior was a grass for one of the movers and shakers in the local CID. As a result of this, any search warrants or operations against the Battersbys had to be seen by this officer. Coincidentally, I'm sure, nothing was ever found at their house, and whenever surveillance was authorised they acted like model citizens.

I'm not saying anything dodgy was going on – I have no idea. It's not unknown for CID lads to tip off sources, and it's technically wrong. But then, they use their sources to hook bigger fish. If their man knocks out a bit of gear now and then, but occasionally hands over someone higher up the chain, is that acceptable? I don't know. What I do know is that we don't live in a technical world. Policing is not, and never can be, black and white, despite the best efforts of some people in the courts, media and Parliament to pretend it is.

Anyway, the upshot was that we were getting nowhere with the Battersbys.

But the National Crime Squad (later merged by the Titanic Deckchair Management Co Ltd into the Serious Organised Crime Agency, itself about to be scrapped for the National Crime Agency) were a different matter, and unbeknown to us mere plods they had decided to mount an operation against them without liaising with the local CID. They had set cameras up opposite Battersby Senior's house, and over the following few months had filmed hundreds of drug deals taking place. When they executed a search warrant, they found several kilos of heroin buried in the rear garden.

Battersby's handler was furious, and so was Battersby. He was held on remand at Nottingham prison for a while, and took the not wholly-unexpected strategy of grassing for England in an attempt to reduce their expected sentences.

Father-and-son teams must have been in vogue around this time. Another duo living close by, Mick and Mitchell Greenwood, sold de-activated firearms to criminals from a disused egg-packing factory. Before 1995, firearms only needed to be de-activated by removing the firing pin and blocking the barrel. These were then sold to enthusiasts without the need for a firearms certificate, and were classed as safe. The Greenwoods – antique dealers by trade – flogged kits to re-activate the weapons, which included the likes of AK47s and Uzi submachine guns, to almost anyone who approached them. After a lengthy undercover operation, they were taken out and jailed for a long time, despite the fact that Mick had a heart condition and Mitchell had been born with cerebral palsy. In fact, Mick Greenwood died in prison.

The Battersbys had been loyal customers of these two, and had stockpiled a large arsenal of weapons in various stashes as an insurance policy. Now they drip-fed information to the police, who could recover firearms from their various caches; by the time they appeared before the judge, they had been responsible for recovering so many shooters that they were almost classed as heroes.

Both of the Battersbys went down for approximately five years, but with time spent on remand and time knocked off due to their talkative ways, they only did a couple before they were back out on the streets.

* * *

WHILE THE BATTERSBYS were away, The Vixen went into partnership with someone else. This new guy was a close associate of the Battersbys, and was a really ugly bastard, with the biggest set of teeth I have ever seen. I called him 'Plug'. He was quite a decent drug importer, and was also into ringing high-class motor vehicles. (Ringing is switching the identity from one vehicle, usually a write-off, to a stolen one of the same type.)

One day, a drug deal went badly wrong for Plug and he was robbed of his Subaru Impreza in broad daylight as he drove through Alfreton. He managed to escape by jumping out of the car before doing what any decent citizen would do in these circumstances – running to the police and reporting the robbery.

The National Crime Squad heard of this and managed to organise for the Subaru to be recovered, but before they handed the car back to a very grateful Plug they planted a tracking device on the vehicle.

On the first operation using this device, a surveillance team followed The Vixen and a local numpty over to Europe and watched as the numpty had thousands of ecstasy pills body-wrapped around him. The Crime Squad then followed the numpty back to Dover where the strike was called in. The lad was travelling on a motor bike and The Vixen was following. The Vixen's role was to be the numpty's minder but he stood back when the lad was challenged by customs officers. While the courier was nicked and held on remand, The Vixen was allowed to escape and stay at large for a short while. Just to see who and what else he led the Old Bill to.

A few weeks later, the local Drug Squad were searching the house owned by the lad's girlfriend when they found a letter he had written to be passed on to Plug in which he thanked him for the £200 reward he'd been paid for keeping quiet about Plug's involvement in the ecstasy job, but went on to say, politely, that it wasn't quite enough compensation for the years he was about to spend in prison. Could Plug possibly increase it to £300? The poor bastard.

The Crime Squad seemed to be enjoying the operation and continued with it. A few weeks later they arrested Plug and The Vixen as they were taking delivery of a large amount of cannabis resin near to Junction 28 of the M1. Things looked rather bleak for the intrepid pair as they were held on remand. But luck was on their side, and they were saved when an officer involved with the operation was himself arrested for drug-trafficking offences, and the Crown Prosecution Service dropped all charges against them.

***

SHORTLY AFTER PLUG'S lucky escape, Battersby junior was out of jail.

Being the type of bloke he was, he wasn't about to go on the straight and narrow and he was soon in business with Plug, and it wasn't long before they had another stroke of luck. This time, it was a bad one.

An undercover operation targeting drug dealers was being conducted in nearby Ripley, where Derbyshire Constabulary is based. Two undercover buyers had managed to infiltrate a local group of cannabis users and were taken to be introduced to their dealer, a man I'll call Shane. Shane was very unpleasant character, with rape, among other things, on his CV. He usually knocked out cannabis and amphetamine sulphate, but obviously he knew other dealers who supplied other types of drugs; the idea was to get him to make an introduction to someone who was pushing heroin.

The two buyers met him and they all got on quite well – well enough to build up a level of trust over a few weeks. Eventually, the lead officer casually asked Shane if he knew where he could get his hands on an ounce of heroin. Rather stupidly, he confirmed that he did, and agreed to put in a few calls. Within 24 hours, he rang back to say that the deal was all arranged for the following day. The two buyers picked him up in their car, which was fitted with hidden video cameras and microphones.

Under Shane's directions, they all drove out of town to a lonely dirt track where they plotted up to wait. And who should appear a short time later, but Battersby junior and Plug, who then proceeded to sell two complete strangers an ounce of heroin, unwittingly being caught on film for posterity.

Talk about stupid.

They were nicked and once more held on remand. Of course, this was professionally embarrassing for Shane, to say the least. In these circles, they often put two and two together and get completely the wrong number, and this all added up to him being a grass. So he packed his bags, said a tearful goodbye to his family and emigrated a full two miles down the road to Codnor, where he rented a one-bedroom flat and started dealing drugs again.

A couple of weeks later, I was asked to visit him to investigate a disturbance at his flat where he had ended up being rushed to hospital. I found him sitting in his grubby living room with a gloomy look on his face and both his legs in plaster.

'What happened to you, then?' I said, although it wasn't hard to guess.

'I heard a noise on the landing,' he said, and winced as he tried to move his left leg onto a box. 'I went out to see what it was and this big bloke wearing a ski mask punched me in the face and knocked me over. Then he smashed my fucking ankles with a sledgehammer.'

'Oh dear,' I said, in my best attempt at a sympathetic voice. 'Why on earth would anyone want to do that to a nice feller like you?'

'I think they must have got the wrong lad,' he said.

I nearly wet myself.

* * *

AT ONE STAGE, I had three outstanding complaints that The Vixen had made about me to Complaints and Discipline.

Known in some forces as the PSD (professional standards) and in the Met as the Directorate of Professional Standards, these are the internal, desk jockey police who watch the real police (though it's never been explained to me who watches them). They love nothing more than to do the legs of officers – particularly those who are close to retirement, because this means you don't get your pension and that saves the force money.

I'm not saying I was totally blame-free in this; I used to really enjoy winding The Vixen up by sitting on the bonnet of my patrol car outside his house for long periods, while he twitched the curtains and shouted abuse at me. It got to the stage where all I had to do was drive past him as he walked down the road and he would immediately ring up headquarters to moan. I was eventually called in by a senior Complaints and Discipline officer and served with a written warning that I was only to have contact with The Vixen if he was committing a serious arrestable offence in front of me – and I was the only officer available to deal.

I thought – and still think – that that was disgraceful. This was a serious and nasty villain. It is the *job* of the police to harass people like him.

The more you put yourself in the firing line, the more shit you attract. No-one complains about bobbies who sit in the nick pushing paper about all day. Still, I could have done more to avoid this grief.

As it was, I kept Complaints and Discipline quite busy. Late one Boxing Day, I was single-crewed in a patrol car in Alfreton while the rest of the section were pissing about with a drunk bloke who was threatening to jump off a six foot wall. A 999 call came in from a woman who said that she had just killed her baby. The only unit available other than me was a carrier-full of specials who were out taking beer off a group of kids, so I took the job and made my way to the woman's house. I knocked on the front door. No reply, so I walked round the back to the kitchen door where I saw a woman holding a kitchen knife, wearing a white dressing gown that was covered in blood. Fearing that her child was indeed dead, I called for back-up and kicked the kitchen door in.

'Put the knife down!' I shouted.

'Fuck off!' she shouted back.

So I gave her a two second blast of CS.

She fell to the ground and I rushed forward to handcuff her. As I got the cuffs on, I noticed that she had slashed her wrists. By this time, the specials had turned up, so I organised a search of the house for the dead child and called an ambulance.

There was no child in the house, and never had been. The poor woman was deranged.

But the following week I got a complaint over the use of excessive force by her 'caring' family – the same people who had left her alone, mentally ill and frightened, on Boxing Day.

Meanwhile, the rest of the section won a Divisional Commander's Commendation for stopping a drunk plummeting to his death off a garden wall. Sometimes there's no bloody justice.

The following week, while on patrol, I heard a shout for urgent assistance from two officers who were being threatened with a knife at Woolworths. I nearly broke my neck driving there, and, as I pulled up outside, I saw groups of hysterical shoppers and staff running out of the shop, screaming. As I forced my way through the crowd, I could hear a racket coming from the far end of the shop. I found a well-handled local scrote pacing up and down between racks of clothes, armed with a long kitchen knife. Two female officers, one at each end of the aisle, were holding their CS canisters out and asking the bloke to drop the knife. But he was having none of it, and was becoming more agitated by the second. Clearly, Cagney and Lacey's tactics weren't working, so I drew my extendable ASP, a metal bar used for smashing windows and, occasionally, hitting people. I raised it above my head and charged towards him, shouting, in the words of many a northern Dirty Harry, 'Let's stop fucking about!'

My first swing missed, and the ASP got tangled up in a load of women's clothing. But I wrestled it free and whacked him in the side of the head; momentarily stunned, he fell to the ground and the three of us pounced on him. We cuffed him and dragged him into the street, where he woke up enough to scream a torrent of abuse towards all the onlookers.

I swear that's exactly how it went down, and I defy you to explain how else to deal with a guy like that. But guess who was the only officer to receive a complaint? It never does to get paranoid, but I had a feeling that my card was marked. If things carried on like this, one day someone in an office on the fourth floor was going to decide I was more trouble than I was worth and cut me adrift.

Luckily, something came along before than could happen.

Chapter 5:

Proper Grafting

I DON'T KNOW WHETHER it was my propensity to hang around scum in general, but as I rampaged through Derbyshire from collar to complaint I somehow caught the eye of the Drug Squad.

In early 1997, when I was 35, I was tapped up by the head of the squad to see if I was interested in joining the Test Purchase Unit. This was a forerunner of the East Midlands Special Operations Unit, which would go on to become one of the best anti-drugs teams in the UK. (EMSOU itself was set up in around 2001, and featured officers from Derbyshire, Notts, Northants, Leicestershire and Lincolnshire. Its formation was a slow process which went on over a number of years, and – as with all things police – was very political, with much resistance.)

The DI wanted to know if I fancied working for the unit as a UC – an undercover cop in the losing war on class A drugs and their suppliers.

There is nothing in the slightest bit glamorous about this work. *Miami Vice* it is not.

What it is, is street grafting. You spend your shifts waiting to score on filthy corners in run-down suburbs in the pissing rain, or going into horrible crack houses, stepping through dirty needles and dogshit, to mix with skanky, hepatitis-ridden whores, borderline paranoid users, and various other people lacking in conspicuous morals, decency, and respect for themselves or anyone else.

Naturally, I jumped at the chance.

Not least because, as I've said, in those days I viewed myself as a bit of an Enforcer. The world was a much more one-dimensional place for me, then. Drugs were illegal, drug dealers and junkies were scum, and it was my job, as a policeman, to target them in any way that I could. It was as simple as that.

Over the next decade and a half, my view on drugs would change dramatically. Today, I bear little resemblance to the Pete Ashton who joined the Job. I no longer think that all drug users are lowlife. In the years that followed my first undercover job, I would get to know plenty of them a lot better than I had when I was just busting them for possession now and then. Many turned out to be ordinary folks, often holding down decent jobs, who just liked a little livener now and then. I was no different from those people myself – it was just that my drug of choice was strong continental lager. Not every heroin or coke user gets hooked – plenty can use it at weekends and hold down a normal job the rest of the week. Even most of those who were properly hooked were victims – weak and stupid, no doubt, but still victims.

As for the dealers, lots of them are nasty, violent, vicious people who deserve everything the law throws at them. But some are just supplying a need – a need that in my view has been created, or at least fuelled, by prohibition. Clearly, banning drugs hasn't stopped their proliferation. When I was a kid, the best you could do in my street was a packet of John Players Specials and a pint of Skol; now you can get whatever you want within five minutes' walk of my childhood home. The price of MDMA has come down over 20-odd years from £30 a pill to a quid, and Chinese chemists are developing a dozen new legal highs every week. All of which suggests that the 'War on Drugs' is not being won.

I'm not saying that drugs are a good thing. In a perfect world, some of them wouldn't exist. Crack, smack and amphet, when used heavily, are utterly incompatible with society, and they wreck bodies, minds, families, and communities. Speed should be a class A drug. I have seen the damage sulphate can do to people, especially when it's injected, as was common when I first transferred to Derbyshire. It did as much damage as heroin, with very little of the bad publicity.

But I really don't think there's all that much harm in cannabis, ecstasy and coke – in moderation, and if taken by adults. I know plenty of people, including police officers who were serving at the time, who have been regular coke users, and who regard cocaine as a clean drug, as long as it's obtained from a decent source and is not cheap rubbish. I've never taken it myself, and I never will – though only in case it's as good as I've been told it is – but I've taken E from time to time, and did so when I was in the police. Often, when infiltrating dealers, a pill would be offered and I would take it. If I were 10 years younger, and I'd been in my early 20s when the acid house scene kicked off in the late 1980s, I'm sure I'd have used E and charlie on a social basis. I've given up smoking, but if I still smoked I'm equally sure I'd smoke weed.

To buy drugs as a UC, I needed to make some changes. You have to think like a junkie, look like a junkie, and smell like a junkie.

The first thing I had to do was grow my hair and stop washing. UC work is not a role you can perform wearing a short back-and-sides and the latest Pringle sweater.

Then I needed a 'legend', or cover story to explain my background and how it is that I'd suddenly popped up from nowhere on a given estate. It's no good creating a new one out of whole cloth, because in moments of stress you'll slip up and tell the wrong lie, and that could have very serious consequences. You need to remember it, and to believe in it yourself, which means painting in actual detail about yourself on the broader canvas. This was the post ecstasy/Thatcher period, when drugs and the Public Order Act of 1986 had combined to knock the stuffing out of the various football firms, so my early legend was that of 'Pete' – you tend to use your real first name – a football hooligan a bit down on his luck, travelling around, buying and selling a bit of this and that, and generally ducking and diving. This was a credible back story and one I could wax lyrical about if questioned. Pretty much everyone I knew outside the Job were football hooligans, and there were plenty of guys like that knocking around at that stage.

I went for a circa 1986 Paul Heaton/Housemartins hairstyle, which was long enough to look unkempt and greasy, and the 'casual' era uniform of Timberland, Stone Island, and Lacoste gear – but a bit old and tatty to show that I was down on my arse. I built my background as originating from the Stockport area, which explained my north-west accent while removing me from Preston. You absolutely do not want these people knowing where you're really from. That can get very nasty indeed.

I needed to be fully conversant with drugs, too. I knew a bit about the field from my time in uniform, but street names, prices, and just general banter differ from area to area so I had a fair bit of learning to do. You can't just blunder into a heroin gang – you have to understand how they operate, and to talk like you're from the streets.

That said, of all the targets a UC can get involved with, drugs are probably the easiest.

It's commercial, rather than ideological – as long as you don't smell of bacon, nobody cares too much about where you're from and what you believe. The political and anarchist arenas are different, and for that reason the very best cops are usually weirdly sympathetic to the people they're turning over. It really helps to know your subject inside out, because it minimises the amount of fake stuff you have to carry around in your head. If you're infiltrating the far right, for instance, it's much easier if you have a working knowledge of the internecine strife in their politics and you've listened to a bit of Skrewdriver and Weisse Wölfe. If you're doing the far left, you need to know your Leninists from your Marxists, to like The Redskins, and to be able to recite the history of the Socialist Workers Party. This book is about my UC drugs career, but years later I trained with the National Public Order Intelligence Unit to go undercover with animal rights fanatics, and most of the other students on the course were hard-core vegetarians (I never quite fitted in, being a fan of the Big Mac). They didn't look or seem to me like police officers at all, and *I* knew that was what they were; I suppose that's the point.

Living the junkie life would often lead to me not shaving or washing my clothes for weeks on end, much to the embarrassment and dismay of my close family. I remember dropping my son Sean off at school before I went onto a job one morning. He was only about eight at the time and there was a parents' assembly that day. He looked up at me with his big eyes and said, 'Dad, would you mind not coming in with me?'

'Why, son?'

'Because you smell funny.'

One thing I soon learned was that the job was done with little or no back-up. Operatives could be deployed for months on end, away from their families, and buyers have to be a certain type to cope with that. Most of them have quirky or strange characteristics that make them different from normal cops, and credibility is king. It can literally be the difference between life and death – or certainly a good result and a good kicking.

Perhaps the best drugs UC I've ever come across was a Cornish lad called Shabby, who I went on to work with a lot over the years. He was mistrusted by a lot of cops, because of his appearance and style, and he wouldn't have made a conventional policeman as long as he had a hole in his arse. But nobody could touch him when it came to drugs buying. He'd been a student in Manchester during the Hacienda days of the 1990s, and he loved the dance scene, and had an intimate understanding of the drug scene that went along with it. He fitted straight into any drug scenario and was instantly credible. He was also very quick on his feet. On one famous occasion, he was on his day off when the police received a report of a suspicious youth picking magic mushrooms in a field. It has been against the law to possess them since 2005, when the government made them a class A drug, so they sent a car. When they turned up they found Shabby with a carrier bag-full of the mind-bending little fungi. (Obviously, I have no idea what he wanted them for... props, perhaps.) He saw the patrol vehicle pull up and a copper get out, and quick as a flash he walked over to the plod, handed him the bag of mushrooms, and said, 'Thank God you're here, officer. I've just been picking these to stop the local kids getting hold of them. You've saved me a trip to the station – can I hand them over to you now?'

Another good buyer I came across was a Sheffield lad called Lee. He loved going to Jamaica on holiday, where he refused to exchange money at banks and would instead meet Yardies down by the docks to get a better exchange rate. He also spoke fluent Spanish; on his wedding day, he took his wife onto the dance floor, while he was still sober, and sang a love song to her in Spanish in front of all the guests. A strange but talented man. The weirdest thing about him was that he passionately disliked all things connected with the police.

Before a likely candidate was let loose out on the streets, he or she had to undergo a five-day Test Purchase Course. This crammed in all the case law, rules and regulations that govern this type of work, as well as a number of exercises where students were assessed by the instructors.

There were eight students on my course from various units around the force area, and the instructors were undercover officers who had been at the game for years. The first day had the usual ice-breakers and tests from the pre-read literature, and then lectures covering street awareness and drugs talks.

On the first evening we had a confidence test in a busy pub. The students had to approach a stranger, who was an undercover officer from London, and engage him in conversation, gleaning as much information from him as possible about his personal life. I couldn't help thinking that in real life you would have been told to fuck off, or worse, but the idea was sound: has this lad got the confidence and ability to approach scary-looking strangers and win them over? After all, that's a big part of the job.

The following day we had more lectures from the CPS on the perils of acting as *agents provocateur*, and other pitfalls. Students were plucked out of class and taken to a room where they were briefed on a scenario: 'Through that door is a flat with a drug dealer in it. We want you to do a cold call and buy a gramme of heroin off him.'

The student would then walk into the role-play, totally unprepared, with invariably hilarious results which were filmed on CCTV. Piss-taking in the evening was a key part of the course, and we were encouraged to drink to excess so that the instructors could assess our behaviour while intoxicated. There's no point in employing an undercover buyer who is prone to fighting or dicking around when he's had a few.

It occurred to me about halfway through one of these nights in the pub, as I chucked another pint of piss paid for by the chief constable down my neck, that I might just have stumbled on the perfect job.

Of course, the role-plays the following day had the added complication of operating with a stinking hangover – another piece of realism. We were faced by street buying and crack house scenarios and the instructors had a great time scaring the shit out of us. Sometimes they'd pull a knife or a shotgun, or even try to get the poor trainee into bed. It wasn't unusual to see students in tears during the subsequent debriefs.

On the last day, each of us delivered a five-minute lecture on a particular piece of complex legislation. and then had to handle questions.

On the Friday afternoon I was told that I had passed the course. I went back to my day job, eagerly awaiting my first deployment.

* * *

AROUND THREE WEEKS later, I got the call to a briefing at Derbyshire police HQ.

It was a freezing Thursday night in February when I met my handler on this job, and many others in the future. He was a big guy called Jazz who had been one of the instructors on my course, and he and I would work together, on and off, for the rest of my career.

Handlers are experienced detectives who have either been buyers or level one UCs themselves, or have successfully completed a national undercover course as an observer with this role in mind. Their job is to look after the interests of the UC before, during, and after a deployment. A decent handler is the buffer zone between the UC and the operational team, particularly the Senior Investigating Officer (SIO). A UC is really just a gun for hire, a resource to be called upon by detectives in a given area to help them crack their harder cases. The SIO, usually a local Detective Inspector, is in charge of the whole operation. Some SIOs have a good understanding of what is and is not possible, and how long it will take to achieve. Some don't – usually those looking to make a name for themselves with a quick spell as a DI before a promotion back into uniform and another rung on the ladder to the top. Jazz kept the good ones in the loop, and the crap ones at bay.

The handler's job is also to give advice on tactics, the law as it relates to the use and deployment of UCs, and generally to look after the buyer whilst he (they are mostly all men, for reasons I'll explain later) is deployed. This ranges from retaining the UC's personal mobile and other effects when he or she is deployed, to dealing with the mundane stuff of daily life that you would normally handle yourself. If the phone rang and it was my mates arranging to meet up for a pint at the weekend, Jazz would answer it and take a message; if a radiator at home sprung a leak, or Carmel's car broke down, Jazz would sort out the plumber or the RAC. The idea is to let the UC concentrate on the job in hand.

He was, and is, a great man – a larger-than-life character who could charm the hind legs off a donkey. On his days off, he was a keen scooter boy and northern soul fan, who also liked sailing. At work, he was a highly professional and competent police officer, and a man I would – and did – trust with my life.

He had worked as a detective sergeant on one of the regional crime squads, and when they were disbanded he served with the National Crime Squad. NCS only dealt with major and organised crime – large-scale drug trafficking, gangland hits, arms dealing, money laundering, kidnapping and the like. So he was a serious operator. In the 1970s and 1980s, he had sometimes flown by the seat of his pants, and on more than one occasion he was invited into the Crown Court chambers for a private bollocking off a judge.

He had pioneered drugs buying whilst part of Derbyshire's HQ Drug Squad, and had a big hand in setting up EMSOU in 2001.

I met him for the first time that Thursday. After introducing himself, he said, 'Let's go and meet the SIO and the other buyers, and then we'll do the read-through of the ACPO guidelines to you.'

These guidelines dealt with what we could and couldn't do while deployed: they were a polite way of saying, if you screw up you're on your own.

'OK Jazz, no problems.'

He smiled. 'Nervous?'

'Me? Fuck, no!'

Jazz gave me a look that I grew to know, which meant, 'You tell even bigger lies than I do. 'But he just laughed, and said, 'What can possibly go wrong?'

He didn't know me too well at that stage, of course.

I was then led down a maze of corridors until we entered a cramped little office housing the HQ Drug Squad. There I met the three other UCs, a rag-tag collection of veteran buyers who warmly welcomed the new boy into their midst. I'd hardly sat down when the SIO entered the room like a whirlwind, dressed in a cream Macintosh and frantically smoothing down his Bobby Charlton sweep-over. To me, he looked, sounded, and acted like a complete nutcase, and when I ended up working for him a few years later I quickly realised that my initial diagnosis had been correct. Let's just say that he was one of the great British eccentrics. But he was also one of the best coppers I have ever worked for or with, totally committed to locking up criminals. (He was recently awarded the Queens Police Medal, and not for polishing a seat or his diversity credentials.)

'Facking take a facking seat, lads,' he said, in broad Southernese. 'And let's have a facking look at this.'

I'm not exactly a prude, and at times my language can be a bit choice, but the SIO sounded like he had Tourette's. We sat down and someone turned a telly on. Immediately, some grainy footage flickered into life. It showed the front door of a pub.

'This is the front facking entrance of the Normanton Hotel,' said the SIO. 'You probably know that it's in the centre of Derby's Asian and West Indian area, and is popular with the facking Yardies. Those cants are using it as a base to deal from. Local CID have had covert observation posts set up above a kebab shop at the front and a private house at the rear, to film the rear car park, for the last four weeks. This is what they've come up with.'

He led us through the video footage of local Yardies dealing crack cocaine and heroin to long lines of punters around the boozer.

'Facking listen in, lads,' he said, bubbling with enthusiasm. 'These fackers will sell gear to *any* facker… They'd even sell it to me if I grew a facking goatee beard and had my nose facking pierced.'

His off-the-wall briefing went on for about an hour, as he bombarded us with names of targets, known vehicles, and areas to avoid. He finished by saying, 'Right, that's it. I want you fackers to deploy at half hour intervals so as to give the last buyer time to fack off before the next facker arrives. You must only score where we are videoing, or else it's a waste of time and facking money and NO FACKER goes inside the facking boozer. If you do, I will be right in behind you, and I won't be very facking happy, because it will blow the job out, and what's more the landlord's a cant and he won't serve me anymore!'

I very much doubted he frequented this particular boozer, but I took his point. The local CID had built up a good intelligence picture of the main dealers. Now it was up to us to box them off.

As my first job, it was – as you might expect – a much smaller affair than others I was later to get involved in. On bigger ops, covert premises were hired, usually a factory unit or suite of offices rented under a bogus company name, within a 10-mile radius of the plot. A large team would be based there – the SIO, an intelligence officer to collate and make available the latest intel on any of the main suspects, an exhibits officer to package the bought drugs, a technical officer responsible for all the covert recording equipment, a liaison officer whose job it was to listen in to any live bugs, in case you needed rescuing, a four man back-up team to carry out that rescue if required, a DS to oversee them and maybe one or two other interested bods. Jobs could take months in the planning, and the UC might be on the plot for several weeks before even attempting to score from the main targets.

This was not one of those jobs. As he wrapped up, the SIO said, 'Well…? What are you facking waiting for? Let's get out there and nail these bastards!'

That was a lot quicker than I had been expecting.

'Get a taxi from the city centre to the hotel,' said Jazz, as we headed out of the room. 'We're looking for crack from one of the dealers. You need to make sure it goes down as near to the doorway as possible so it's captured on video.'

It was a very nervous Pete Ashton who was dropped off later that evening with an hour to kill before I was due at the Normanton. The plan was to send four buyers in. The other three were all Nottinghamshire lads who had been doing this type of work for a few years.

I decided that I needed a bit of Dutch courage, so I nipped into a local boozer for a few pints. An hour later, I jumped into a taxi outside Derby bus station and asked the driver to take me to the Normanton Hotel.

'Alright, pal,' he said, looking at me with narrowed eyes. 'That'll be three quid, please.'

You know you're going somewhere dodgy when cabbies ask for their money up front.

As I sat in the back of that car, I felt like I was hyperventilating. I'd never been so fucking nervous in my life, and I include those times in the Falklands when I'd thought the Argie special forces were about to freefall onto my position and slit my throat. The streets outside were a blur of lights, people huddling in doorways against the cold and passing traffic: all I could think of was getting in there, buying my rock and getting out, without being stabbed in the process.

As always, when you're dreading arriving somewhere, the journey ended all too soon. The cab pulled up outside the Normanton, and as I got out I saw that there was a Rastafarian stood in the door way. Buoyed by several pints of Stella, I grabbed the bull by the horns and approached him.

'Can you sort me out with a rock, mate?'

The Rasta looked down his nose at me and grinned. 'Wait here, my friend,' he said, and disappeared into the boozer. A few minutes later he returned, and handed me a small Clingfilm wrap with a pea-sized crystal inside. I gave him twenty quid which he palmed straight into his pocket.

The weight lifted from my shoulders. *Was that all there was to it?*

I relaxed and felt my confidence growing, and decided to stand and have a chat with the guy for a few minutes.

'Are you going to stay for a smoke, my friend?' he said.

'I'd love to, mate,' I said. 'But I can't. Me woman's waiting for me to get back with the gear… If she sees I've smoked some already, she'll hit the fucking roof.'

He chuckled and nodded. 'I've never seen you around before. Where you from?'

I fell back onto my legend. 'I'm from up north,' I said. 'I've only been down here about a month. I'm working on the new football ground they're building. I'm shacked up with my bird in Spondon.'

'No problems,' he said. 'Listen, my name's Leroy. If ever you need to score again just come down here and ask for me. I serve up 24/7.'

I said my farewells and made my way back to base.

Each time you score as a buyer, you return to the covert premises and go down a hypothetical circular conveyer belt until you come out of the other side, ready to deploy again.

The first thing you do is place the drugs in an exhibit bag, sign and seal them, and hand them over to the exhibits officer. He or she documents them, and hands them on to an officer responsible for taking them directly for analysis – in those days by the now-defunct Forensic Science Service – to establish whether or not they are real drugs.

This is essential, for two obvious reasons.

The first is evidential: is it crack, and if so how much cocaine does it contain? Purity and weights differ from dealer to dealer, area to area, and time to time. It's usually around 25% pure, though purity never really concerned me out on the street. It was either banging gear or shit gear; any talk of 'purity' would raise suspicion from the people I was mixing with. One thing you could guarantee is that you would get less than you had paid for. Let's say a rock was a 'twenty', supposed to weigh 0.2g: it would always be less that than when bought directly from a street dealer, and even less again if another junkie had bought it for you, because they would skim a bit before handing it over (and then they would usually expect another 'official' smoke for sorting you out in the first place).

The second reason for the analysis is security: before you deploy again, you need to be sure you haven't been skanked. Rip-offs are obviously not unknown in this world, and it's important for credibility that you react as a junkie would if he'd gone home and tried to snort brick dust. It takes time to get an official report, so if you need to go out again before the formal result is returned, the resident Drug Squad officer can field-test the exhibit, though only for intelligence purposes and to allow the UC to re-deploy.

The conveyer belt process in full is: briefing; ACPO guidelines; issuing of drugs money; collection of props such as a small amount of cannabis or a crack pipe (usually something like a small pill bottle, with a tube sticking out of the side and gauze over the opening of the bottle, on which where the crack is placed) and any covert technical equipment; deployment; return with exhibit; debrief; pocket book and statements. At times during bigger and busier jobs in the future, I would go through this process many times a day.

I actually found myself quite liking Leroy – probably because he had served me up rather than tried to stab me on my first deployment, but also because he had that laid back, likeable West Indian way about him. It wasn't just me who felt like that; at the debrief, I got talking to a female officer who had been manning the OP above the kebab house. 'When I saw Leroy dealing to you all I almost wanted to shout out of the window at him not to do it,' she said. 'I've known the daft bastard for years and I've actually got a real soft spot for him.'

It was an early introduction to one of the issues inherent in undercover work – the possibility of getting too close to the subjects.

In every force in the land, female officers have fallen for the bad boys they're supposed to be nicking, and have ended up having to leave the Job. In undercover work, you can obviously get very close to your targets. This is more of an issue for cops working on political and protest movements. As I've said, their sympathies often tend towards the people they are working on, and it's not at all unheard of for them to 'go over the side.' The most famous case is that of Mark Kennedy, who infiltrated climate change protestors and other groups over a period of several years. Kennedy, a Met UC who started out in drugs buying before moving into the political arena, had affairs with at least two of the women he was supposedly investigating, and was only uncovered when one of them found a passport in his real name among his personal effects. It's hard to imagine how he got so sloppy as to leave that lying around, but it's almost impossible to keep your game face on all day, every day. His unmasking led to the abandonment of a major trial, and to all sorts of panic and recriminations in the undercover world.

In drugs work, at least there wasn't much chance of falling for one of the targets. You can have free sex every day – if skanky street hookers are your thing. But the actual world of importing, wholesaling and retailing drugs is an almost entirely male environment. Women don't tend to get involved in either selling or buying at any serious level, so there's no point sending in female UCs on their own – it would just look weird. The female UCs – and there are obviously some very good ones out there – are usually used as the male officer's 'girlfriend'. In the early days, especially, when bag cameras were more common, a woman carrying a bag aroused less suspicion than a man. Additionally, for some reason a couple arouses less suspicion than a lone male; and if the woman is good-looking (and they usually tapped up the prettiest WPCs for the job for this reason) she can also work as eye-candy to distract the dealers.

Anyway, much as I liked Leroy's easy manner, I didn't feel bad about helping to nail him and his mates. In fact, I never had any problem befriending and then 'betraying' anyone – I never felt any remorse or regret. Mostly, this was because I worked on the nasty shite end of the market, but even with the likes of Leroy I was always too busy enjoying the buzz of the chase to worry about it. And I never lost sight of which side I was on.

Of course, you don't stand out the front of a shitty hotel in Derby on a perishing Thursday if you're a serious player. Leroy was only a pawn in the game, to be used and abused by those higher up in the trade. One of his roles was to act as a mule; some years later, while he was flying from Jamaica to Heathrow with a stomach full of cocaine-packed condoms, one of them burst and he became ill. The plane re-routed to Miami but he was dead on arrival. I was a little bit sad when I heard about that. It's no way for anyone to go.

But back on that night, he was the man who had dealt me my first score. After a few minutes, we shook hands and I walked through the terraced streets to where the back-up team was due to pick me up, with a head the size of Salford. I was grinning from ear to ear, wanting to tell the world what a shit-hot buyer I was: it was like I had conquered Mount Everest. The buzz that I got from buying that little lump of cooked coke and baking soda stayed with me for years.

The Normanton Hotel job came to an abrupt end for me when I turned up to score one night and a dealer who had previously sold to me blanked me.

When I pressed him, he replied, 'Just fuck off back to the police station.'

Being young and naïve, I was mystified as to how we'd been blown. I later discovered that a local officer had told his main informant not to deal drugs to strangers outside the Normanton, as they were police. This is a constant background issue when you are running undercover ops, ostensibly unbeknown to the bobbies working the area day-to-day.

There is some outright corruption, obviously, where local cops have been recruited by criminal elements through bribery, or perhaps blackmail, but this is rare. There is a slightly greyer area, where lads have grown up with each other: one joins the police, the other becomes a drug dealer. The officer might be as dedicated and honest as they come, generally, but then he overhears something and decides to help his mate out, for old time's sake. (This is why, for a long time, some forces had very strict rules against people policing their home area, and looked hard into the background and connections of all potential recruits before taking them on. These rules have been relaxed in recent years, which in my view is a very bad thing.) And then there are the detectives, who rely on informants to pass on the titbits and scraps of intelligence which help them to clear up crime in their area. This is the lifeblood of basic CID work, and unsurprisingly, they are not keen to see their snouts taken out of circulation. In a way, it's even reflected in official policy: you help the police, you get a reduced sentence at court. Over the years, a few CID lads have brought it back a stage, so their men never got to court in the first place.

As I was to find out, we'd be fighting a constant battle to ensure that cops who weren't involved in our operations didn't somehow get to know about them. Over the next few years, once EMSOU was formed, a system was put in place to cover undercover operations. Officers involved in the running and planning of these jobs were made to sign a legally-binding document that forbade them from discussing the operation with anyone not involved, and they were officially placed on a 'confidential operation' as a cover for their absence from their usual place of work so as not to raise any suspicions back there.

From our point of view, obviously, it didn't matter how or why the shite heard about what we were up to; it just spelled death to our work. More to the point, the whole experience had brought me down to earth with a bump. I suddenly saw how quickly this type of thing could go wrong, and it wasn't a huge leap to imagine what might happen if you were behind locked doors with some of these people, and they had been tipped off that you were Old Bill.

But, despite this obvious risk, I was already hungry for more. I loved the challenge and excitement that this kind of work brought: it beat anything I'd done in uniform, TSG included.

Over the next few years buying became just about the most important thing in my life, after my family. And my family found out that sometimes even they had to come second to my undercover work.

* * *

IMMEDIATELY BEFORE ANY deployment, the full team would meet for a briefing to outline the day's objective. The intelligence officer would read out any recent information relating to the job or the targets. These sessions were open forums: each member of the team was encouraged to offer suggestions as to how to gain the best results. At the end of the briefing, the UC would go into a separate room to be issued with his drug money and expenses, and to be instructed formally on his day's objectives by the SIO. On each occasion, the UC would sign an APCO contract underwriting the official rules governing undercover work. These effectively say that UC must not act as an *agent provocateur* – in other words, while it is not illegal for him to join an existing conspiracy he must not incite or procure a person to commit an offence that he would not normally have committed.

Then the UC would pick up any covert recording equipment that might be required. This stuff comes in all shapes and sizes, and it's a lot better now than it was. We had vehicles that were wired for sound and video, with multiple cameras recording the front and back seats and feeding through into a recorder stowed under the spare wheel. A casual observer had no hope of spotting the lenses – I knew they were there and even I couldn't see them half the time. We carried bag cameras – literally, a video camera in a bag, not the classiest piece of kit and something that made me feel vulnerable to discovery – and body cameras powered by batteries taped to the small of your back, with on/off switches on cables sewn into your jeans pocket. And we had attachments for recording phone calls, and 'smart phones' which came in a few years later.

The latter looked like a standard mobile, but was actually a radio transmitter – it was on permanent 'send' with someone back at base tasked with listening in – and was important for both evidential and safety purposes. We were not always deployed with them. The use of all body-worn covert recording devices was strictly risk-assessed, and they were only used when we were going after specific targets and we felt that the dealer was comfortable with the buyer; additionally, we also needed a proper mobile, a job phone to call the dealers on, and having two 'mobiles' in your pocket looked a bit suspicious. Junkies normally spend every available penny on smack, and don't have a pot to piss in, never mind a brace of Nokias. So they were only handed out at crucial points on big investigations, when the risk of raising eyebrows, or the risk to the UC, was outweighed by the evidence they could generate. Whenever you had a smart phone, the liaison officer would be tuned into it in case things turned violent – a very real possibility with some of our targets. (Of course, it was also a 'spy-in-the-cab'. You never knew who was listening to you back at the covert premises, and lots of the older buyers like me, who had operated without them for years, hated them for this reason. The law is black and white, especially with regards to UC work, but out on the street it was anything *but* black and white, and sometimes jobs had to be helped along a little, in ways I'll come to later.)

On some ops, the operations team* would dream up a codeword that the UC could say to initiate a rescue by the back-up team. On one job, for reasons known only to themselves, they came up with 'Bookstand'. I'm not even sure that's a proper word, and even if it is I don't know how you're supposed to slip it in during a drugs buy. Throughout the job I had difficulty in remembering it; whenever I tried, for some reason I would come up with the word 'coat-hook'.

I imagined being in a crack house with a shotgun aimed at me and stuttering, 'Nice coat-hook you've got there... My mum used to have a coat-hook just like it... She got it from a market stall that specialised in selling *COAT-HOOKS*.'

Meanwhile, the liaison officer and back-up team would be listening with puzzled expressions, saying, 'Do you think he means "bookstand"?' before shrugging and putting the kettle on.

At the back of my mind, I always thought that if I needed rescuing I'd make it clear without the use of anything fancy like that, anyway – probably by shouting something like, 'Aaaarrrggghhhhh! Fucking help!'

But bearing in mind that I may need these blokes to save my bacon from time to time, I decided to take it all as seriously as I could.

The last, vital thing to do before setting out was to get rid of anything that contained your true identity or indicated that you were a cop. Mark Kennedy can tell you what happens if your passport is found; wallets, cash cards, personal mobiles – they all had to be left behind in the care of the handler. New UCs were thoroughly searched before setting off, in case they were patted down on the streets by dealers. I devised my own plan to discourage them from checking down my underpants. I just wore the same pair for every deal, and after a few months no-one went anywhere near them.

* * *

EVERY UC HAS to cut his teeth on little jobs, usually aimed at recreational drugs, before getting involved in long-term infiltration work. The idea is that you prove your worth on smaller fry before getting in with really dangerous, hardcore scum.

I was sent to Sandiacre, a little town about half a mile off the M1 near Derby. The targets were a couple – I'll call them Dave and Sandra – who were dealing cannabis and amphet on a small scale from their home. The idea was I'd cold-call their house and buy a small quantity of dope.

'This'll be nice and easy,' I thought, as I set out on a Friday lunchtime to get to know the area. After a quick scoot round the town, I ambled up to the dealers' door and gave it a tap. I was met by a clinically obese woman in her mid-20s with a skinny little kid attached to one of her legs. Sandra, I presumed. No point in fucking about. 'Alright, love,' I said, trying to strike exactly the right note of shiftiness. 'Can you sort me out with a G of blow?'

She raised her eyebrows. 'What?'

'Cannabis, love. I want a gramme of cannabis.'

'I know what fucking blow is, love,' she said. 'What I'm asking is, who told you to come here?'

'A bloke in the boozer said you could sort me out.'

'Fuck off.'

The door was slammed in my face. As it turns out, cold-calling *isn't* easy – whether you're selling insurance or buying drugs. (Nowadays, it's really only used at shit-or-bust moments, but in the 1990s it was still a common tactic.) Disappointed, I dawdled off up the road to the pre-arranged pick up point. At the debrief we decided that we should try again the following Friday, but using a slightly different approach.

'Why don't you double up with Kenty and have a few beers somewhere first?' said the SIO. 'You'll hopefully meet up with some locals who can make an introduction.'

Kenty was a mate of mine, an ex-Met body-builder who would sadly die some years later when he crashed his car on the A38 just outside Derby early one morning. The church was rammed – he was one of those kinds of blokes.

We decided to plot up in the Alexander Club, in those days a grotty working men's club frequented by the local lowlife. We got stuck into the Carling Black Label and had a look round. A group of druggies were playing pool, so we wandered over and put our names on the board. Two hours and a dozen pints later, we were shit-faced, we'd lost a lot of games of pool, and we had been told to fuck off by the druggies when we'd clumsily tried getting them to score for us. We had also spent all our expenses. But we were undeterred.

'Let's have a fucking go ourselves, eh, Pete?' said Kenty.

So we staggered up the road and I stopped behind the dealers' garden wall for a much-needed slash while Kenty knocked on the front door. As I opened the garden gate, I saw Kenty slurring away to a small, skinny bloke, who turned out to be Dave, the fat lass's other half. But their opening exchanges were disturbed by a loud clatter and a curse as I fell headlong over a dustbin that was in the middle of the garden path. I landed just a few feet away from them.

Dave stepped over and helped me to my feet, laughing. 'Fuck me,' he said. 'You've had a good day, mate!'

At this very moment, his other half waddled out. 'You need to get rid of them fuckers!' she said.

'They're only after some gear,' he said. 'We can sort them out.'

He had clearly taken a liking to us, but his wife's antennae were more sensitive. 'We don't know who the fuck they are,' she said. 'They could be coppers, for all we know. Come in, and shut the fucking door.'

'Coppers?' said Dave, with an incredulous grin. 'They ain't fucking coppers. *Look* at them. They're pissed out their faces. Coppers can't drink on duty, can they?'

The big lady looked at us, armed folded. Kenty was leaning against the door frame with his head, and I was on the path in a mess of chip papers and empty beer cans. She softened. 'I didn't think of that,' she said. 'You'd better come in then, lads.'

We followed the dynamic duo through their kitchen, was piled with unwashed plates and take-away cartons, into the living room. A bucket bong sat in the corner, and used syringes were scattered on the floor among children's toys. Two scrawny kids aged about three or four were sitting, blank-eyed, on the settee watching television. Things like that helped me understand why I was doing what I was doing.

'What you after then, lads?' said Dave.

'Any chance we can get a quarter?' said Kenty.

Dave dug in his pocket and pulled out a block of cannabis resin, about four ounces or so, wrapped in Clingfilm. He opened a drawer and pulled out a blue velvet box containing a set of brass scales. He put the resin and the scales on top of the television, cut a small lump from the main block using tin snips and placed it on the scales. He snipped off a few more bits of resin until he was satisfied that we had a quarter of an ounce; then he wrapped that up in a new piece of Clingfilm and handed it to Kenty, who passed him twenty quid in return.

We nodded to the wife and kids and weaved our way back to the front door, trying to avoid sticking ourselves on any of the needles.

'Come back anytime if you want a smoke,' said Dave at the front door. 'Or if you want any whiz. Thirty pound a gramme for base, a tenner a gramme for cut.'

'Whiz' is amphetamine sulphate, or speed; 'base' is a purer version, and 'cut' is base speed chopped up with bulking agents to make it go further.

'Nice one,' I said, shaking his hand.

He shut the door, and we staggered off for a debrief.

Over the next few weeks, we scored resin and base frequently from skinny Dave and his fat missus, letting them get themselves deeper and deeper in.

Eventually, the decision was made to nick them and turn over their house. Kenty and I knocked on the door and the fat lady answered. 'Got any blow, Sandra?' I said.

'I'm sorry, love,' she said, looking up and down the empty street. 'I'm out at the minute. But I've got a nine bar on its way so if you come back in a couple of hours I'll be able to sort you out, like.'

A 'nine bar' was a nine-ounce lump of cannabis resin: if we recovered that, it would be excellent evidence of dealing.

'Alright, love,' I said. 'We'll see you in a bit, then.'

We left and reported this intel to the DS who was running the op. He was champing at the bit to execute the search warrant.

'If we just hold fire for an hour or so we'll get them with a bit of weight,' I said.

But he insisted on going straight ahead, to avoid paying his team overtime. The raid found no drugs apart from a bit of resin stuck on the tin snips. Dave and Sandra denied dealing for financial gain, and said that they passed small amounts on to close friends whenever they had some in. At court they were given community service orders because the judge believed their version of events. If the operational team had waited as I'd asked they would have recovered a decent amount of gear and things would have been very different for Dave and his tubby lover.

* * *

WE HAD A FEW cock-ups in the early days. One weekend I was off duty at home when I got a phone call telling me to get to HQ Drug Squad as soon as possible for an urgent job. The target was a guy called Waitey, a very scary second-generation Jamaican and a well-known drug dealer who had given the Derby Drug Squad the run-around for many years. He lived the high life – lots of bling and designer clothes, top of the range cars, and beautiful women hanging off him. He was once spotted in the sauna at a Derby health club surrounded by his cohorts while one of them held a mobile phone to his ear for him to speak into, like something out of *The Godfather*. But he was extremely switched on, and although his activities were well-known that's a different matter from proving them to a jury.

He had jetted off to the West Indies on holiday, and had handed his mobile phone – and thus his business – over to a young lad called Vinney. This was something of a leap of faith, as Vinney was quite new to the game, and a bit soft. Before leaving, Waitey gave his protégé clear instructions: do not sell any gear to strangers, as they are more than likely to be cops. That was sound advice, but what neither man knew was that one of Waitey's existing regulars was a police informant.

After dealing with Vinney, the informant called his Drug Squad handler to fill him in, and a job was quickly put together by a DS called Jim Skinner. Jim was the epitome of the quiet dog that bites – a man of few words who was big into kick-boxing, and very well respected, both as a firearms officer and a thief-taker. Sadly, he passed away a few years ago after he fell sick on a firearms exercise and was found to be absolutely riddled with cancer. Another sad loss.

This might be their 'in' to Waitey. If they could turn Vinney over, maybe that would lead them to the big man? Jim and a Drug Squad buyer called Nick hatched a plan which involved Nick ringing Vinney and pretending that he was a regular customer: 'Hello mate… Who's that? Where's Waitey? Oh, is he? Well, I need to score…'

Vinney took the bait, and twice sold Nick some crack. On the third occasion, he engaged Nick in conversation as they were sitting in a car. 'So how long have you been scoring off Waitey, then?'

Nick was taken off guard, and just blurted out the truth. 'I've never scored off him.'

Vinney sat bolt upright in his car. 'I thought you said you was a regular customer of Waitey's?'

Nick, thinking on his feet, said, 'No I said my *mate* was a regular of Waitey's.'

Vinney, probably starting to feel quite ill, said, 'Fuck this. Before I sell to you again you'd better bring your mate out.'

'Yeah, sure,' said Nick. 'No dramas.'

Hence the phone ringing in my kitchen.

I changed into my greasy, filthy buying gear – which was kept in a bin bag in the garage – and headed down. The DI met me with his usual scowl and a wrinkled-up nose. 'Christ,' he said. 'You don't half stink.'

I took my brief and went with Nick to Gregory's Pub in Spondon where we put the call in. Vinney was very hesitant when he realised that it was Nick on the phone, but appeared an hour or so later and

I was introduced to him. He asked me a couple of simple questions to test my legend, and seemed physically relieved. He smiled, served Nick a rock, and drove off waving cheerfully.

A week or so later Waitey returned from holiday and asked Vinney how business had gone. When Vinney mentioned that he had sold to Nick and his 'mate', Waitey went ballistic and told him to get used to porridge. Word got back to the Drug Squad that Waitey was back, and Nick put a call in to him pretending that he thought he was ringing Vinney. He got a frosty reception but managed to agree a meeting in the centre of Derby. Nick was dropped off at Derby bus station and waited for an hour or so until Waitey pulled up in a BMW soft top, and ordered Nick into the car before driving round Derby for a while, testing his story, and asking him about his mate who used to score off him – i.e. me.

Waitey was extremely aggressive, and Nick genuinely feared for his safety, but he was eventually dropped off without any gear and told to bring me along if he still wanted to score. The following day, I met Nick for a game of pool and a think. The plan we came up with was that I was a mate of a Derby junkie, a customer of Waitey's who we knew was currently languishing at Her Majesty's Pleasure. We decided that I should tell Waitey that I'd hung around the corner while my mate scored off him. It was a long shot but it might just work. Then again, it might not.

We put a call into him and he told us to call back in one hour, repeating this little game for a few hours before finishing the last telephone call with, 'This isn't the Drugs Helpline, so fuck off!'

Despite some pissing around, the Drug Squad eventually arrested Vinney and Waitey, and they were charged with conspiracy to supply crack cocaine. Which was a shame. In those days, the Drug Squad was a self-contained unit of experienced detectives who managed their own cases – especially a relatively small job like Waitey and Vinney – and only really brought in CPS on the larger, more complex conspiracies. Nowadays, most nicks have resident CPS solicitors on hand to handle all cases, advising on the law and how to proceed; this can be a pain in the backside, but it might have helped on this occasion. To prove a conspiracy, there must be at least two people involved, and unfortunately there was very little evidence against Waitey. The Squad also screwed up by not hitting Vinney with a separate charge of supplying. If that wasn't enough, they also made a number of errors related to identification. The judge kicked it all out and both men walked free from court.

Waitey got his comeuppance a year or so later when he broke his own cardinal rule and sold to a stranger, who turned out to be an undercover cop. When he was arrested, they found 10 rocks of crack cocaine down his sock. The cop asked him about his involvement in the supply of drugs and Waitey denied ever touching the stuff.

'So how do you explain all that crack we found in your sock?' said the officer.

'Erm,' said Waitey. 'Er… I don't really know.'

Not the best answer. This time he went down.

Chapter 6:

Nottingham Vice

ONE COLD AND INHOSPITABLE morning in February 1999, I was sitting in the Drug Squad office when I was introduced to my partner for the next few weeks.

I was feeling under the weather and wasn't exactly full of the joys of late winter, but I perked up when I saw 'Tina from Heanor' – a bleached blonde with a big arse, big tits, and a loud, grating voice that reflected her upbringing in Heanor, a rough old place a few miles west of Nottingham. Tina was rougher still – never a bad thing in an undercover copper – and I soon found out that she was game for anything, a very effective operator who had recently passed her course and had been assigned to me for her first job. She was a great pleasure to work with.

Our briefing was due to take place at West Bridgford in south Nottingham, not far from Trent Bridge, so we jumped in a car and made our way there. On the way we firmed up our legend – I was an unemployed layabout and she was my bird – and chatted about this and that.

I was keen to put Tina at ease, but I needn't have bothered: she knew Nottingham well from her childhood, and pointed out lots of landmarks as we drove through the Radford Road area. 'I've had fucking nightmares about that place,' she announced, pointing out a Kentucky Fried Chicken shop. 'We used to go to the pictures and stop off on the way home for chicken and chips, and we'd sometimes get mugged for our fucking food!'

Confident that I was working with no shrinking violet, I arrived at the briefing, to be met by the Nottinghamshire liaison officers, Dave, a likeable DS, and Steve, an experienced UC and a man after my own heart. We were briefed about Saint Anne's, an estate in the centre of Nottingham where heroin had all but taken over. Addicts stumbled through the streets and walkways like zombies, and used needles lay scattered around the playgrounds and the doorways of the numerous blocks of flats.

Dave handed us a list with dozens of names and mobile numbers on it. 'Work your way down that till you get someone who's prepared to supply you,' he said.

Half an hour later or so, Tina and I were dropped off in the estate in an unmarked Job car, with magnetic minicab plates stuck on the side which had been borrowed from a contact of Dave's at a taxi firm. We shuffled towards a telephone kiosk, both of us chattering our tits off in the freezing grey air – I had suggested Tina wear very skimpy clothes, because addicts are chaotic people who don't always think to dress up warm, and because we'd look the part better if we were shivering and appeared to be withdrawing from heroin. I was only in a t-shirt and jeans myself; we were chilled to the bone.

The first two numbers I dialled were unobtainable, but the third – to a lad known as 'G' – was answered after a number of rings. It was a pretty succinct conversation.

'What you saying?' *What do you need?*

'Two white and two brown?' *Two rocks of crack, and two wraps of heroin.*

'Where are you?'

'St Anne's.'

'Come to the Kentucky Fried on Radford Road and bell me again.'

The phone went dead. I turned to Tina. 'There's good news and bad news, mate.'

'Go on?'

'The good news is he's going to sell us two £5 bags of smack and two rocks,' I said. 'The bad news is we're off to your favourite KFC.'

We jumped on a bus to Radford, Tina muttering under her breath that she couldn't believe where were heading. When we arrived, we joined the queue of junkies at the telephone kiosk outside, and when it came to our turn I put the call into the dealer. He told us to wait, so we did – for an hour.

'It's not like it is in the films, this,' said Tina, stating the obvious as we stood shivering in a shop doorway, watching the usual procession of pregnant, buggy-pushing teenagers, dead-eyed druggies and hooded youths with Staffie dogs.

Eventually, a thin, sallow-faced lad approached us. 'You waiting for G?'

I nodded, and we followed him deep into the estate until we came to a communal concourse at the base of one of the blocks of flats. There, parked next to a stack of bins, was a blue Ford Escort with steamed-up windows and a deep bass rhythm pounding from it. As we approached, the doors opened and four black blokes jumped out and encircled us. They were dressed in padded puffer jackets, tracksuit bottoms, designer trainers, and woolly hats. I felt the now-familiar clutch of fear in my stomach, and a shot of adrenaline rushing through me. I moved myself so that my back was to a nearby wall, pulling Tina towards me. One of the blokes, a big gold tooth at the front of his mouth, said in thickest Jamaican, 'What ya sayin'?'

'Two white and two brown.'

'Ya blood clot! *You're a used Tampon.*

'G told us to come here.'

'Lash me! Ya Babylon? Batty Bwoy!' *Blimey! Are you a police officer? Gay boy!*

Meanwhile Tina was moving seamlessly into her role – or so I thought. She already was bent over almost double, clutching her stomach, and shivering all over. Now she let out a low moan.

'Ya alright?' said one of the four. 'You roastin'?'

'Roasting' was the local slang for withdrawing – from 'roast (cold) turkey'.

'No,' she said. 'I'm fucking freezing!'

The Yardies all burst out laughing, staggering around and clapping their hands in that show of mirth peculiar to West Indians. Tina had totally defused a tricky situation, and one of the men served us up with the gear. 'You take care of her, man,' said one of them. 'Get her a coat, innit.'

With that, they jumped in the car and sped off. Nice chaps.

Dave came out to pick us up in the bogus minicab, and we'd started a pretty happy debrief when Tina, sitting in the back, noticed another minicab heading up our arse and flashing his headlights. Dave had already clocked the car and was putting his foot down to get away, but further down the road the minicab was joined by two more, and they started trying to box us in and stop us. Dave jumped a red light and screeched up outside West Bridgford nick, and the chasing cars also pulled up. Within a few moments, Dave was surrounded by angry minicab drivers demanding to know who he was. It turned out that they were from the firm whose magnetic signs Dave had borrowed. The drivers had never seen Dave or the car before so they assumed he was a bandit using their name. The taxi plates were ditched after that, and we resorted to relying on local buses.

Over the next few days, we scored off a dozen or so dealers. It was like shooting fish in a barrel: quite often, we didn't even have time to get to the telephone kiosk before we were approached and offered gear. One was a West Indian called Jay who spoke in a near-whisper and was introduced to us by a junkie. He wore expensive designer clothes, and took a massive shine to Tina – he insisted on giving his mobile number to Tina, not me.

'I reckon he wants me as his white trophy,' she said, laughing.

The following day, she was on annual leave so I doubled up with another new buyer called Paul, a particularly convincing lad who looked as if he had been on smack for years and was in the latter stages of AIDS. I put a call into Jay and he asked me who I was.

'I'm Tina's boyfriend.'

'Where's Tina?' he said.

'She's sick at home.'

'Next time you ring, you tell me you're Tina's brother,' he said. 'I don't want to hear no "Tina's boyfriend".'

'Yeah, right-ho, mate.' Maybe she was right, after all.

Jay told us to make our way to a nearby petrol station and wait for him. 'I'll be there in about an hour,' he said.

Paul was wearing a bag camera over his shoulder which he had already activated, and we decided to leave the video running because the remote control was dodgy and we wanted to make sure we filmed Jay when we scored. As we stood by the garage, we were joined by a group of crusties, new age travellers, and a big pack of mongrel dogs. They were waiting to score off another dealer, and had been told to wait at the same place as us.

It was all going so well, until one of the dogs curled out the biggest turd I have ever seen on the forecourt of the garage. The cashier came out, screeching at us all, and was met with a barrage of abuse. She stormed back into the garage where I could see her picking up the phone and jabbering into it. I knew what was coming next, and, sure enough, within five minutes a patrol car had pulled up and two coppers were putting on their hats and plodding over to us.

'We'd better do one, Paul,' I said. I was carrying a flick knife down my sock to scare off anyone who might try to rob or attack me, and if they found that I was getting nicked. More importantly, I didn't want the two PCs to find the video recorder in Paul's bag. As I've said, undercover operators need to be as undercover from the local police as they do the local villains. 'Meet me back here in 10 minutes?'

I jogged off one way, ditching my knife on the way, and Paul legged it in the opposite direction.

I walked around for a bit, until I thought the coast would be clear again and I returned to the garage. Jay was already waiting for me, but Paul was nowhere to be seen. It transpired that he had got lost: all he ended up with was film of himself running round in circles in the centre of Nottingham. I scored off Jay without being able to record it, but it turned out OK. When Jay was later arrested, I had to attend an ID parade to pick him out. That's not always the easiest thing to do – this was a guy I'd met a couple of times some weeks earlier – but I needn't have worried. There were 11 guys all looking either bored or amused, and one whose bottom lip was trembling and whose knees were practically knocking together.

* * *

THAT JOB CARRIED on for some time, with loads of targets, lots of little ops and strikes. There was plenty of work to be done, too. People think Nottingham is a nice sort of place, the home of lace, a largely female student population, Robin Hood, and the ghost of Brian Clough. There's some truth to that: parts of the city are beautiful. But the bits the police mostly work are not. I spent my time on the sprawling estates, with their urine-stinking underpasses, vandalised playgrounds, and concrete tower blocks crawling with dealers and customers.

One such place, the Meadows Estate, sits in the south of the city, not far from the Notts County and Nottingham Forest football grounds and Trent Bridge cricket ground. Home to around 8,000 residents, with a higher than average number of ethnic minorities and young people, the Meadows isn't the worst-looking place. But it was still a hotbed of gang-related gun crime and drug-dealing, much of it run under the control of the notorious Colin Gunn. Gunn lived further north, on the Bestwood estate, but his empire of guns, extortion, and drugs stretched all over the place. At this point, he was at the peak of his powers, and was making the transition from dealing amphetamines, ecstasy and cannabis into heroin, crack and coke, which he was moving in serious weight. A 6ft 4in steroid-abusing, cokehead maniac, he was a very unpleasant man indeed. One guy who had fallen foul of him was driven out to a remote country lane, where his hand was nailed to a bench and he was doused in petrol as Gunn stood next to him, lighting matches and threatening to set him on fire. It's impossible to overestimate the fear he had engendered in the local criminal underworld, never mind the law-abiding locals; this fear made it almost impossible to get people to give evidence against him. Added to that, he seemed to have a spooky ability to stay one step ahead of the local cops; despite his driving round in a Porsche Cayenne with the personalised number plate P10WER, they never seemed to be able to catch him at it. It later transpired when he was eventually taken down – and jailed for the rest of his life – that he had bent officers on his payroll, including one PC who he had recruited *before* he joined the force.

For now, all we could do was chip away at his empire and hope for a lucky break. I was pulled in to West Bridgford police station to get a briefing on Diamond Back Two, a job that had been running for about a month but was making no real headway. The previous buyer was a local Nottingham lad who had become paranoid about being sussed out by the dealers. So me and Nick – from the Waitey job – were parachuted into the estate to see if we could make some progress.

First off, we drove around the place in a little Fiesta that was wired for sound, with a camera in the steering column. But after a few circuits it was obvious that we were spooking the gangs of teenagers standing around on the street corners, so we ditched it and walked through the estate on foot. As we approached a phone box, we saw a bloke in dirty tracksuit bottoms and hooded coat hanging up and marching off at speed, pushing a pram. There was a real purpose to his step, and Nick and I looked at each other with raised eyebrows. We followed him, but he lost us in the labyrinth of footpaths running through the estate. We mooched around for a bit, trying not to stand out too much, and as luck would have it we bumped into him again about 10 minutes later. He had obviously just scored, because he looked a lot happier than previously.

Nick walked over to him, hunching his shoulders up and trying to look like a heroin addict who was clucking, and desperate to stick a needle in his arm. 'Hey, mate,' he said. 'Can you help us? I just need to get hold of some gear, know what I mean?'

He did, indeed, and obligingly gave us the number of a dealer called Shakey. Shakey was well known to the local police. He was mixed race, with very pale skin and freckles, and he was part of a street robbery gang who mugged people on the underpasses around the estate. He'd just walked on a nasty robbery in which he'd stamped on an Asian lady's head and left her for dead. He was the sort of bloke, in short, who it would be a pleasure to fuck up.

We put a call in to him and, after a very brief Q and A, he accepted us. 'You know The Poets Corner?' he said.

I did. It was a horrible local boozer built in the 1970s.

'There's a shop behind there where they sell papers and sweets and that. Get outside there and I'll come and meet you.'

It only took us a few minutes to make our way to the spot, but Shakey had beaten us to it. As we walked cautiously across a piece of dogshit-strewn waste ground behind the shop, we saw a bloke standing by the wall, baseball cap pulled right down over his eyes and jacket collar pulled up over his nose so that we couldn't see his face. He beckoned us over and held out his hand. Nick placed a ten pound note on his upturned palm, and the lad pointed towards a crushed cigarette packet that was lying on the floor nearby. The packet contained two £5 bags of heroin.

The next morning, I put another call into Shakey. 'Mate,' I said. 'That gear was fucking spot on. Can you do us some more?'

This time he told us to make our way to the footbridge over the River Trent near the Globe pub. As we walked onto the footbridge we saw a lone figure standing in the centre of the bridge looking out over the river. I assumed that this was Shakey, so we walked over to him. He was wearing the same jacket but this time he had a scarf wrapped around his face and a leather baseball cap pulled down over his eyes. Nick handed him the dosh and Shakey pointed at a crisp packet that was on the floor at his feet, before walking off.

We had scored again, but on neither occasion had we caught Shakey's face. At the debrief we sat scratching our heads as to how we were going to engineer scoring without him covering his face.

'Is there any point scoring off him if we're never going to ID him?' said Nick.

'It's only twenty quid,' I said. 'We might as well give it one more go, and then go for a buy-and-bust?'

A 'buy-and-bust' is what it sounds like. An arrest team are on standby, with a surveillance team also deployed to observe the deal. As soon as it goes down – or the suspect appears, depending on the operational requirements – the UC gives a pre-arranged signal (placing a baseball cap on your head, for example) and the arrest team moves in. As a rule, buy-and-busts are only done when the address or the identity of the suspect is not 100% known. The advantage is that he is nicked there and then, which removes the necessity for an ID parade. The downside is that it exposes the UC, and potentially blows him or her out in that area.

'Yeah,' said Nick. 'Hopefully, there'll be DNA on the wrappings, and that and the mobile phone evidence will be enough to convict him.'

We headed back off on foot into the estate in search of gear. As we hung around a telephone kiosk on the edge of the estate, we saw a young kid circling us on a pushbike. He was dressed in the uniform hooded top and baseball cap, and as he cycled past I said to him, 'Can you sort us with two white and two brown, mate?'

The kid pulled up and pointed towards an underpass. 'Wait over there and Prentice will come to you,' he said.

We did as we were told and walked over to the entrance to one of the many underpasses. We waited there for about 15 minutes, and eventually a kid on a mountain bike cycled up to us.

'What you after?' he said.

'We're after two white and two brown.'

The lad dug around in his trackie bottoms and served us up. I gave him the money and said, 'Can I get your mobile number, mate?'

He gave it to me and said his name was Prentice.

The following morning we were joined at the briefing by another detective who ran a number of informants on the estate.

'One of my lads was speaking to a kid called Prentice last night,' he said. 'The word is, Prentice reckons he sold gear to a pair of cops.'

This caused a bit of a flap. In the end, we decided to go back out onto the estate to gauge the feeling towards us, and we were about as popular as a clown at a funeral. Every junkie we approached legged it, and whenever we walked past groups of kids on street corners they would make siren noises.

Clearly, we had been blown out, and we were going to get nowhere near Shakey or Prentice.

(We didn't see Prentice again, but he made the news a few years later when a 14-year-old girl called Danielle Beccan was gunned down as she walked home through the estate. It was a random attack and part of an ongoing feud between gangs from rival estates. Prentice – so-called because he'd been an apprentice barber, his real name was Junior Andrews – was sentenced to life imprisonment for firing the shots, with a recommendation that he serve 32 years before being considered for release. To give you an idea of how rough it was in the area, Danielle lay bleeding in an alleyway for 45 minutes before an ambulance got to her, because the paramedics required back-up from armed police. She died some hours later on the operating table at Nottingham's Queen's Medical Centre.)

Exactly how we'd been blown, I don't know. It could have been a tip off from inside. More likely, he was just a bit more switched on than some.

Two new buyers were brought in to work the Meadows, and Nick and I were re-located to the area of Nottingham train station to target dealers working there. We had a quick walk around the station, and saw a Rastafarian *Big Issue* seller by the steps on the main road outside the concourse. We walked up to him and asked him if he could help us to score. He wasn't interested – at least, until he'd sold the dozen or so magazines that he was holding. He was a likeable bloke, though, and we hung around with him for a bit while he told us stories about how he used to live in the Stoke Newington area, and score on Sandringham Road, which he called 'the front line'. I later used a lot of his stories as my own when I went onto more difficult jobs, and had to natter away to dealers and junkies for hours on end.

After half an hour or so, we did a few more desultory circuits of the station and eventually wound up standing by a slip road, waiting for something to happen. Before long we were approached by two young white kids, no older than 15. One of them walked straight up to me and said, 'Are you after business?'

'What kind of business?' I said.

'Do you want a blow job?'

'No, I don't. Fuck off!'

'We're after a couple of rocks,' said Nick.

'You got any change?' said the kid. I gave him a handful of coins, and he ran over to a phone box while his mate stayed with us.

'If we score for you, are you going to let us have a smoke?' said the mate.

'Look, son,' I said. 'I'll give you a fiver and you can do what you want with that, but we want the rocks for ourselves.'

Soon, the other kid came running back. 'You got twenty quid?' he said.

Nick handed over the dough and he ran off again. Ten minutes later, he re-appeared and beckoned us to follow him. We walked for a few minutes until we got to a rough old boozer. There were a couple of rooms at the back, grubby and sparsely furnished with just a single bed. There was loads of burnt foil on the floor. This was obviously where these two rent boys brought their punters.

'Here you go,' said the lad, handing over two tiny rocks wrapped in loose-fitting Clingfilm. It was obvious that he'd skimmed quite a bit of gear off them before returning to us. The youths pulled out crack pipes and began preparing them, so Nick and I beat a hasty retreat before we were invited to a communal pow-wow.

We later passed their details on to the local police in order that they could get social services involved via some kind of referral under the juvenile offender policy, but I never saw the two rent boys again.

I came across plenty of young kids, buried in the filth and murk of the drugs world, over the years. I found it very sad, particularly as a father myself. They didn't really stand a chance; usually the offspring of junkies, the majority of them were on a one-way ride through the care system and into prison. I used to compare them to my own kids. They were amazingly streetwise compared to my lads. The other very obvious difference was in their size: they were all scrawny and sickly-looking. I mentioned this to Kenty one day, when we were buying in Sandiacre. He pointed out that normal kids eat wholesome food, while those we came across were brought up on crisps and oven chips.

Meanwhile, the two new lads who had been brought in to cover the Meadows fared even worse than we had: on their first day on the estate, a gang of local hoods ambushed them with baseball bats and fucked them off good and proper. It was a very scary experience, and potentially very nasty, and the job was then knocked on the head for a bit.

Later, we learned that there had been a competing long term undercover job running in the area which had just had its strike day, and everyone was a bit spooked. In that general atmosphere of paranoia, Prentice had probably put two and two together and been lucky. Once the word was out that the Five-O were around, everyone went to ground. Of course, competing UC operations should never happen. Before you start a job, senior officers are supposed to flag the area/targets with a national supervising agency. This was originally the National Drugs Intelligence Unit, later the National Criminal Intelligence Service, and now SOCA (though it's about to change again). In theory, this will highlight any potential 'blue-on-blues', but obviously, cops being cops, they like to keep info close to their chests, so cross-overs will always happen.

I only came across it on two other occasions. One was in Middlesbrough, when I was working for South Yorkshire Covert Ops. (I know, Middlesbrough isn't in South Yorkshire: we were a bit lost, which just about sums up the job.) It came to light that Cleveland were running a buying job at the same time, targeting the same group of Yardies, and their Chief Constable politely told us to fuck off back down south and leave it with them. The other occasion was when I was waiting to score off an elderly Nottingham Jamaican called Pops – a surprisingly major-league dealer who I'll talk about later. I was approached by a female who asked me if I could help her get sorted with a rock. She was obviously a cop, or so I thought, so I told her to fuck off. It turned out she was an ex-bobby who was working as a private investigator on behalf of the local council, which was trying to get evidence of drug trafficking against Pops so that they could evict him.

* * *

INFILTRATION CAN BE VERY difficult at the best of times, especially in the close-knit communities which we usually worked. People had lived on these estates for generations.

On one estate just outside Nottingham, a heroin job had been running for a couple of months with little progress. The scene was a 'closed market' – a situation common to small towns, where all the druggies and dealers know each other, and there is no or very little transient drug market. Because of this, the whole thing looked nigh-on impossible to infiltrate, but we were having a go.

The local team had obtained a house in the middle of the estate and wired it up. The television in the living room contained a camera that could be activated by the TV's remote handset, and the kitchen and front door areas were also fitted with covert CCTV. Two female buyers from the Sheffield area with big reputations had gone in – their cover story being that one of them had been re-located by social services to escape her bullying boyfriend (me, as it happens), the other lass being her mate who had tagged along. It wasn't the best legend in the world, but in these situations you sometimes have to work with what you've got. They had got nowhere, so I was approached to play the part of 'Joanne's' bullying boyfriend. My brief was to turn up once or twice a week and knock her around a bit; the hope was this would buy her some credibility, and maybe even sympathy.

I started to appear now and then, and after a couple of visits we engineered a scene where I had a shouting match with my 'girlfriend' in the street. We made sure I was seen by the locals to drag her over to my car, throw her in and drive off. In order to get the best effect, I waited until all the mothers and baby-fathers had picked their kids up from the local primary school – those who actually bothered going, that is. In front of the usually assortment of skinny blokes pushing prams and buggies, overweight mothers in rip-off tracksuit bottoms and Lonsdale tops, and under-nourished tykes, I screeched to a halt outside our house and jumped out of the car. Slamming the door shut behind me, I charged up the garden path, stormed inside and, after some realistic shouting and crashing and banging about, reappeared a few minutes later dragging my 'lass' with me, while her terrier dog ran after me barking and snapping at my ankles.

'I told you to go to the fucking cashpoint today and call me when you had the money,' I shouted.

'I've been ill,' she screeched. 'You're hurting me... Let go of my fucking arm!'

I opened the car door, pushed her in, and screeched off again down the road.

'Well,' said my colleague, smoothing her hair, once we were out of sight. 'That went OK, I think, Pete.'

Back at the house, my bird's mate was dragging the dog back inside the house and mumbling her apologies to the neighbours, who were standing shaking their heads in disgust about how the tone of the area was being lowered by these out-of-towners. This all had the desired effect of getting the jungle drums going; whenever I turned up in the future, I could see curtains twitching from our neighbours' houses. We were starting to be accepted.

One day we were having a walk round the estate and had stopped to buy a few bits and pieces in the local shop, when we noticed a group of smackheads huddled together looking up and down the road, obviously waiting to score. Joanne walked over to the group, leaving me glowering on the other side of the road. She asked one of the kids for a light, and then said, hands shaking, 'He's told me to come over and see if anyone can help us score a ten bag. If I don't get him any gear he's going to kick the shit out of me.'

A couple of kids glanced over at me; another agreed to help her. She was not acting as an *agent provocateur*, because the kids were themselves druggies who were waiting to score and divide the gear up between them, and the offence of supplying was therefore already 'in being'. They would have dealt drugs, whether we were there or not.

A few minutes later, an old green BMW drove past and parked up on a bit of waste land nearby. The kids ran over to it and were all served up by a bloke in the front passenger seat. The boy who had agreed to help us score called Joanne over and handed her a bag. 'If you ever need to score again, just ask me,' he said.

As the weeks progressed, the girls started getting known by the local drug users and dealers. I would score for good measure whenever I appeared in the area. The main den of junkies lived in a small semi-detached house on a local housing association plot, where the tenant, a skinny kid called Spider, with a butterfly tattoo on each cheek and a spider's web tattoo covering all of his neck, knocked out his gear. We began scoring there on a regular basis.

One Monday morning, I went over to the plot on my own. I'd been on a Stella bender over the weekend, and I felt like my brain was coming out of the front of my forehead – it was the worst hangover I'd suffered in many a year. I pulled up outside Spider's house, knocked on the door and was invited into the living room. There were about 10 junkies in there, all chasing the dragon. The room was full of heroin smoke, and I inhaled a lot of it as I waited. By the time I was served, I was feeling a bit woozy, and, as I staggered from the house to my car, I had difficulty focusing on my key to get it in the lock of the door. Once behind the wheel, I dialled the operational team on my mobile to let them know that I was on my way back. As soon as I pressed the button to end the call, I sat back in the chair and relaxed. It occurred to me that my hangover had all-but gone. In fact, I was feeling quite nice and chilled. Maybe there was something to this heroin!

At the debrief, when I had trouble focusing on my pocket book, it was sussed that I'd inhaled a fair amount of heroin; the job was rapidly brought to a close.

Officially, this was on health and safety grounds, though there is no health and safety risk involved in what happened to me. What it *actually* was, was a case of our Complaints and Discipline Department causing problems – not for the first, or last, time. Dave, the DS in charge of this op, was about to retire, and was almost paranoid about PSD. He was absolutely adamant that nothing even remotely suspect was going to occur in anything he was involved in, and having a cop blasted off his face on smack constituted something remotely suspect.

For instance, on another operation he was running I was out in the Radford area of Nottingham, just testing the market against a new dealer, and I successfully bought a rock off this character. Unfortunately, as I walked back to pick-up, the bloody thing dropped through a hole in my jeans pocket and was lost. I explained this to Dave on de-brief, and he sent me back to the plot to search for it. I was out there for hours on what amounted to a fool's errand: this was an area in which a junkie would have seen the rock fall from 200ft, and picked it up before it had even hit the floor.

So Dave was taking any opportunity he could to bosh jobs. But, by then, the operation had half a dozen or more dealers boxed off, and there comes a time where – if you keep going back again and again looking for gear – you may end up being seen as an *agent provocateur*. A dealer says, 'This big, scary bastard was at my door every day, badgering me. I didn't want to sell him drugs, but I was scared of him. What did they expect me to do?' At which, PSD's ears prick up, and, depending on how tight the operation has been, you may be in trouble.

* * *

UNDERCOVER OFFICERS HAVE to be psychologically assessed annually, basically to check their sanity. It always seemed to me that the purpose was to tick a box and protect the organisation, rather than the individual. The assessors were a well-meaning bunch, but difficult to take seriously sometimes and much closer to the social services end of the spectrum than law enforcement. I had a very nice Asian lady as a welfare officer for a time; the main part of her training seemed to have been to ensure that, whenever I answered a question, she smiled sympathetically and said nothing for five seconds, presumably to embarrass me into saying something further. I'm not entirely sure that I was the ideal subject for this type of counselling. I had a session shortly after that case ended. It went something like this:

'How are things at home?'

'Fine, thanks.'

Smile, and five second pause. 'Really?'

'Yeah.'

'Do you have flashbacks?'

'No.'

Smile, and five second pause. 'Really?'

'Yeah.'

'Do you sleep OK?'

'Yeah.'

Smile, five second pause, and added earnest look. 'Really?'

'Yep.'

'How often do you drink alcohol? '

'Very rarely.'

'Really?'

'OK, you've got me there. I drink a few pints and a bottle of whiskey every night.'

I could almost see the eyes of the kind and well-meaning welfare officer light up at this opening. This was what she'd been hoping for: now she could get to the bottom of my fragile state of mind. She didn't even smile and wait for five seconds. But she did look much more earnest.

'Really? Why is that, do you think, Pete?'

'Well, I think… I mean, I'm not sure, but I think it's probably because I support Preston North End.'

Chapter 7:

Derby Win

THE NEXT FEW YEARS were a blur of similar jobs, and towards the end of 2002 – by now, I was working for EMSOU – I was given a rest from Nottingham.

I'd been over-exposed, having done lots of buying in the city and its satellite towns over the last three or four years, so I headed up Brian Clough Way and back over to Derby to look for business on the other side of the East Midlands. I soon came across one wily old bird who was generating his own little crimewave as one of the city's most prolific house burglars. The bloke was called Richo, and he lived in bedsit land off the Normanton Road. This had once been a very classy area of Derby, full of large Victorian houses in tree-lined streets., but now it had mostly been turned over to squalid flats filled with the benefit underclass and illegal immigrants, salted by a smattering of smaller-end dealers. Richo was one of these, but his main job – his vocation – was burglary.

Every morning, he would set off on foot towards more salubrious parts to screw the houses of working people. He got stop-searched from time to time, but the tools of his trade were never found on him: it turned out that this was because he kept the screwdriver he used for forcing windows rammed up his backside.

He was becoming a bit of an irritant to the chief as his crime wave gathered pace. There's always more than one way to skin a cat, and I was tasked, alongside my mushroom-picking mate Shabby, with spending a few days a week around the Normanton area, with the aim of buying heroin off Richo and getting him off the streets for a while.

We quickly got in with the right faces, scoring at will, and within a couple of weeks we were known to every dealer in the neighbourhood – *except* Richo, who wouldn't come out to play. As the point of the operation was not to infiltrate the drug fraternity, but to get Richo put away, we decided to visit his flat.

It was a lovely day, and the street was lined with emaciated, pale blokes, all stripped to the waist, who'd come blinking out of the dark to enjoy the sun and drink a few bottles of White Lightning. We stopped to chat with those we knew, and a wizened old crone pointed us in the direction of Richo's flat and told us to whistle up at the front first floor window. So off we toddled, to spend the next 10 minutes trying all different types of whistles and hoping he'd appear. Eventually, a face popped out.

'What?'

'Richo?'

'*What?*'

'Are you Richo?'

'*Who?*'

'Richo!'

'Why?'

'Can you do us a ten bag?'

'What?'

'Look mate, are you Richo?'

'*Who?*'

'Is there anyone else up there we can speak to?'

'Why?'

'We've been told you're the bloke to see round here for smack. Can you help us?'

'Smoke?'

'SMACK!'

Fucking hell. It was like pulling teeth, and it didn't get a lot better.

For the next half hour or so, we sat on the garden wall outside Richo's; every so often, a face appeared at the window and quickly ducked back inside when we looked up. Eventually, a young kid aged about 13 walked out of the house and nodded for us to follow him. He led us to an alleyway at the end of the street and produced a small paper wrap.

'Here,' he said, holding out his grubby little mitt up for the money that Shabby handed over.

This wasn't enough to get Richo, by a long chalk, but it was a start. We were in.

Back at Jazz's office, we opened the wrap up to check the gear. But instead of seeing the powder we were after, originating from the exotic plains of Afghanistan, Turkey, or Pakistan, what we found had been produced in Accrington. Fucking brick dust.

In the drugs world, everybody gets skanked now and then, and there's no point in worrying about it. What *is* important as an undercover buyer is how you deal with it. You have to react as a junkie would, so we went back the next day to do a bit of shouting and sulking and generally register our displeasure. Shabby parked directly outside the house and I jumped out, slamming the door and whistled as loudly as I could up at the window. Nothing happened, so Shabby sounded the car horn in long, loud toots. Still nothing. We chucked handfuls of gravel at the window, and then I alternated between hammering on the front door and shouting 'Richo!' at the top of my voice.

Eventually, a straggly-haired witch – the mother of Richo's baby – stuck her head out of the window. 'Yeah?'

'Is Richo in?' I said.

'No.'

'What time is he due back?'

'Dunno. Why?'

'He skanked me yesterday, and I'm not fucking happy!'

'He ain't here.'

'Well, ring him and tell him I want a fucking chat!'

The witch disappeared and we sat on the wall to wait. Around midday, just as we were about to bin it, Richo and another two scruffy gits walked round the corner. Shabby and I went to meet them in the centre of the road.

Richo beat us to it. 'Alright lads,' he said. 'I hear you think I ripped you off yesterday. Well, it had nothing to do with me, but here's your money. Now, I'd be very grateful if you'd fuck off and not bother me again.'

This was actually something of a result. At least he knew we weren't to be fucked about. We jumped back in our motor and rushed back to Jazz's office, to ponder exactly how we were going to get this little shit off the streets. It was already developing into something of a shared obsession.

Shabby came up with a plan. 'We know Richo's not averse to a bit of handling [stolen goods],' he said. 'Plus, he sends that bird out shoplifting baby clothes for their kid. What if we spread the word that we travel around the Midlands selling stuff at car boots? Maybe knock some tat out in the area, to look realistic.'

It wasn't a bad plan. We started mouthing off about our little business, and cruising about with a car boot full of baby clothes, tinned milk powder – plus some booze, cartons of fags and tobacco, courtesy of a useful contact in Customs and Excise. The idea was that if we sold enough cheap fags and baby clothes in the area, word would eventually get to Mr and Mrs Richo, and hopefully they'd pay us a visit.

In order further to reinforce our cover, we recruited a new buyer called Kerry. Her role was to look wasted in the back seat of the car. Criminals have limited imaginations, and for some reason they seem to think undercover cops don't come in threes. But the job dragged on for days, and then into weeks, much longer than we'd hoped. I was desperate to get a result, to the point where I was getting pissed off with Richo and thinking about him nearly every minute of my day. I spent my nights tossing and turning, and generally allowed my home life to suffer for the buzz of the chase.

This was when I began to understand how – after three or four years of constant buying – the role was getting under my skin.

Halfway through the job, I had two weeks off to go on a family holiday to Disneyland, but even that seemed like an inconvenience: I wanted to be with Shabby and Kerry, and was actually glad to fly home. I went out straight away with Shabby, just cruising around the area, and as we turned into Normanton Road I saw a likely-looking bloke in his mid-20s standing on the corner. We stopped, and I said, 'Do you want to buy some cheap fags, mate?'

He walked over and bought a couple of packets. As he walked away, I called him back. 'Hey, mate, do you where I can buy some ganja?'

He turned back. 'Of course, I fuckin' do.'

Sweet.

He jumped into the back of the car – obviously a trusting sort – and guided us to a block of flats in Gerrard Road. As we pulled up, I said, 'Do you want me to stay here or can I come with you?'

The lad laughed. 'Fuck me!' he said. 'They'll serve anyone here. Come and have a look.'

I followed him up a few flights of stairs to a flat with a large steel door, with a small slit cut in the door, almost like a letter box. The lad hammered on the door. A minute or so later, a quiet voice spoke through the letter box. I couldn't hear what was being said.

'What's happening?' I asked.

The lad turned to me. 'How much do you want?' he said.

'A quarter,' I said.

He leaned back towards the slit and gave my order. A couple of fingers appeared through the slit, and the lad motioned me to pass my cash through. A minute later the fingers reappeared with a lump of resin. This was a pretty secure way of dealing: hide behind a fortified door high up in a block of flats and deal through a slit so that nobody can see you. Class.

Over the next few months, I paid this flat a visit once a week to check that it was still functioning and to allow them to see me. It was so easy that, back at the office, we discussed using the flat as a live buy for students on the next course.

The lad who had taken me there was called Guardy. He was a local crackhead and ne'er-do-well – just the sort of person I liked to get to know – and he'd given me his mobile number. He seemed happy for me to call him any time, and he turned out to be quite useful. A few days later, I showed him a bag full of snide designer jeans that we had robbed from a police property store. I say 'robbed': the operational teams were forever raiding the stores before jobs started and 'acquiring' lots of goodies that had not been claimed, and which were due to be auctioned off – laptops, mobiles, bikes and so – for use as props by the buyers to help us infiltrate and gain credibility with the local lowlife.

'Do you know anyone who can take these off my hands?' I said.

He jumped in the back of the car next to Kerry, and took us to an Afro-Caribbean takeaway a couple of miles away. Shabby and I followed Guardy in. There were a couple of women cooking patties or stirring goat curry, and a group of West Indian blokes just sitting around chatting.

'Is Jinksy around?' said Guardy, to a girl who was sweeping up.

She motioned to a room behind a curtain at the back of the shop, and we headed through. There were a few settees and chairs scattered about: it looked like a rest area for the staff. Sitting on one of the settees was a small, bald, black bloke in his mid-40s. He was wearing leather trousers, shades, and a designer top, and had a row of gold teeth at the front of his mouth. This was Jinksy, the takeaway's proprietor – among other things. He puffed out his chest, and said in a light lisp, 'Nice place, eh? I'm buying the Paki shop next door and knocking it through. There's going to be a hairdresser's on one side and a clothes boutique on the other. I'm gonna call it Jinksy's Emporium.'

It was a bit like Starsky and Hutch at their first meeting with Huggy Bear, and Shabby was stifling a laugh. I thought I'd better keep the mood reasonably serious. 'I've got a load of jeans in the boot of my car, mate.' I said. 'Do you fancy having a quick look at them?'

'Yeah, sweet.'

I went out to the car to pick up a slack handful of snide black Armanis and headed back inside, plonking them down in front of Jinksy. He rummaged through them, selected a couple of pairs, and paid me. Back at the office that evening, the SIO sat up when Jinksy was mentioned. It turned out that this guy who we'd assumed was just another local dickhead was actually very well-connected to the regional heroin and crack cocaine supply network. We had a new target.

The following week I made it my business to bump into Jinksy and his son as they sat outside a café on Normanton Road eating their dinner. We chatted about nothing much for a while, and then I said, 'Can I talk to you about a bit of business?'

'Sure,' he said, standing up. We wandered off down the street together. I suppose he was expecting me to talk about Jinksy's Emporium, but instead I asked if he knew anyone who could sort me out some weed. He grinned from ear to ear. 'Meeeeeeeee!' he said. ' Meeeeeeeee! When do you want it?'

'Today?'

'Go to my place at five,' he said.

And so a few hours later, I made my way to the takeaway and was shown through to the back by one of the girls. Despite his comical appearance and manner, he did seem to command a fair amount of respect on the street, and you don't get respect by being a twat, so I stayed on my guard; when he handed me a bag of shit, home-grown weed, half of it seeds and stalks, I took care not to complain too much.

* * *

WE CARRIED ON SCORING off Guardy every few days, although his crack habit was beginning to spiral out of control and he was committing street robberies to fund it. He was still a good source, and through him we had marked a number of dealers. But I hadn't forgotten the main objective of the operation, which was to get that toe rag Richo off the streets.

Kerry carried on sitting in the back of the car looking wasted, with a body camera strapped to her, getting some very decent covert footage of a growing number of deals. Most of the action still centred around Normanton Road. One day we came across a kid named Karl. I'd wandered up to him to ask for a light, holding up my fag with shaking fingers, and he asked me where I normally scored.

'Usually at the Normanton Hotel,' I said, calling on the memory of my first-ever buy, several years earlier. 'But I'm keeping out of there just at the minute because I owe somebody some money, if you know what I mean?'

Karl grinned. He did know what I meant. 'Come with me,' he said. 'I'll get Owl's number for you.'

'Owl' was a new name on me, always a good thing. We walked for about a mile, with Kerry hanging just behind and filming, until we came to a large, terraced house. Karl opened the door and ushered us in. The place stank of mustiness and old heroin smoke, and, as we walked into the main room, junkies began appearing from nooks and crannies like the zombies in the *Thriller* video.

'Broad, man,' said Karl. 'Broad' was someone I did know – he was a junkie I'd seen begging a few times in the city centre. 'What's Owl's number?'

'Man, I can't give you that,' said Broad, though he relented when Karl explained that I'd promised to let them have a bit of heroin in return for helping me out. 'OK,' he said. 'I'll take you to see Owl. But she'll have to wait here.'

I looked at Kerry, wedged on a stained sofa between a pair of blank-eyed zombies. She gave me a look that said, 'If you leave me here, I will kick you so hard in the balls that you will be pissing razors for a week.'

'No,' I said. 'She's got to come with us. She's my bird, I ain't leaving her here.'

Broad's insatiable need for heroin overrode his loyalty to Owl, so the three of us made our way to a nearby street where I let him ring his feathered friend on my mobile phone. Twenty minutes later, a Nissan pulled up, a young Asian kid behind the wheel.

'This is Owl, man,' said Broad.

Owl served us up without any fuss. 'You can call me direct from now on,' he said, 'but don't ring me on Friday afternoon 'cos I'll be in the mosque.'

Our back-up team had never heard of Owl, so I was asked to keep buying off him past the normal three clean buys – enough for the CPS to consider running a case – so that they could find out who he was and where he lived.

We continued to bump into Karl and Broad, who were always keen to introduce us to fresh dealers. Since Karl was less important, he was nicked after a while and charged with the supply of controlled drugs.

He hanged himself in his prison cell while on remand. At the time, I didn't really give that much thought: shit happens. Recently, though, I find myself thinking about it more. If I hadn't targeted him he wouldn't have been remanded and maybe... I must be getting soft in my old age.

We moved towards strike day, when the various dealers we'd infiltrated while trying to get to Richo were going to be taken down – the likes of Jinksy and Owl.

We scored off Jinksy frequently, but only cannabis. Whenever we broached the idea of stronger drugs to him, he seemed less than enthusiastic, despite the suggestions of our intelligence. Eventually, we nicked him but his lawyer got him off on a technicality, using some spectacular delaying tactics until the judge lost patience and threw the case out when he was presented with some incomplete paperwork from the local police. I used to ask myself why we bothered.

Good old Guardy had been arrested for a number of street robberies and was on remand, so we planned to visit him while in prison after the strike day. The slimy Richo was nowhere to be seen, and so soon enough the only person I was still scoring off was Owl and a kid that Broad had introduced me to called Garry, whose diverse portfolio of business interests included a little pimping and the occasional burglary. He initially served me up with a decent bag of heroin, which was a bit of a coup because the operational team wanted him off the streets due to his other activities. But it took me weeks to get my second and third buys, and by the time it came to strike we didn't have a clue where he lived, so we decided to do a buy-and-bust on him and Owl. But it was hard work. Every time I called the number Garry had given me, a woman answered it and screeched, 'Fuck off!'

Finally, at about 11am one day, I managed to speak to Owl. He agreed to sort me out with some heroin, saying he'd be with me in 10 minutes. So I put a call into some of the Derby drug squad lads who were attached to the operation, and who were plotted up in a nearby car park.

'It's Pete. Owl will be in the normal place in 10 minutes.'

'OK.'

'Can you let the eyeball know? As discussed in the briefing, I'll stick my baseball cap on as the signal that he's sorted me out, and I'll chat him up till you arrive.'

The 'eyeball' was a detective sitting in an observation van 50 yards away. As soon as he saw the transaction was complete, he would call in the strike. While the cavalry drove round like The Sweeney, I'd keep Owl talking about some stolen gold which I supposedly had for sale.

'No probs, mate. Good luck. Oh, and by the way, we've been talking… You do know you look like you've spent the last six months buying pork pies not heroin, you fat bastard?'

'Fuck off.'

'And you, sweetheart.'

Owl turned up and I leaned into his car and scored. Then I put the baseball cap on my head, and dug my hand into my pocket. I pulled out a couple of heavy gold rings and a chain that we'd borrowed from a police property store. 'You interested in buying some of this stuff, mate?'

His eyes nearly popped out of his head. 'Let me see them?' he said.

I dropped a ring in the footwell of his car and, as he bent down to search for it, the four Drug Squad cars screamed into view. The poor bastard didn't know what had hit him. As the four cars boxed him in, I stepped back from his car and watched as eight Drug Squad officers swarmed all over him and dragged him out. As he was being led away to a marked police van, I stepped forward to the arresting officer and said, 'This person has sold class A drugs to me on eight occasions.'

This identification at the scene usually removes the necessity for an ID parade. Owl's face was a picture of total disbelief, and I later heard that he spent the next hour or so sitting in the custody area, waiting to be booked in, shaking his head, and repeatedly saying, 'Pete can't be a copper! He just can't!'

All of which did my ego no harm whatsoever.

Half an hour later, we were on Garry's case.

I walked through a prearranged point where a surveillance team was waiting for me; they were going to follow me to my usual meeting place and make the arrest when he turned up. We had plenty of evidence to charge him without scoring off him again; we were only buying-and-busting him because the operational team didn't have a clue where he was living. If they had, they would have just busted him at dawn at his home address.

I knew all of the team, but they were well-hidden – I only spotted one of them as I walked through the car park and made my way down Normanton Road. I called Garry's number and, miraculously, he answered it.

'Hello, mate,' I said. 'Can you sort me out with a ten bag, please.'

'Er...' he said. 'Look, can you call me back in a few hours?'

'Wait, mate,' I said, injecting a note of panic into my voice. 'Don't hang up! I'm desperate, here. I need that shit. Look, I've got some gold rings for sale, if you're interested?'

This got his attention. 'OK, he said. 'Be by the usual park gate in 10 minutes.'

I always met him on a bench just near to a small park on a side street off the main drag. When I put the phone down, I called the DS to update him.

'Just be aware, Pete,' he said. 'The intelligence is that Garry is down on his arse. There's every chance he's intending to mug you for the rings.'

I wouldn't have particularly minded this challenge: mind you, it helped that the odds were slightly stacked in my favour, with a 12-man surveillance team following me.

As I turned the corner near the park, I saw an old man with a walking stick and a trilby sitting on our park bench. *Shit!* All I could do was to stand near the gates and wait for the old geezer to fuck off. After what seemed like hours, I saw Garry walking towards me with a striking purpose to his step. He walked past me, beckoning me to follow him into the park. But that would have blown my surveillance team out so I shook my head.

'Nah mate,' I said. 'Come here.'

He walked back to join me by the park gates, an irritated expression on his face. 'Sorry, Garry,' I said. 'It's just that Kerry's got the rings. She'll be with us in a couple of minutes.'

I then put my baseball cap on the back of my head to initiate our second strike.

Then, to my surprise, the old man jumped off the park bench and launched himself at Garry – as an electrician who had been working on a nearby junction box jumped up and grabbed him round the neck. The cleverly-disguised old man turned out to be Malc, a lad in his 40swho I'd known for years; the electrician was a copper called Brian who I also knew well. I hadn't recognised either of them. Unfortunately, Garry didn't see the funny side – and he particularly didn't take the fact that I was a copper too well. He struggled violently, and I had to help restrain him with a few well-placed kicks until the rest of the squad arrived.

Within a year, 13 dealers had been arrested, charged and imprisoned, and Shabby, Kerry and I each received a Chief Constable's commendation. A major success... Except for Richo. He never featured again; it turned out he was always one step ahead of us, and I had seen him for the last time.

I did see Broad though, when we were having a piss-up in Derby after strike day. He'd been arrested but bailed, and was begging with a little mongrel dog next to him. I walked over to him, threw a few quid in his hat, and wished him good luck. Sadly, he didn't seem to see the funny side: his language towards me was choice, to say the least.

And this job was to prove my swan song in the Normanton area: it was decided that I had been over-exposed and was burnt out.

Chapter 8:

Life and Death

I WASN'T UNHAPPY to be out of there. The longer you stay in one place, and the more people who are nicked, the thinner your cover gets.

I was also ready for a new challenge, so I was pulled out of there to work on an infiltration in a little place called Swadlincote, a run-down old pit town in the middle of some nice south Derbyshire countryside. The main problem there was in an area called Newhall, a run-down patch largely made up of council estates and housing association complexes. A relatively small, closed market heroin scene operated from dealers' houses. Mostly, they would score just enough for their own use and to supply a small circle of customers about three times a day. Once the dealers 'had' – the local drug slang for having gear, and being open for business – the users would appear from their nooks and crannies to make their purchases and then disappear again.

When they weren't buying gear or shooting up, they were out working to get the money for their next fix. By 'working', I mean carrying out shed breaks, house burglaries, car thefts, and the occasional robbery – in fact, anything they could do to get their hands on the money to feed their habits. We're talking a fairly tight-knit bunch of junkies, but they were sending the local crime figures through the roof. So the number crunchers had decided that the local proactive team should put a buyer into the estate to remove, or at least reduce, the drugs problem.

Previous undercover operations had failed. As I've said, it is not easy to infiltrate insular communities. It's not like straight life, where people move in and out of the area for work, or because they've got married, or bought a bigger house. In places like this, there's very little transient movement. People who are born there very rarely leave until they're carried out in a wooden box, and outsiders hardly ever move in. Everybody knows everybody else, and new faces are instantly spotted and challenged.

I suppose that's where the skill of a good UC comes in. By now, the jobs I was working were full-on operations, with a major operational team set up in a temporary office around 10 miles away. In this case, we were plotted up in a covert office in the grounds of Repton, an expensive public school attended over the years by, among others, Roald Dahl, Jeremy Clarkson and assorted MPs and Archbishops of Canterbury. I'd moved away from my Paul Heaton/football casual look, and had taken on the appearance and demeanour of a 1980s throwback skinhead. I got a few funny looks off the staff, turning up dressed as a shaven-headed Nazi every day, with my scruffy little mongrel dog Scooby trotting along next to my maroon Doc Martens.

Looking back, my skinhead phase was another sign that I was getting a bit too deep in to this undercover lark. As ever, I needed to be able to talk the talk, not just look the part, so I'd spent a lot of time researching the extreme right wing, and along the way I'd somehow actually managed to get into the white noise music these bozos listened to. Thanks to Napster, I got obsessive about Blood and Honour-label bands like Skrewdriver and No Remorse, who did catchy little numbers such as *Barbecue in Rostock*, which celebrated the burning down of a block of flats that housed immigrant families. It was a very long way from the ska and reggae that I've always loved. I stress, I was never a Nazi, or anything close, but the more I researched the more interested I became. I remember devouring, and enjoying, Andrew MacDonald's book *The Turner Diaries*. This book, written under a pseudonym by the American white supremacist William Luther Pierce III, is the graphic story of a race war in the United States which features, among other delights, the ethnic cleansing, by mass hangings, of Los Angeles. The Oklahoma bomber, Timothy McVeigh, was supposedly inspired by it. It's not healthy bedtime reading.

But I digress. I was assigned to the Swadlincote operation to act as the main buyer. The plan was for me to do all the ground work, add a female buyer to act as my girlfriend, and eventually another male buyer who we could bounce off. Slowly, slowly, catchee monkey was the order of the day, so there was no pressure for me to start scoring too soon. Initially, I just got my face seen. I was playing a chancer who drove around in a white Astra van and bought mountain bikes to sell at car boot sales – a legend that I had used elsewhere. I started by posting flyers through people's doors with my mobile phone number on; that would get my face seen, and hopefully some of the junkie burglars would take the bait and ring me to try and sell their stolen goods.

I had a housing association flat not far from the main drugs hot spot, so I quickly set about moving in and meeting the neighbours. I was using Scooby as a bit of additional cover. He was a veteran of a number of drugs jobs, and it's fair to say that he looked the part.

My van had all the usually technical equipment installed, including a camera in the steering column with which I could film any front seat passengers. I was all set up – and the good thing about Swadlincote was that it was only about an hour and a half drive from home, which meant that I could get back to see my family most days.

Carmel was pregnant again, after suffering a recent miscarriage, and she was quite on edge about the pregnancy. Not that I really noticed. I was throwing myself totally into planning and preparation for work. I was obsessed with advancing my undercover reputation. By now, I had taken part in quite a lot of UC drugs ops around the country – apart from Derby and Nottingham, I'd worked a lot in Manchester, Middlesbrough, Sheffield, Stoke, London, and Salisbury. I'd also been involved in a big buying job in Iceland in 2001, which was quickly followed by one in Aldi. (Old undercover joke.)

Along the way, I'd had a lot of success, including commendations from a number of chief constables. A lot of people queued up to tell me how good I was at this game. I was only too ready to believe them.

In the early stages of the Swad job, I often walked past a street called Chrysanthemum Court. When the weather was warm, residents would sit on their steps, drinking and watching the world go by. One of the houses usually had a few locals and schoolkids hanging around, no matter what time of the day it was – always a good indicator. One day I was on my travels with Scooby, when his doppelganger ran out of this house and began jumping all over him. The other dog was chased by a woman with straggly black hair, no front teeth, and wearing the uniform of snide Juicy tracksuit bottoms and some sort of sportswear t-shirt. 'Come here, you little fucker!' she screamed, dragging her dog away. Then she turned to me. 'You're not from round here, mate.'

'Nah,' I said. 'I've just moved in to one of the flats in Haden Court.'

She gave me a toothless grin. 'So you're the one everybody's talking about? The word is, you're dodgy.'

'Nothing dodgy about me, love,' I said. 'My name's Pete.'

She seemed happy to give me a chance. 'I'm Gail,' she said. 'This is my daughter, and that's my fella.' She indicated a scruffy kid and a bloke who was sitting on the step nursing a can of cheap cider. I smiled, nodded my hellos, and went on my way.

Later that day, I mentioned Gail to the intelligence officer in the team.

'She's well-known,' he said. 'No front teeth? Yep, she lost them when the Drug Squad raided a dealer. He reckoned Gail was a grass, and when he was released he went straight to her house and punched her in the mouth.'

She wasn't a grass. That's life, I guess.

Over the next week, I made it my business to bump into Gail frequently. I would often ended up sitting on her doorstep, sharing a cup of tea or a can of Three Hammers. I began drip-feeding her my legend, waiting for the right moment to broach an interest in drugs. One day, when the chat turned that way, I said, 'I had a bit of a problem with the smack. But I've been off it for a year now. I just do a line or two these days.'

When you chase – smoke heroin – you lay the gear out in a line on a piece of tinfoil and apply heat underneath with a lighter, sucking the smoke up with a tube. The amount smoked would usually depend on how heavy the user's habit is: 0.1 of a gramme would normally do about two or three lines for someone with my supposed habit.

'I just split up from the missus,' I said, 'so it helps me get through the shit times.'

'Oh,' said Gail, with a sad look. 'I'm sorry to hear that, love.'

She was a sympathetic soul, and quite likeable; for a brief moment I felt a twinge of regret. But she was my way into the local heroin market, and you can't make an omelette without breaking a few eggs. A week or so later, I bumped into her, doing my best to look like I was withdrawing.

'You alright, Pete?' she said. 'You look terrible.'

'I'm back on the gear,' I said, 'and my van won't start. I'm having a walk round trying to get a quick fix so I can get my head straight before I get the van sorted.'

Gail hesitated. Then she said, 'Have you tried Pogo?'

'I don't know him.'

'He lives at number 11. If you have any problems, tell him to give me a ring.'

'Oh, thanks, love,' I said. 'That's fucking great. You're a star. I owe you one.'

I hurried off to Pogo's, feeling the usual knot of apprehension in my stomach as I got near. This was new territory, and potentially a major leap forward in the case. I was moving from passive stranger to someone showing an interest in the heroin market: make-or-break time. To add to which, I also didn't know who or what Pogo was; he could have been the mad axeman of Swadlincote, for all I knew.

I knocked on his door and waited. Eventually a young kid with ginger hair answered the door. He was deathly pale, so much so that I nearly checked his pulse.

'Is Pogo in?' I said.

'That's me,' he said. 'What do you want?'

'Oh, mate,' I said. 'Gail said you could help me out. I'm after a score?'

He thought for a few seconds. 'I'll have to use your mobile,' he said. 'I haven't got any credit on mine.'

I handed it over. I couldn't believe my luck: he was going to dial the dealer's number into it. After speaking for a minute, during which I tried to appear not to be listening, he handed me back my phone and disappeared into his house. Then he re-appeared in a nylon parka and led the way without another word. We weaved through a warren of streets to a row of shops just off the High Street. On the right hand side of the shops was a dirt track with a few back gardens leading to it. I handed Pogo a dirty, screwed-up tenner and waited by a small wall as he walked off up the alleyway. A couple of minutes later he bounced back round the corner with a yellow-toothed grin, and handed me a small tin foil wrap.

'Here you go, mate,' he said. 'Never call my uncle, or try scoring off him without coming to me first. He's paranoid.'

Nice one. Pogo. Not only had he scored for me, he'd given me enough information for the operational team to identify the dealer. He was instantly shaping up as an excellent pet junkie.

That day, my new 'girlfriend' also arrived. She was a buyer called Haley, who was fresh out of the tin after completing her course. She was a nice kid with long blonde hair who wasn't afraid to 'scuzz down' and let her appearance slip for the job. She was quite skinny, too, and easily looked the part of a smackhead.

A few days later, Pogo introduced me to another dealer, a lad called Sharpey, who stepped into the breach when his uncle ran out of gear. Sharpey seemed happy to serve me up, and gave me his mobile number. This was also an opportunity to introduce Haley. After a few calls, a girl who answered his phone told me to come to their house if I needed sorting. I decided to take Haley along to score and we parked up outside Sharpey's house. I knocked on the door and we were taken into a living room. Despite it being a warm day, the gas fire was going at full blast and we could hear dogs scratching and yelping on the other side of the kitchen door. Haley and I sat on a settee and the girl opened the kitchen door, whereon two pitbulls sprang from the kitchen and jumped on the settee where they began sniffing and growling at us. I think they could smell Scooby on me because they wouldn't leave me alone. The girl disappeared upstairs leaving us with the attentive guard dogs.

'You OK?' I said to Haley.

She managed a smile. I don't think she was a dog girl.

About five minutes later, a skinny, nasty-looking little shit who I'd never seen before strutted into the room. He looked to be of gypsy stock, and I later found out that this was the case – though he lived in a house so was known as a 'settled traveller'. He picked up a large wooden stake which he forced down between the front door and the second stair leading upstairs, effectively locking us in and stopping anyone forcing the front door open. I gave Haley a squeeze on her arm to reassure her as the bloke walked back into the living room and dropped a small tin foil wrap on top of the fireplace.

'There's your focking smack,' he snarled. He then picked up a large roll of tin-foil from the kitchen table and threw it down on the settee between us. 'And you'll be needing that!'

He was trying to intimidate us, and make us smoke the gear there and then.

'Why do I need that?' I said.

'Because you're going to have a smoke of the gear that you're so keen to focking buy.'

This is a constant issue for UCs. Real junkies are usually so desperate to get their hands on the crack or smack they want, and reluctant for various obvious reasons to carry it around on their persons, that they don't waste much time smoking it, shooting it up or tooting it, often on the spot. Obviously, we're not supposed to do that, and we face a constant battle to appear convincing. Some people can get away with it, and some people can't, and there's no easy answer as to why that should be. I think it boils down to Richard Gere's advice in *Chicago*: razzle-dazzle the bastards, they can't see with sequins in their eyes. So you look, act, talk, and smell the part. You come across as somebody who takes no shit, *ever*. You know your commodity inside out. And, if necessary… well, you probably *do* need to be prepared to smoke a bit of something from time to time.

The dealer thinks he's being smart by passing a spliff around. If this new guy's a cop, there's no way he'll take a draw on that, right? Wrong. Many's the time, if I'm honest, that I've smoked cannabis in a junkie's flat. This is what I meant earlier, when I talked about helping a job along. The suits in the offices don't like it, and were always talking of bringing random drugs tests for all UC officers. My view was, they could try it – but they'd quickly find themselves down on UCs. Because no actual junkie – anywhere, ever – is going to turn down the offer of a free toke. You might as well lay your warrant card on the table. I'd have smoked crack or heroin, too, if I'd had to. Luckily, I was always able to get out of that, one way or another.

On this occasion, I did it with the 'take no shit' approach. 'Who the fuck are you?' I said, narrowing my eyes.

'I'm the man with the focking smack, son. Who the fock are you?'

I fancied knocking the little twat through the wall, but I didn't want to upset the pitbulls. Just then, as luck would have it, the girl heard the raised voices and came back into the room. 'Leave it, Gaz,' she said. 'Let them out.'

The bloke held my stare for a few more seconds, and then reluctantly moved the wooden stake from the door. I slowly stood up and Haley followed me out of the house.

As we passed her, the girl said, 'Sharpey won't be around for a few days, so there's no point calling. And by the way where's my money for the gear?'

I forced a smile, and handed her a note. Then we made our way back to the van, both pumped with adrenalin. As I drove off, we burst out laughing. It had been quite a baptism of fire for Haley, but she'd kept cool when it mattered.

Over the next week or so we carried on trying to score off Pogo's uncle and Sharpey, but with slow progress.

* * *

BACK IN THE REAL WORLD, meanwhile, Carmel was due to go for a scan to see how the latest pregnancy was developing. I booked the afternoon off and went home to take her to the hospital. As we waited outside the room, I felt nervous. Ever since the miscarriage, I dreaded these days; I just wanted to get this appointment over with and to be told that everything was OK. The midwife ushered us into the room, Carmel got up onto the bed, and the midwife switched on the machine. She did the usual preamble, asking how Carmel felt as she applied the gel, and then began searching for the heartbeat. After a few seconds she stopped talking and began concentrating more.

Carmel said, 'Is everything OK?'

The midwife screwed up her face, concentrating. Then she looked at Carmel. 'No,' she said. 'I'm sorry, love, but it's not. I'm afraid there's no heartbeat.'

My own heart sank. I felt physically sick. I looked at my wife: she just stared straight ahead, saying nothing.

'I'll leave you alone for a while,' said the midwife. 'Then the doctor will pop along and have a chat to explain what will happen next.'

She walked away, and we sat in silence for about an hour. Eventually, we were joined by a nurse who escorted us through empty corridors. I wonder now if they had left us for so long in that room to allow all the other happy expectant parents time to leave before walking us to the doctor's surgery.

I needed to make a phone call to sort out childcare for our two kids, and was asked to do that in the car park. As I left the maternity wing, I walked past a group of heavily-pregnant mothers having a smoke by the main doors. I wanted to kick them up their arses – them and the junkie bitches who turned out kids by the half dozen. We didn't smoke, or fill ourselves with smack, and we'd just lost our baby: these selfish bastards were doing fine. It just wasn't fair.

After I had rung a friend, I made my way to the doctor's surgery where I found Carmel waiting alone. I tried to comfort her, and tell her that everything would be OK, but I was wasting my time. The tears hadn't come yet from either of us, we were both just in a state of shock. I sat and waited, sighing from time to time, for what seemed like an eternity. Finally, a doctor appeared. 'There are two options,' he said. 'The first is a tablet which will make the foetus leave eventually. The second is an operation to remove the foetus immediately.'

'I'll have the operation,' said Carmel. She just wanted to get things over quickly.

She hadn't eaten or drunk anything, so she was taken straight in. An hour or so later, I walked alongside her trolley to theatre, and kissed her goodbye outside the theatre doors.

We'd agreed that I'd get back to the kids. I went to my car, sat behind the wheel, and cried like a baby. After some time, I managed to pull myself together and began driving home. I had to pull over three times on the way when I broke down in tears again.

Later that evening I walked back into the ward at visiting time, and my sadness turned to anger. The ward was full of noisy parents, grandparents and children, all marvelling at their new babies and playing happy families – in the same room in which my wife lay unconscious in bed. I pulled the curtain closed around her and stood holding Carmel's hand for the rest of visiting time. She was well out of it, and I have to admit that I was relieved when the nurse told me it was time to go.

I went back home and rang our parents with the sad news. I also spoke to my handler, Jazz, to tell him that the job needed to be put on hold. This was the first time in years that I had managed to get work in some kind of context, and it took a tragedy like this to help me to realise just how much my family meant to me. I should never have forgotten that, even for a second. I went through a bottle of whiskey, a few beers, and a box of tissues, as I sat there feeling sorry for myself and ignoring the telephone. My mind went back to an incident that had happened years earlier during the ambulance dispute in East London. We had been called to a flat to a report of a miscarriage, and on arriving we were met at the front door by an Asian bloke who let us in. As we entered the living room we saw his wife standing sobbing, with her skirt pulled up by her waist and blood all over her legs. On the floor at her feet was a still-born baby. We needed to get them in the ambulance and take them to hospital so I asked the father if he had anything I could carry the baby in, at which point he produced a Tesco carrier bag. Black humour is a well-known coping strategy in the emergency services, and after this incident we cracked all kinds of sick jokes in the ambulance. Years later, it didn't seem as funny, as I sat at home alone, nursing a glass of Bushmills.

The next day I drove to the hospital with a thick head and brought Carmel home. Her mother came over from Ireland to be with her and to help start the healing process. I went back to work – too early. I thought that the best way I could cope was to throw myself into the job, rather than moping around at home. But my fuse was a lot shorter than usual.

One day I went to score off Sharpey, and, to my annoyance, the gypsy – Gaz – came out of the house and sat in the front passenger seat of my van.

'You can drive me to the stash to pick up the gear,' he said, aggressively.

I wanted to punch his fucking lights out there and then, but that wouldn't have been a good idea with the covert camera running. So I started driving, and the twat began giving me the third degree. Splendid.

'How long have you been on the gear, then?'

'Four years, on and off.'

'You don't focking look like much of a smackhead!'

'What does a smackhead look like?'

'Not like you.'

The more he went on, the angrier I got.

Swadlincote is the world capital of speed bumps. You can't go for more than 50 yards without having to slow down. As he gave me more and more of a hard time, I started driving faster and faster and hitting the speed bumps without slowing. Eventually, I was racing over them, and every 50 yards we were taking off and he was smashing his head into the roof of the van.

He'd shut up long before we pulled up outside his house, and started concentrating on surviving the journey. He was well shaken-up by the time we stopped, and he never gave me a hard time again

– other than skanking me a few weeks later. But, hey, life's too short to hold grudges.

Speaking of which, I had started to notice that my van smelt of urine. I mentioned this to Bob, the technical officer. He started chuckling to himself. Scooby didn't like being left in the van, and it turned out that every time I left he would cock his leg and urinate on the gear stick – all clearly captured on camera. Bob had been watching this for weeks without telling me. Crockett and Tubbs never had to put up with that sort of shit.

* * *

POGO'S UNCLE WAS still my main source, but he was difficult to get to. He would only sell through Pogo, or a middleman couple called Rob and Cat, a middle-aged pair who lived in a flat that would have done the set of *Steptoe and Son* justice. They spent most of their time in bed, holding court to a motley crew of users who needed them more than they liked them. They would deign to get up if someone knocked on the door wanting to score. Cat usually did the work; Rob was discouraged by the fact that it would have meant him getting dressed. Almost every time I saw him, he was wearing nothing but the same pair of Y-fronts.

On one rare occasion when he was dressed, he decided to take me to a new dealer. As he sat in the front of the van, I turned on the video, using the switch which was out of sight next to the steering column. He obliged me with a magnificent bout of carefree boasting. 'When I first moved here I was the main smack dealer in the area,' he said, airily. 'I used to have junkies queuing up round the block to score off me. I was on a fucking fortune. We used to move half a kilo a week, and then we started cutting the gear with blockers.' These are chemicals which block the body's opiate receptors and do not allow the opium 'hit' to take hold. 'As soon as they hit… whack! Instant fucking rattle, and they'd be back at my door wanting to score again!'

I sat there, nodding and laughing along, thinking, 'The judge is going to love you, mate'! It's always nice listening to them putting together the preparatory work for the prosecution.

He was an old lag, though, and he had been round the block a few times. I'd gone round to score off them again, in another attempt to get closer to Pogo's uncle; as Cat got out of bed to get dressed in her mismatched assortment of rags and knock-off fashion gear from the previous decade, Rob looked at me thoughtfully and said, 'There's something not right about you, Pete. You don't look like a smackhead, you never stay for a smoke after we've scored, and you disappear for days at a time.'

I laughed it off with some shit about saving the gear for later, but he wasn't the first to question my legitimacy in the area. I decided it was time to cut to the chase, and try to draw Pogo's uncle out. Cat walked back in looking like a scarecrow and I took a deep breath. 'Any chance you can get me a teenth, Cat?' I said. 'Only, I'm going car booting so I'll be away for a few days.'

A 'teenth' is 1/16th of an ounce, or about 1.75 grammes – not an insignificant purchase and one that could either draw me in closer or blow me out. On these sorts of jobs, I usually bought a number of 'points' – 0.1 of a gramme – or, at the very most, half-teenths. Street junkies who are regularly putting away teenths of smack are emaciated and wasted, because they don't spend any money on food. My build and appearance, the product of much lager and many kebabs, were such that it would have looked highly dodgy if I had tried buying more on a regular basis.

She called Pogo's uncle who said he would sort it, but we would have to ring him again in two hours' time. So later that day I picked Cat up and we made our way to Four Lanes End, where I dropped her off with my money. When she re-appeared, she looked like she had just seen a ghost – he'd obviously given her a hard time about wanting a relatively large amount so suddenly. I began driving back through Newhall and held my hand out for the gear.

Cat started gagging, and eventually she coughed up a lump of tin foil, plopping it, covered in saliva, into my upturned palm. I nearly threw up, and I can clearly be heard on the surveillance video, retching all the way to her place and trying to stop myself puking all over the dash board. When we got back there was a kid there dressed in British Gas overalls. I got to know him over the next few days and, one time when we were scoring together off another dealer, I noticed he went as white as a sheet as the dealer approached. He actually looked like he was about to faint with fear. After we had scored, I said, 'You OK? What was all that about?'

'Yeah,' he said. 'I'm alright. Buying drugs off these people scares the shit out of me. I hate it. I'm a pretty straight person, really, it's just the heroin... I want to stop, but I just can't. I'm in tears about it every morning when I wake up.'

It was a sad case, and I felt sorrier for him than I expected.

The emotional side of my job, and the Job generally, is hard to put a finger on. I'd just turned 40, and I was burning the candle at both ends, I know that. I had a pretty shit home life because of the recent miscarriage, and that was eating away at me. But I couldn't give Carmel and the kids the time they needed. I was obsessed with work. Every waking moment was spent thinking about drugs and drug dealers, or dealing with the stress of leading a double life in their presence. I was also getting very frustrated with the current operation. It was extremely difficult to get any forward momentum in such a close-knit community, but the SIO was making no allowances for that. Instead, with his own head full of budgets and overtime and grief from *his* bosses, he was putting more and more pressure on us to get results. In this line of work, you're only as good as your last job, or your last fuck up, and I was desperate to make this one work.

I was on a cycle of sleepless nights, too much booze, and too short a temper, and I was pedalling the bastard like Lance Armstrong on crack. As we moved towards the end of the job I was feeling shattered and very much on edge. I was losing my rag at the slightest thing – the SIO asked me one day if I had PMT. It all came to a head one Sunday, when Carmel, the kids and I went to visit relatives in Preston. We all went with some of my brothers to a local pub for a bite to eat, a few beers, and to watch the England v Sweden match at the start of the 2002 World Cup. The pub had a children's play area, as well as a big, widescreen TV, and I noticed a few known faces from the local football firm, which set my nerves jangling. Still, there was nothing to be done about it – I just hoped it didn't kick off.

Unfortunately, it did. It started as scuffles, and, when Sweden equalised to make it 1-1, a full-scale punch-up started in the car park. I watched as the groups ran *en masse* to the back of the pub where the outside children's play area was. My two boys were playing in there, along with lots of other youngsters, so I rushed out to check that they were OK. As I got to the play area, I saw two dickheads fighting on the floor about six feet from where my two sons were screaming in a plastic ball pit.

At that moment, all the tension, anger and energy that I had bottled up for weeks exploded, and I completely lost it.

I ran over and kicked the one on top in his head as hard as I could. He staggered to his feet and ran off, and I ran after him. I caught him by a kiddies' climbing frame, and smacked him a few times in the face – heavy, solid punches. He managed to get away and legged it into the pub. As I chased him, my eldest son, Sean, walked into his path. The wanker picked Sean up and threw him out of the way. I was now spitting with rage. He made it into the dining area, near to some of his mates, but I caught him again and was onto him, punching and kicking him to the floor. As he lay there, I picked up a big menu blackboard and smashed him over the head with it.

A load of screeching women from his party came running up to me, and made enough fuss to cause me to come to my senses and back off. I went into the toilets to clean myself up, and when I came back out I saw, to my absolute horror, a number of uniformed police officers talking to Carmel. She was giving them Sean's name, and making a formal complaint of assault on his behalf. But the water was muddy enough that, to my intense relief, the police agreed not to pursue the matter, and instead to give words of advice to the hooligan.

But it could have been a job loser for me. I had to get a grip.

* * *

BACK IN SWADLINCOTE, the strike day eventually came around and a few doors were put off their hinges.

The arrests went well into double figures. We never did get the uncle, but Pogo got three years, and Rob and Cat got five-and-a-half each. Apparently, Cat didn't cope well with her incarceration and for the first year or so refused to leave her prison cell unless a warder could coax her out.

Sharpey got three-and-a-half years and Gaz the gypsy got three. According to newspaper reports, Sharpey had an extra six months banged on top after security at Derby Crown Court found him in the court toilets trying to stuff a Kinder egg full of heroin up his backside. Brilliant.

Then there was kind-hearted, toothless Gail. Halfway through the operation, when I had been back and forward with Carmel, another buyer called Kurt had been brought in. He had concentrated on Gail, with a view to getting into the pills and powder scene. She developed a bit of a soft spot for him, and one day she had spilled her guts to him, boasting about how she would give her daughter cannabis at night to help her sleep, and that she gave cannabis and amphetamine to local schoolkids in exchange for their dinner money.

Oh dear.

Kurt recorded the whole thing on the body camera he was wearing. Three years imprisonment for Gail, and her little girl taken into care.

Not that it's really in my job description to offer helpful advice to drug dealers like Rob and Gail as to how to avoid prosecution, but I have to say that it's rarely a good idea to brag about your operation, and how big a dealer you are or were, when there's a stranger or new associate listening. You never know whether your words will come back to haunt you: judges really don't like it.

Chapter 9:

The Leicester Smack Trade

OVER THE NEXT few years, my work took me all over the country, though I mostly focused on the East Midlands. Sooner or later, most buyers burn out. It's dangerous, stressful and just plain weird, constantly pretending to be someone and something you're not.

Looking back, I think maybe I was on the way to becoming the fake me. I was lucky not to get arrested for some of the stunts I pulled and I was going off like a firework over trivial matters. I was getting careless and daft, too. After one Saturday night session at my local boozer, I came home and swallowed a gram of Sputnik resin that I had for a prop on jobs (there are dozens of varieties of marijuana, and Sputnik is a fairly strong hybrid of two other strains, Apollo 13 and Black Russian). I spent a very strange Sunday in orbit; I remember spending much of the morning sitting on my bed sniffing a freshly-washed bath towel, absolutely amazed at how fantastic it smelt. By teatime, things had gone very much in the opposite direction, and I crashed back to earth. To be honest, it scared the arse out of me.

On another occasion around this period, I was deployed to Manchester with another officer – I'll call him Kev, he's no longer in the police – to target a group of dealers who were pushing pills and powder out in the local pubs and clubs. The Operational team had provided us with a house on an estate nearby and we had spent a few weeks getting our faces known and testing the market. One Friday night, Kev and I were tasked to look at a couple of target venues – a pub and a nearby nightclub. A local detective had been tasked to pick us up after the deployment, so there was no problem with us having a drink or three to look natural.

We hit the boozer first. It had a long bar, a raised area where karaoke singers and DJs did their thing and a pool table in a smaller side room where the dealing was reported to take place. So after buying a pint each, Kev and I pushed our way through the crowds and wedged ourselves in by the pool table. I could smell cannabis immediately, and at least five or six people were openly smoking long, exotic-looking roll-ups.

I downed my pint, got halfway through a second and decided to approach a couple who were sharing a spliff. 'Any idea where I can get a bit of that?' I said, nodding at the joint.

They nodded over to a bloke in his late 20s who was standing by a small hatchway that served as a bar. He had shoulder-length hair, and was wearing a Stone Island jumper and a pair of Henri Lloyd jeans, and was deep in conversation with a couple of giggling birds. The three of them were sharing a spliff, so I made my way over and said, 'Any chance of a pull on that?'

The bloke – who turned out to be called Kirky – looked at me, shrugged and handed me the spliff. I had a long drag of it, held the smoke in for a moment and then involuntary coughed it out – much to the amusement of the three of them.

'Hey mate,' said Kirky, in a broad Mancunian accent. 'It's fuckin' bangin' gear, innit?'

I took another pull, just to prove I could, and handed it back. 'Cheers pal,' I said, making sure I didn't choke again, and weaved my way back to Kev. I felt very light-headed, and a bit sick, but a couple of mouthfuls of lager improved me no end. We gave it five minutes, until the girls had left and Kirky was standing by the bar alone, and then I walked back over to him. 'Mate,' I said, 'can you sort us out with a quarter of that?'

He looked at me. 'You don't want to buy a quarter until you've sampled it properly, mate,' he said, and with that he placed a large lump of cannabis resin and a packet of Rizla papers on the bar. 'There you go stranger,' he said. 'Fill your boots.'

Using four Rizlas, the tobacco from a B&H and the corner of the block, I rolled myself a fat one, trying to keep my hands steady as I did so. I wasn't a practised maker of joints, but it was a skill you had to learn – normally using tobacco only, of course. Eventually, I glanced up with a look of triumph and noticed Kev had joined us.

'What you waiting for mate?' said Kirky, with a grin. 'Spark up!'

I looked at Kev and said, 'You'd better get the beers in, chief.'

Before I knew it, half an hour had become an hour and then two; after a few more pints and joints, I was feeling an incredible sense of friendship towards both Kev and Kirky. I remember thinking that they were the two funniest and most sincere blokes I'd ever met; I was laughing at anything, and chatting to anyone who came near. Kirky eventually sold me that quarter ounce of resin and left me to it. Kev spent the rest of the night playing pool with a woman who'd also bought some dope off Kirky, while I trapped her other half by the jukebox and spent an hour or so delivering a lecture on Ska music generally, and the Two Tone label in particular.

Before we knew it last orders had been called and we had been booted out into the street, where we staggered off in search of a chip shop.

I decided now was a good time to call Jazz.

Jazz (very sleepy voice): 'Hello?'

Me: "JAZZ MATE IT'S FUCKING ME WE'VE FUCKING SCORED ME AND KEV WE'VE FUCKING DONE IT WE'VE GOT A FUCKING QUARTER OF A FUCKING OUNCE MATE!'

'Really? That's… great, Pete. I'm pleased for you. But it's not the first time you've ever scored, mate, so why are you ringing me at midnight to tell me?'

'I'M RINGING YOU TO TELL YOU I FUCKING LOVE YOU MATE AND I'M TELLING YOU AND THIS ISN'T DRINK TALKING MATE I'M TELLING YOU I WOULD FUCKING KILL FOR YOU!'

'Mmm. Listen Pete, you go to your pick up point and I'll get the liaison officer who is ON DUTY TO PICK YOU UP? Have you got that?'

'KEV SAYS HE LOVES YOU TOO MATE!'

'Fuck off.'

At times, my head was all over the place. My marriage had certainly suffered. All I wanted to talk about was buying drugs, and developing my cover story and knowledge of drugs. I was changing with the pressure of the work which, from 2001, was more long-term infiltrations. I know that Carmel would say I was not the person she had fallen in love with. She wanted me to jack it in and get back into uniform, and we talked long and often about this.

My argument was always that, because of the overtime involved in buying, and the annual special priority payments for officers doing this kind of work – £1,750, which was a lot of cash at the time – we were financially much better off. What I didn't say was that I had turned into a kind of junkie myself, hooked on buzz of the work. When an operation finished, or I was at home for a rare weekend, or away on a bit of holiday, I was twitchy and irritable, and craving excitement.

I was lounging around at home one morning after end of the Swadlincote job, trying to relax my way through some of the annual leave I had stored up. I was mulling over a long and fraught chat I'd had with Carmel the night before. It had been the usual story: she wanting me to knock the UC work on the head, me wondering how we'd make ends meet if I did. I'd sort of convinced myself that she was right – surely I did want out? The whole thing was running round my brain, bumping into all the images of dealers and crackhouses and smackheads that otherwise filled it, when my phone rang.

It was Jazz. After the usual chit-chat, he came out with it. 'Pete, we've got a big heroin infiltration on in Leicester… You interested?'

'When and how long?'

'Next week, for seven months.'

I thought about it – for a second or two. 'Sure – no problem.'

Did I want to quit this fucking job, or not? I had my answer.

The following Monday morning, Jazz picked me up from home and drove me down to a big detached house on the outskirts of Leicester. It had a set of office units attached to it, and these units were rented out by local small businesses. The police team I was being attached to was masquerading as an engineering firm. When we arrived we were met at the car by my liaison officer, Rick, who led me into an office away from the back-up team. We didn't hit it off, at all. 'I don't want any unnecessary contact between you and the remainder of the team,' he said, and proceeded to run through his own CV. He'd spent time as a Level 1 UC himself, and seemed to think he was the dog's bollocks when it came to undercover work. I got the distinct impression that if I'd personally taken down the Medellin Cartel, Rick would have had a story to top it. I looked at Jazz, and he just shrugged. It was going to be a very long seven months.

Next I met Phil, the SIO and a DI within Leicestershire Police. He turned out to be a cracking bloke, and promised me his full support. The back-up team consisted of four PCs who would stay close by whenever I was deployed. This lot were a good bunch – handy lads, as keen as mustard and always up for a laugh – though sometimes they were a bit odd. The operation ran through the summer, and one day when the weather was hotter than Rio De Janeiro they relieved the boredom with a little competition. They wound up the windows in their car and turned the heaters on full blast and sat, parked up, in the blazing sun: the first one to bottle out and get out of the car lost. But I had no doubt they'd be there if I needed them. It's important that you feel comfortable with the guys you're working with and, Rick aside, I did.

Leicester has always had a decent-sized heroin problem, with the drug coming in from two main sources. The Asian dealers in the city's large Indian and Pakistani community import their smack directly from Pakistan, Afghanistan, and Turkey, often hidden in bales of textiles or agricultural produce. The main white dealers, in areas like Beaumont Leys and the neighbouring Mow Acre, usually buy their gear from wholesalers in London and then distribute it through a network of young kids on the estates.

My operation was targeting the big white operation on the Beaumont Leys, a shitty, 1960s housing estate made up of concrete tower blocks and grey, semi-detached houses, inhabited by a mainly white underclass with a smattering of first and second generation immigrants to leaven the mix. The kids all wore street labels, usually tracksuits and baseball caps, and they were always knocking about. Unemployment was high, as was the crime rate and drug abuse. The estate had a high percentage of heroin and crack cocaine dealers, between them moving millions of pounds-worth of product each year; as usual, they had all known each other since birth and the suspicion and mistrust with which strangers to the area were treated was worse than anywhere I'd been before.

The first thing to do was to move into a flat on the estate and start to get a feel for the area. I was after the keys to a little one-bedder a good distance away from the shopping precinct where a lot of the drug dealing went on, and preferably in a cul-de-sac – so that, when I was there, I could better monitor the comings and goings.

To get the flat, I had to go through a formal interview at the local council's housing office. These had been set up for me by someone in Leicestershire Police who had an inside contact in the department. This contact was officially signed up to the job; going through the motions of being interviewed and allocated a flat, as though I was a normal member of the public, would make my presence look kosher, and guard against the possibility of the wrong side having their own contacts in the same department who might check me out and find that I'd got my flat via some secret route.

On my first appointment, I walked into the main reception area and joined a queue of seven foot Somalis wearing bright robes. The lady behind the counter was having a heated conversation with the leader of the group. 'This is a perfectly good house we have allocated you, so why don't you want to accept it?'

'We do not like the area. It is dirty and full of naughty English boys.'

I could understand the Somalis wanting to live near their friends, rather than among Leicester's indigenous scum, but the council lady was unsympathetic. 'This is the only house available, so take it or leave it.'

When the big Somali protested, she snatched the keys back off the counter. 'Move aside please,' she said. 'I need to serve the next client. Next!'

Next was me. Hesitantly, I stepped forward. 'Hi,' I said. 'I've come for an interview. I don't mind where my flat is as long as it isn't in Somalia.'

I was given all the relevant forms and, crucially, the keys to my pad. We were in business.

I spent the next few days moving furniture in and making the place look lived-in. Once I'd done this, I began cruising around the local drugs hotspots that the intelligence officer, Sara, had identified for me. I was using my usual cover, that I bought and sold mountain bikes for weekend car boot sales. That gave me a sensible reason for being out of the area for days at a time, when I was actually on annual leave. I was driving my wired Astra van, and had a smart phone. I also took Scooby, the great gearstick-urinator. In some ways, that was a pain in the arse, but he looked the part around the estate and I looked less like UC Old Bill with him around.

So I set off round Beaumont Leys, being pulled along by Scooby, in search of anyone who looked like a heroin user and who might be prepared to introduce a total stranger to his dealer. And, as luck would have it, my pet junkie appeared almost immediately, in the shape of a young lad who I saw hanging around a phone box on the shopping precinct, showing flu-like symptoms – which, in the middle of summer, is one of the classic signs of your standard issue junkie. He was a skinny kid in his early 20s, with a spotty face and dirty blond hair, wearing a padded jacket and the ubiquitous tracksuit bottoms and baseball cap. I approached him. 'Are you looking to score, mate?' I said.

He looked like a startled rabbit caught in the headlights, and shook his head.

'Want a fag?' I said, offering my packet of Lambert and Butler. 'Look, I'm new to the area. I've just moved down from Manchester, and I'm struggling to get any gear.'

He took a fag and we both lit up.

'I buy and sell bikes, by the way,' I said. 'Here, have one of my flyers.'

I handed him one of the A4 sheets I was sticking up on any flat surface I could find, offering cash for wheels. If I was in luck, he'd screw his neighbour's shed that night to sell a bike onto me so he could get the readies together for his next day's supply of smack.

'Ta,' he said.

'Look,' I said, 'you know what it's like. I've been off the gear for a bit, I'm only doing the odd line or two. If you hear anyone knocking any out…'

Slowly, he started to relax. He told me his name was Wayne, and eventually admitted that he was waiting to score off a bloke called Kev. 'I'm a bit short, though,' he said.

'I don't mind subbing you a few quid if you can sort me out?' I said, and handed him my mobile. He dialled a number, told someone that he wanted two bags, before handing me my phone back and telling me to follow him. I couldn't believe he was taking me along to meet his man this soon: more sensible junkies usually took my money and made me wait round a corner, and often did a runner. He led me to an underpass, where we waited for about 15 minutes. He'd become quite talkative, quizzing me at some length about my habit, about how I took my smack, and where I normally scored. I was prepared for all of it: any undercover buyer needs to have an encyclopaedic knowledge of whichever commodity they're purchasing. Wayne's head suddenly looked up as a fit-looking bloke walked towards us along the underpass. The newcomer, another white kid in his early 20s, had an athletic build and a boxer's nose. Wayne nodded to him and he walked over to us. This, evidently, was Kev.

'How much you after?' he said.

We both asked for a ten bag, and he reached down into his sock, pulled out a small Clingfilm package and removed two small wraps for us. He looked at me a bit closer, then, and said, 'Never seen you before mate, where you from?'

'I've just moved onto the estate from Stockport.'

'I know Stockport,' he said. 'Who'd you score from there?'

'This black kid called T?' I said.

You can score from a black kid called 'T' in every town in the country.

'Right,' said Kev, nodding. 'Just get my number off Wayne and I'll sort you out.'

What a result! My first outing, and I already had an intro. Plus, I had Wayne. From now on, he'd be able to reference me into any other dealers I came across. The end result, invariably, would be a shoeing once the dealers started getting nicked. But that's just the way things go.

I made my way back to my flat and called Rick to let him know that I had been successful, so he set up a debrief at the office. As I relayed the events of the day, I was surprised by a cheer that went up from the back-up team. It turned out that Kev was the main dealer on the estate, and that the local cops had been after him for years. They'd been hoping to catch him at it; they couldn't believe their luck – and it *was* just luck – that he'd fallen at the first hurdle.

After the debrief, we had a bit of a chat and a laugh, and then Rick summoned me into my private room at the covert premises where the back-up team ran the 'engineering business'.

'I told you,' he said, 'I don't really like you having the crack with the back-up team. It's not healthy to build up a relationship with those officers.'

I couldn't believe what I was hearing. 'I think you're talking bollocks,' I said. 'If I need help, I want those lads to like me enough to actually want to come and dig me out, rather than hold back because they think I'm some jumped-up prima donna who deserves a good kicking.'

The following day, I headed back out onto the Beaumont Leys with Scooby to try to make contact with Kev and buy more heroin, waiting until the same time of day as our first encounter to ring him. He answered quickly and told me to wait in the same underpass, which I did. I started to get nervous when I noticed a number of junkies gathering, and looking at me with some suspicion. Soon enough, Kev appeared on a mountain bike and the junkies swarmed over to him. I joined the queue, and when it was my turn I exchanged my drugs money for a small bag of smack. I made my way to a safe area, and reached for my mobile to tell the back-up team that I had scored again.

That's when things went wrong, and I dropped a major bollock.

In recent years, when I've delivered courses about street culture and buying to potential undercover officers, I go on at some length about the need to learn how to operate all the equipment you have, until it's absolutely second nature. This is why. On this occasion, I hadn't completely familiarised myself with the phone I had been issued. I dialled, and the phone was answered by a bloke. I said, 'It's Pete.'

'Alright, Pete?' said the voice.

'I've scored off Kev,' I said, 'and I'm ready to be picked up.'

'Who the fuck's this?'

'It's Pete,' I said, feeling uneasy. 'Why – who's that?'

My uneasiness was not helped by what came next.

'It's Kev.'

'Oh fuck!' I said. 'Sorry, mate. I thought you were Wayne.'

It was the best I could do in that instant.

I hung up, and then I nearly threw up. What a dickhead. Undercover rules dictate that I should now return to the covert premises and explain to the SIO and the rest of the team that, due to my fuck up, the job had to be scrapped. If there had been other UCs out there with me, that's exactly what I would have done. But as I was on my own, and the only person at risk was me, I decided to keep my mouth shut and carry on as if nothing had happened. If Kev suspected me of being Old Bill, I was in the shit. But, frankly, the alternative – of looking like policing's biggest twat in front of Rick and the rest – was even less appealing. If I scrapped the case, that was a major operation, with a huge team and all the associated expense, down the toilet.

What made matters worse was that this had happened on a Friday and I wasn't due to deploy again until Monday. I spent the weekend mentally flogging myself for my incompetence. Anyone can make mistakes, but going out without checking the kit was unforgivable. I also had plenty of time to ponder my impending doom at the hands of a drug dealer in a Leicester underpass. Kev was a seriously violent individual, and I wasn't happy to go out entirely unarmed. I no longer carried a knife down my sock, but I had to have something on me. I fished out an old football sock and dropped a lump of concrete into it, knotting the open end. I had a weapon, of sorts, if I needed it.

On the Monday morning, I travelled down to Leicester, bright and early, hiding my home-made club under the front passenger seat of the van. The plan, despite my screw up, was pretty straightforward: I was off to score, or meet my maker. I'd made this mess and it was up to me to clear it up, if there was any clearing up to do. When I arrived I dialled Kev, my heart thumping.

He agreed to meet me. Was there a note of suspicion or aggression in his voice? I wasn't sure.

I waited by the underpass for almost half an hour, sweating. And, as so often when you're expecting the worst, it all went fine. Kev turned out and met me, and in the two minutes we spoke he made no mention of the phone call.

Maybe he believed that I really *had* been trying to phone Wayne. Maybe he had been so wasted over the past 72 hours that he'd forgotten the incident. Or maybe he was now suspicious and keeping an eye on me. I thought the latter was the most likely, but there was no need to start whirling that concrete-filled sock round my head.

Later that day, I was walking through the estate when I bumped into Wayne and stood around chatting with him for a few minutes. He was very concerned about the geopolitics of the Middle East, and the US strategy in that region, the War on Terror, and the likely increased volatility that implied for the global economy. In short, he was pissed off that the invasion of Iraq was interrupting the free flow of heroin into Leicester. But he perked up when he told me he was scoring off a girl called Tracey. 'She does banging gear,' he said. 'I'll let you meet her if you like?'

Never being one to look a gift horse in the mouth, I hassled him into taking me to her straightaway. Tracey lived with her family in a semi-detached hovel deeper into the estate, where she operated as part of an established cottage industry. The system was that a smackhead would collect your money on the door and tell you to return an hour later. You would then retire to a nearby children's playground with the other junkies and while the time away talking about whatever took your fancy, which tended to be heroin. An hour later, you returned and were shown into the living room by one of Tracey's many children, to join the junkies ahead of you in the queue who were sat on the floor passing around spliffs.

The first time I was allowed into the inner sanctum, one of Tracy's lads cast a critical eye over me and announced, 'The first time I saw you I thought you was a copper.'

At which point everyone in the packed room turned to look at me and a few junkies nodded and grunted in agreement. Then the little nuisance carried on. 'Do you want to know why you're different to the rest of these?'

'Go on.'

'Because these are all sweating, and you ain't.'

Not quite correct. If the little git had taken time to run his hand up my spine, he would have found enough sweat to float the QE2.

'And your van.'

'Yeah?'

'You sell mountain bikes, yeah?'

'Yeah.'

'So how come you've had the same fucking bikes in the back of it for the last two weeks, then?'

Mentally, I cursed myself again. *Careless bastard. Another* fuck up. The tangle of bikes served two purposes. One, as basic props. Two, to make it hard for anyone who broke into the van – or stopped me, in the case of the local police – to get to the spare wheel compartment and find my recording equipment. I hadn't expect anyone to notice that, despite my legend, I didn't actually sell any of them. But some of these junkies have very fucking sharp eyes, even if they look dopey. *Careless,* careless *bastard.*

'I sold two last week,' I said, fronting it, 'and I'm getting rid of two more later on, so you've got that wrong, youth.'

He was about to say something, but the moment passed with the timely arrival of Tracey bearing gifts. I was forgotten about as we all queued up to be handed our smack.

I got out of there, and the first thing I did was change the bikes for some new ones out of the property store. It was a timely reminder. People often questioned my identity, and I shouldn't be making it easy for them. I was probably going to be OK, though. These folks are suspicious one minute; the next they're so wasted that they don't even know who they are, never mind you. Ultimately, they're ruled entirely by the desperate need to get their next fix, so other issues quickly become peripheral. But I was still acutely conscious that I had now made a couple of schoolboy errors inside a fortnight, and getting your cover blown can, and sometimes does, lead to extremely bloody consequences – as we will see shortly. I had to stamp out this complacency.

A lot of dealers don't seem to comprehend the length of time involved in a major operation: if they haven't been busted after a couple of weeks, you can't be police. Over the coming weeks, Tracey's family accepted me – even Mr Sharp Eyes – and didn't bat an eyelid when I turned up. I used to sit there, chatting, and waiting for the smack to be delivered. One particular day, I noticed that the house was full of stylish new furniture and I mentioned this in passing to Tracey.

She gave me a knowing smile. 'All the asylum seekers are getting flats round here,' she said, 'and they're all being kitted out with IKEA stuff. If I need anything, I just get one of the lads to get it for me and I pay them with a ten bag.'

That explained the large number of skinny youths I'd seen scurrying around with Scandinavian dressing tables and such like.

A couple of months in, I was happy that my cover was relatively safe with both Kev and Tracey. I felt they trusted me enough not to pat me down – and therefore that it was safe enough to introduce covert body cameras into the operation. Covert cameras had developed since my early days, and had shrunk from being about the size of a shoebox – usually carried in a bag or strapped to the small of your back – to much smaller things that could be stuck down your underpants. There still seemed to be an appetite in the police for using the big cameras, probably because they were bought and paid for, and still worked, and the people making the financial decisions didn't have to use them. But it seemed daft to me to take risks when there was better equipment available. Not long before this, a test purchase operation was being conducted in Chapeltown in Leeds, and the buyers were using a bulky camera that was strapped to their bodies. The officers, who were working in a pair, had scored off the dealer a number of times and felt confident that the dealer was happy with them. They were ready to get video evidence. One officer wore the camera and his job was to step back from the deal and film the transaction while the officer without the camera approached the dealer. The pair called the dealer and were directed to an alleyway in the centre of Chapeltown where they joined a queue waiting to score. The dealer appeared and began dishing out the gear in exchange for money. But as the UCs approached, for some reason he became suspicious of the junkie in front of them, and patted him down. Now he was spooked, and insisted on patting down the officer without the camera, and then approached the officer who was wearing it. The officers followed procedure and split up, running from the scene. The dealer and his mates chased the bloke who was wearing the camera deep into bandit country, and when he became lost he went into a shop for help. But the gang of dealers dragged him out of the shop and down an alleyway where they found the camera. They then kicked the living fuck out of him. It took the rescue team 15 minutes to find his unconscious body and call an ambulance.

This, and incidents like it, had encouraged technical officers to insist on the up-to-date kit being available at every opportunity. I was working around another buyer, Lee, and he and I had been issued with the smaller versions after we'd pointed out that, if we were deployed with the larger, obsolete version and we came to harm after being compromised, when smaller, more covert versions were available, EMSOU had better have very deep pockets.

* * *

SOME WEEKS INTO the operation, Lee was moved in to work the neighbouring Mow Acre estate, and we began bouncing off each other and using each other as references. Lee had successfully infiltrated a family of heroin dealers called the Rourkes, and over a period of weeks obtained enough video evidence to have them boxed away. But this was an opportunity to broaden the operation and I was introduced to them as a crackhead, to explore the possibility of them introducing me to a crack dealer.

One day I met one of the Rourkes outside a pre-arranged telephone kiosk. He got into the passenger seat of my Astra and directed me towards the centre of Leicester, doing his best to fight off the attentions of Scooby while I drove through the busy lunchtime traffic. As we pulled away from some lights, Rourke said, conversationally, 'So, do you ever got stopped by the police?'

'I've never had no problems with them,' I said.

Talk about tempting fate. Thirty seconds later, a traffic patrol car drove past us and quickly spun round to follow me. The police driver put on his blues and indicated for me to stop. At this stage, Rourke was flapping like a budgie and frantically stuffing a bag of heroin down his sock.

I pulled over and waited. One of the bobbies approached my window and leaned in. 'Can you turn the engine off please, sir?' he said.

I did as I was told, knowing what was coming next. 'Can I have your name and date of birth and home address, please?'

'Pete Ashton,' I said, 'January 18, 1962, and I live at number 12, Pitchens Close.'

This was tricky. There was no Pete Ashton – certainly not one with my face, a driving licence, or car insurance. I knew his next move would be to check me out on the PNC, and that at that point he would find out that I didn't exist. Then I'd be nicked.

The other officer was checking out Rourke's details, and while they were waiting for the answers from the PNC they started going through the vehicle with a fine-toothed comb. This made me even more twitchy; I didn't want my cover blowing, to the cops or the Rourkes, and had to hope that the jumble of bikes might put the PC off from being too thorough. One thing I was certain of from my own years in uniform – they would be setting his antennae twitching.

Just as my cop started making as though to drag one of the bikes out, his oppo came over, ear to his radio. 'You're catching the bus, chief,' he said to Rourke. 'So you can clear off.'

Rourke couldn't believe his luck, and he scurried off down the road with a sock full of smack and without so much as a backwards glance. 'Can you come and sit in the back of the patrol car, please?' the bobby said to me. I did as instructed, and he left me unsupervised while he returned to chat to his mate by the Astra. I took the opportunity to speak into my smart phone. 'I'm about to get arrested,' I told the back-up guys. 'Stand by.'

Sure enough, a minute later the cop returned to me, and slapped me in handcuffs. 'I'm arresting you on suspicion of handling stolen goods,' he said. 'I am detaining you to ascertain your correct identity because I believe you've given me a false name and address.'

No shit, Sherlock – promote this boy, and move him to CID now.

I was desperate to avoid the van being impounded, or Scooby being put in the kennels – or, worse, left in there alone for a few minutes to allow him to piss on the gearstick.

'Look,' I pleaded, 'if you take me to my flat on the Leys I can show you my paperwork to prove who I am.'

They agreed, and there followed a slightly farcical series of events. One of them went over to the Astra to drive it behind the squad car, but returned slightly shaken as Scooby had leapt at the window with bared teeth unwilling to let him in. Then I was placed in the back of the Astra with Scooby on my lap, and me handcuffed to the front. Everything seemed fine until PC Plod sat in the front and Scooby became a foaming mass of fangs again, and launched himself at him. Being cuffed, I couldn't stop him and the poor copper had to fight Scooby off unaided.

Eventually order was restored and we headed to my flat, where Scooby was locked in the bathroom and the cops had a good look round. Unsurprisingly, they raised their eyebrows somewhat at the burnt foil that was scattered all over the floor – props I had left around to fool any junkies who might break in to check me out.

I produced my housing association paperwork, but the cops were still having none of it and said they were taking me to the station so that they could put me on a Livescan machine so they could take my computerised fingerprints. This wasn't good, at all, because all police officers have their fingerprints taken when they join.

My cover was now in serious danger. I was going to have to put on a show at the nick so that they would stick me in a cell; this would buy the back-up team more time to think of a reason to get me released without blowing the operation. I hoped that they hadn't been making a brew when I'd alerted them to my predicament via the smart phone.

I was walked out of my flat in handcuffs – which, to be fair, did my image in the area no harm at all – and placed in the back of the car. When we arrived at Beaumont Leys police station, I was relieved to see Sara, the intelligence officer, standing by the back gate pretending to have a fag. She caught my eye, and I relaxed in the knowledge that at least they knew where I was, and were hopefully making waves to get me released.

Rick wasn't around – not great, for a liaison officer – but unbeknown to me a girl called Lindsey from the back-up team had sped over to Leicestershire Police HQ to try to arrange my release with someone important.

This arrest – and I was only surprised it had taken this long, given I was driving a dodgy van and living the life of a criminal – was as much of a risk to the operation as my misplaced phone call. As in the Colin Gunn case, corrupt officers can pass information about ongoing operations to suspects; no local officers were to know that the job was running until the strike day, when all the troops would be gathered to bash down doors and pull people in.

As the two burly traffic officers took me into the custody area I was still unsure of my predicament so I went ahead with plan A to avoid the computerised imprint. I walked straight up to the custody sergeant, stuck my nose six inches from his, and shouted, 'I want to make a fucking complaint!'

The custody sergeant took a step backwards. 'OK, sir, calm down. Just let the officers explain why they have brought you here.'

But I was on a roll. 'Calm fucking *down*? Don't tell me to fucking calm down. I've been assaulted, and I want to see a doctor.'

Cue two puzzled traffic bobbies looking at each other, mouths agape.

'You can see a doctor after we take your prints,' said the custody sergeant.

So I carried on. 'I'm not doing a fucking scan. I want to make a complaint now!'

After another five minutes of this, I managed to find myself standing in a cell wearing a paper suit and a blanket over my shoulders and holding a polystyrene cup of cold tea. Mission accomplished, sort of.

All I had to do now was to wait to be sprung. If it took much longer, and I was asked to do the scan I'd need to really kick off. Within 10 minutes, I'd finished my tea, and within half an hour I'd finished reading some custody leaflet about 'rights for detained persons'. I was bored, with a capital B. But I've hung around enough custody areas in my time to know not to start pressing cell buzzers or rattling the hatch on the door for attention, even supposing I'd wanted them to remember I was there, so I just sat back and wait for my hopefully imminent freedom.

A couple of hours later, as I lay in my cell, getting increasingly fed up with the smell of piss and sweat, unbeknown to me Lindsey and a Leicester superintendent were having a chat with the traffic officers who had nicked me. They told them that I was a known criminal who was being followed by a surveillance team, and that they needed me to be released as soon as possible so that their operation could re-commence.

The traffic cops, and particularly the custody sergeant, were more than happy with this, and an hour or so after being nicked I was kicked out of the front door of the police station, wondering how much the outside world had changed during my time inside. Not much, as it turned out.

I made my way back to the operation headquarters in the business park, to have the piss taken out of me by the rest of the team, and another day drew to a close.

* * *

THE NEXT MORNING, I contacted Rourke and picked him up by the phone box. He didn't mention the previous day's drama, just directed me to the centre of Leicester, where we parked and made our way to the shopping precinct. He explained that we were due to meet a man called Ezra who would sort me out with as many rocks as I needed. As we sat on a bench outside JD Sports, I noticed that Rourke was shivering and sweating and finding it hard to stay still. He was obviously rattling. He was talking skittishly about the street dealer's favourite subject – heroin – and if I closed my eyes I'd have though I was sharing a bench with a Jamaican, not a skinny white kid from the East Midlands.

All of a sudden, he jumped to his feet and walked, Liam Gallagher-style, his jeans hanging off his arse, over to a mixed race bloke who had appeared through the crowd with a group of black kids. This was obviously Ezra. There was some shaking of hands and nodding in my direction, and then Rourke brought him over to me.

'Ring this number in a couple of hours, yeah,' said Ezra, handing me a piece of paper with a mobile number on it. 'I'll sort you out.'

Rourke then rolled off with Ezra, and I made my way home with another useful target.

Over the next few weeks, I saw Rourke's health decline sharply as his heroin addiction took over. And he was getting more desperate. On one occasion, he ripped me off for twenty quid which I gave him to buy a rock of crack from a new dealer. He spent the next few days avoiding me. He wouldn't come to the door if Lee and I knocked, and if we sat outside his house in our car he just hid in his room. One day, we bumped into him and his older brother in the city centre. He looked a bit shaken, though it was probably mostly that he was off his face on smack.

'I want my money, man,' I said, menacingly.

'Alright, alright,' he said, holding his hands up defensively. 'Go to the bus stop near my house, yeah? I'll see you there in half an hour and give you the money.'

Half an hour later, as Lee and I sat near the bus stop, a bus pulled up. Within seconds, the headlights began flashing and a mechanical voice inside the vehicle shouted, 'THIS BUS IS UNDER ATTACK!'

Then the two Rourke brothers jumped out and ran towards their house, each carrying a couple of money bags. Lee and I looked at each other, and burst out laughing. They had just robbed a bus to pay a copper back the money they owed him. Outstanding!

'We'd better get out of the area before the police arrive,' said Lee, still grinning.

Over the next few weeks, I repeatedly rang the number that Ezra had given me. He never answered it when I used my own mobile, and when I used a public phone box he would answer but make some excuse when he realised it was me. He obviously didn't trust me, and so we decided to cool it with him and begin looking in a different direction for crack.

By now, it was a couple of months into the operation and we had a good number of dealers boxed off with at least three clean buys caught on camera. It was important to be careful when we had enough evidence, and to stop buying at the right time: to do otherwise ran the risk of our being accused of acting as *agents provocateur* by the defence. We had to play this quite carefully, too, though. Dealers get pissed off and nonplussed when you stop scoring off them, particularly when they see you knocking about, clearly still in the market, and they're selling perfectly decent gear. There were some awkward moments when we'd bump into a junkie and press-gang him into taking us to score with him, only to discover he was taking us to a dealer who was already boxed off from earlier in the operation. You could end up in a farcical situation where you'd have to make up some reason for not wanting to score off a dealer who was known to be selling banging good shit. On one occasion, I said I didn't like the dealer because I thought he was 'a chutney ferret'. This was the first thing that came into my head, and I'd dragged it from the deepest depths of my consciousness. It dated back to my time in Derbyshire as a uniform. The Derbyshire Complaints and Discipline Department habitually emailed all supervisors within their force a weekly bulletin on what was politically acceptable within the workplace. One such bulletin revolved around a case in Brighton, where an employee of the council sued his employers because he was gay and one of his colleagues called him a 'chutney ferret'. This cost Brighton Council a few grand. Complaints and Discipline picked up on it and emailed all supervisors forbidding the use of the term. This email was read out on all briefings to police shifts when they came on duty; predictably, a previously obscure term for a gay man very quickly became the go-to word for almost anything and anyone in the force.

***

ONE DAY I BUMPED into a couple of junkies, a bloke and a girl, who seemed to know me from somewhere. I assumed they were lovers – they were holding hands. The male asked me, 'Where are you getting your grips from these days mate?'

'Grips' was a new one on me, but I assumed he meant heroin. 'Tracey,' I said.

'Oh, right,' he said. 'Listen, we're scoring off a lad called Pinkey these days. Do you fancy coming in with us? That way we can get a bigger lump and share it?'

Even junkies understand economies of scale.

I already knew Pinkey from when I'd been scoring off Tracey and her family. Tracey knew I had a car, and she had asked me one day if I would take her and her bloke into the centre of Leicester to score. I did that and arranged to return later to pick them up. This gave me the chance to stick a video tape in the recording equipment hidden under the spare wheel, and hopefully obtain some decent evidence. I returned a short time later and a little skinny bloke jumped in the front passenger seat while Tracey and her fella climbed in the back seats. The skinny bloke was Pinkey.

'Head for Leicester railway station,' he said. He seemed quite chatty and, with the Achilles heel of many a dealer, began boasting. 'I'm making a grand a week these days,' he said. 'Sometimes two or three. You don't wanna use no-one else. I'm the main man round here.'

As we drove past the railway station he directed me through a series of terraced streets in an area that was predominantly Asian. Then he told me to pull over next to an old cinema that had been converted into a mosque. He started mumbling into his mobile phone and then muttered a few more directions to me. We moved off and parked up in a nearby street and waited for about half an hour, during which Pinkey began giving me the third degree about who I was, where I came from, and if I had a heroin habit. I told him I did about twenty quid's-worth of smack a day.

But he was dubious. 'I tell you what,' he said. 'Once we've scored, we'll drive somewhere quiet and have a smoke together.'

Fucking marvellous. I hate it when that happens. We were eventually approached by an Asian bloke who shook hands with Pinkey and handed over a Clingfilm package in exchange for a bundle of notes. Pinkey then pulled a set of gravity scales from up his sleeve and attached the package to the clip on the bottom.

'Oh, man,' he said, looking at the Asian bloke with a disgusted expression. 'There's too much of this shit wrapped around it. I can't see how much gear there is.'

With that, he unwrapped the package as the guy explained that it was banging gear. He had a bizarre Jamaican accent, and I couldn't help thinking that this was a fine testimony to multicultural Britain: white junkies buying heroin off young Asians with Jamaican accents. He was hopping from foot to foot, and clearly wanted to rejoin his mates, who were strutting their stuff round a Nissan Sunny, all dressed like Ali G. I half-wanted to point out that it was supposed to be a comedy. But Pinkey wasn't to be rushed, and carefully weighed the heroin, while I filmed him on my covert camera on the steering column of the van. Tracey and her fella were still sitting in the back, while Scooby jumped up and down and barked at everyone who walked past.

Eventually Pinkey seemed satisfied, and the mood lightened a little. He bumped fists with the Asian dealer and then told me to drive back to Beaumont Leys. To my relief, he seemed to have forgotten about our planned communal smoke. I was never at my best after that sort of thing.

I dropped him off near his flat, and he leaned back into the car to speak to Tracey. 'Give it an hour before coming round,' he said. 'I've got to go and pick the kids up from school.'

Heart-warming. He was obviously a caring parent who took his family responsibilities very seriously. I then dropped Tracey and her bloke back at their house, refusing the kind offer of a cup of coffee and a spliff.

At the debrief that day, I'd heard a lot about Pinkey from Sara, the intelligence officer on the operation.

'He's a sly little bastard,' she had said. 'We've been after him for years. Be on your guard when you're with him. He carries a knife and he doesn't mind using it.'

But since that first meet, four weeks had passed and I hadn't seen anything of him. Here was my opportunity to get into him, courtesy of this pair of lovebirds.

All of this flashed through my mind; I tried to look like I was weighing up the pros and cons of the offer from the two junkies, before eventually saying, 'OK, I'll get in with you, but only if I can come with you to score.'

They agreed and we made our way through a maze of alleyways towards a block of flats. The bloke spoke into an intercom by the communal door and a voice told us to come up. We went up to a flat on the third floor. The door had a steel gate across it. The lad knocked on the window and the door was answered by a teenage girl who, almost predictably, looked like death. She was totally spaced out, and we followed her into a living room to join six other junkies all smoking heroin off tin foil.

I was hit by a wall of pungent sickly smelling smoke and my eyes began watering.

Pinkey appeared from the kitchen area and greeted me like a long-lost brother. We followed him into the kitchen where a bloke was cooking up on a spoon.

He pulled a large tin foil package from down the front of his tracksuit bottoms, picked up a small cardboard scoop and ripped a piece of tin foil from a roll. Then he opened the package, scooped some of the brown powder inside onto the smaller piece of foil and folded it before handing it over to me. The junkie who had brought me to Pinkey's flat then handed over the money. I held my breath and we walked back through the smoke-filled living room.

Once out of the flat we hurried to a nearby park and went into the public toilets, the floor of which was carpeted with burnt tin foil and used syringes. I handed the junkie the tin foil wrap, he unwrapped it and began transferring heroin onto a Rizla paper that he rolled up and handed to me. The girl had followed us in, and was fiddling in her bum bag for her works (injecting equipment). I took my share of the score and left.

It was all very squalid, and as I wandered back across the park, the doubts I had before I'd been commissioned on this seven-month operation suddenly came back to me. I was 42, and had just split a bag of heroin with two kids who were probably that age between them, although they looked a lot older. I just felt, at that moment, that I was too old for all this shit.

Over the next few weeks, I met Pinkey on a number of occasions and bought heroin off him each time, getting most of the deals on either a body camera or the car camera. One time, he even dealt to me in the living room at his ex-wife's place in front of his kids, while he was supposedly babysitting for them. On that occasion, he was highly indignant about a recent court appearance. 'I got robbed, yeah,' he said. 'I told the police I wanted to press charges, and when I was giving evidence at Crown Court the defence barrister said I was a drug dealer. I said, "Even if I am a drug dealer, which by the way I'm not Your Honour, does that mean I deserve to be robbed?"'

I'd heard about this from Sara, who had been in court. She'd told me she nearly fell off her seat when she heard him say this, knowing the evidence we had stacking up against him.

Not long after that, we busted him. Perhaps ironically, he was up before the same judge. He was sentenced to five years.

Chapter 10:

Stick or Twist?

THE COMES A POINT in all operations when you begin to struggle targeting fresh dealers. You end up buying off one dealer too many times, or spending forever looking for fresh dealers, and sometimes an SIO will bring the job to a premature end and make do with what has been achieved so far.

We had just about reached this point in Leicester, but, as I walked through the estate scratching my head, who should walk round the corner but my old mate Ezra. I decided to grab the bull by the horns and crossed the road to greet him. 'Alright, Ezra, how's it going?'

He tried to place me. 'I don't know you, do I? What do you want?'

'One of the Rourkes introduced us a few weeks ago,' I said. 'You let me have a fix.'

Ezra played dumb for a bit while he weighed up the risks of getting involved with me. All dealers have to balance the potential danger of being turned over with the need to grow their customer base. Eventually, he said, 'What's your name?'

'Pete Ashton, mate.'

'Right, ring me from the phone box near the Rourkes' house in an hour.'

I left it for a bit longer than an hour, to look like I wasn't too efficient, and he told me to come to his house to pick him up. Five minutes later, he was warily climbing into the front passenger seat of the Astra.

'Drive into Leicester,' he said, and for the next quarter of an hour he quizzed me – who I was, where I was from, what I knew about drugs, how long I'd been using. 'Who do you normally score from?' he said, finally.

'I usually go through the Rourkes,' I said, as I pulled up outside their place.

'Wait here,' he said, and he went into the house.

While he was gone, I rang Paddy, the technical officer.

'The back-up team's just round the corner,' he said, reassuringly. Paddy was always on the ball.

I hung up just as Ezra was leaving the house. He plonked himself in the front seat and looked at me. 'Everything's OK, Pete,' he said. 'What you saying?'

'A twenty quid rock, mate.'

He spat a small Clingfilm package onto the palm of his hand – they do have some filthy habits – and then handed it to me. 'Stick that in your gob in case we get stopped,' he said. Spit-dealing and carrying drugs in body orifices are recognised ways for dealers and users to carry gear around, as they knew we were not allowed – thank goodness – to do intimate body cavity searches, and it was a lot of hassle to get a doctor to do one. I also knew that Ezra was flexing his muscles, but my hepatitis jabs were up to date and he looked clean enough. I stuck the rock in my mouth, and we drove off.

From then on, I carried a spare bit of Clingfilm to wrap the rock in, just in case he insisted I mouth it again. But he never did, and within days I had the three clean buys I needed. And we picked him up in a very clean strike, with no resistance or violence. In fact, when he was arrested he insisted he had always known I was a copper – he claimed he'd just been playing along, and had only ever sold me little stones in Clingfilm and that I must have exchanged these for crack cocaine later on. This held little water with the judge, who gave him four years.

* * *

BUOYED BY THIS unexpected bonus, we decided to carry on. There was still some fertile ground nearby. The New Parks estate is a spit away from Beaumont Leys so it became a natural progression. It was a case of getting out and about again, so off I went, with a new UC called Becky for company.

We weren't pulling up any trees. Becky was refusing to scuzz down, and given that she was an attractive, well-groomed kid in her mid-20s, and dressed like a PR executive, that was a severe handicap. She was on the Atkins diet at the time, and had to drink a large amount of water. She always had a litre bottle of Evian stuck to her lips, and Evian is not the smackhead's drink of choice. She was also playing the part of my girlfriend, which I thought looked a bit ridiculous: sadly, not many fat, middle-aged heroin-addicted skinheads in old Astra vans pull middle-class foxes.

I had asked the SIO to take her off the job but he wasn't up for that. He wasn't the one having to convince people he was a junkie, I suppose. But, hey ho, Becky was a nice person and a good girl to have around, so I was happy to give it a go.

We were sitting in my van outside a phone box waiting for something to happen, when a strange-looking girl came running up to make a call. She was wearing an oversized car coat, a big floppy Paddington Bear-style hat, and a big pair of specs. She was also missing half her front teeth. She looked like Sue Pollard's chalet maid Peggy from *Hi de Hi*, but in a kind of smackhead way: it was an unfortunate appearance. We watched her having problems getting the phone to work, so I wound down my window. 'Are you scoring, love?' I said.

She was clearly desperate for heroin, because she came straight over and accepted my offer of the use of my mobile. I sniffed a chance. 'If I chuck a tenner in can I come in?'

At that, the frantic chalet maid jumped straight into our vehicle – quite scary, if you think about it. 'My name's Cheryl,' she said. 'Do you know where the railway station is?'

We drove off in that direction while she chattered away. In fact, the only time she stopped talking was when she was coughing down Becky's neck; I had to stifle a giggle as Becky shuddered each time it happened. At one point, Cheryl was coughing so much that I picked Becky's water bottle up.

'Have a drink of that, love,' I said.

Cheryl gratefully did. The look I got from Becky was priceless, and I smirked all the way to the station.

Until Cheryl leaned forward to Becky and said, 'You're a pretty young thing, love… Are you his daughter?'

It was Becky's turn to grin then. I could picture Paddy listening to this back at the covert premises and laughing his cock off.

We eventually pulled up behind the station and Cheryl borrowed my mobile to ring the dealer. Ten minutes later, an Asian kid pulled up in a Nissan, and Cheryl jumped out of our van and ran over to him. A few minutes later she ran back over. 'Drive back to the New Parks,' she said, and all the way back she carried on babbling and coughing; she was starting to get on my tits, though I consoled myself by looking at Becky wincing.

At Cheryl's block, I followed her out of the van while Becky stayed put. The flat was a shit hole on the first floor. As I followed her inside, she pointed to a bedroom, the door to which was barred. 'Kev [her boyfriend] is rattling in there,' she said. 'He'd love to shoot up but all his veins are fucked so he has to toot.'

The place was full of junkies. I later found out from Sara that a Nigerian crack dealer called Ben operated from the premises as a master forger. He had a number of computers set up in Cheryl's flat where he knocked out copies of just about anything, from passports to driving licences. He was also a crack dealer and a skilled deception merchant who had given the local police the runaround for years. Cheryl began dishing the gear out to the waiting posse. I joined the back of the queue, and was eventually served up with a very small bag and left, declining the offer of a smoke.

One problem with junkies is that they have too much time on their hands. When they aren't taking gear or getting the money together to buy gear, they usually sit around talking about gear and the drug scene in general. Years of substance abuse brings on paranoia, and this led to distrust from the New Parks crowd. Sara, the intelligence officer, who ran just about every grass in the area, later told me that, after I'd left, they conducted a council of war.

'I reckon that bloke Pete is a copper.'

'Why?'

'Ziggy from Howden Close reckons he was nicked by him once for burglary.'

'I don't know, he doesn't look like Old Bill to me.'

'Why don't we ask him next time he comes here?'

The following day I parked up outside the block of flats and pressed the buzzer, after a few minutes a man's voice asked me who I was.

'It's Pete. Is Cheryl in?'

'Pete... er, hang on.'

A minute or so passed and Cheryl's scatty, if direct, tones came over the intercom. 'Are you a fucking copper?'

'No,' I said, trying to sound offended. 'Of course, I'm not a fucking copper! Do I smell like bacon to you?'

Etc etc. I got served, eventually.

We played around with Cheryl for a week or so but the damage had been done and it was bloody hard work. I scored smack off her about six or seven times and I managed to get Ben to sell me crack cocaine twice. I always got the third degree whenever I turned up and although the atmosphere was never threatening I was anything but welcome.

It had been a long, hard operation and my patience was beginning to wear a little thin. I had mixed with shit for months – actually, years on end before this particular foray – and, once again, I started to seriously consider binning this kind of work. But the SIO still thought there was more juice to be squeezed out of this particular lemon. So we carried on. There wasn't really a shortage of targets: we were just running out of dealers who didn't know each other too well.

We started buying off a couple called Michelle and Jason. They were a charming pair, completely off their faces all the time. They used to tell their punters to wait in the car park of a local supermarket, and you could tell when they were about to appear because the car park filled up with dodgy-looking people in clapped-out cars. Michelle and Jason would then announce their arrival in a cloud of burnt rubber and exhaust fumes. They were always so out of it that they could hardly see what they were doing. Catching them was so easy it almost wasn't fun.

No such luck with a couple of Asian brothers we went after called Sammy and Baz, who sometimes sorted Cheryl out with her gear. They were quite well-to-do, and had been privately schooled, but instead of making the best of the education they had been given Sammy sold heroin and Baz dealt in crack. I had Sammy's mobile number because Cheryl, with her weapons-grade dippyness, had used my phone to ring him more than once. But her suspicion of me had gradually turned to dislike, and she bad-mouthed me at every opportunity. I couldn't use her as a reference to Sammy – I needed another way in. There was a lot of head-scratching over the final weeks of the operation; to a degree, we wanted to try something new to relieve the day-to-day boredom. So somebody came up with a cunning plan, which involved getting a custody sergeant and gaoler signed up to the operation. Sammy was dealing some chunky quantities of heroin every day on an industrial estate. We knew his vehicle, and that he usually visited in the late morning or early afternoon. On the day we picked, a marked police car manned by two lads from the back-up team stopped Sammy as he drove onto the plot. They conducted a stop and search under the Misuse of Drugs Act 1971, and found a small package containing four wraps of heroin. Bingo. Now we could get him into custody, where a cell-block introduction could take place; this would give me some instant credibility, and, we hoped, allow me to start scoring off him without involving any of the New Parks crew who thought I was dodgy.

Sammy was duly nicked and taken to Beaumont Leys police station where he was interviewed and bailed, pending the results of the forensic examination of the drugs. He was then placed in the holding cell in the custody area while the paperwork was being sorted out. Holding cells usually have glass fronts, so that the occupants can be monitored by the custody staff, and they often contain more than one prisoner. On this occasion, as luck would have it, there was another prisoner there – a balding Lancastrian called Pete.

I was also being 'bailed' on drugs charges, and in the spirit of expediency we were kicked out of the front door together, where, being a chatty sort of con, I engaged him in conversation. 'What you been nicked for, mate?'

'Bastards caught me with me stash of heroin, brudda,' he replied.

'Fuck me. The bastards got me for the same thing, mate. Now I'm fucked. I need me gear!'

'You rattling?'

'No, but I fucking will be soon!'

'You got any money?'

'Yeah, why?'

'Go to the corner of Monk Street and me brethren will get ya sorted.'

'I only need a ten bag to see me through,' I said.

While they only usually dealt in bigger amounts, he agreed to help me as a fellow victim of police over-exuberance. So we went our separate ways, and I put a call in to Paddy back at the covert office at the business park. The back-up team were put in the area, for what it was worth – they were a very good bunch of lads, but there was no getting around the fact that they were three big, short-haired white blokes and one big, short-haired black bloke, all wearing body armour and sitting in a car in the middle of bandit country. So they had to stand off a good distance from the plot, to avoid spooking the targets and making my job impossible. They were almost always a few minutes' drive away, should I need help, and, with the best will in the world, whatever was going to happen to me would have happened by the time they got there.

I also hadn't been given my smart phone, due to the nature of the day's work. It wasn't only drug dealers who would be suspicious about a junkie with two phones: the local plod would certainly have smelled a rat very quickly, and a cursory examination of the device would have shown them what it was. Beaumont Leys was a very busy nick, and there was every chance that some copper not involved in the operation might see it and suss me out.

I made my way slowly to Monk Street, a grotty road that had alleyways running behind the terraced houses. There was a corner shop at one end, so I hung around outside there to wait for Sammy. As I stood there, a Nissan Micra containing four Asian lads drove past and turned the corner. Then a young kid appeared and told me to go into the alleyway behind the houses. I put a quick call into Paddy to let him know where I was going, and then headed in to the alley. It was empty, so I hung around at one end until a young bloke came out of a back yard and beckoned me. As I ambled over, a group of five Asian men sprang out from the yard and pushed me up against the wall. Four of them held my arms and pinned me down to stop me from moving whilst the fifth began patting me down.

'Who the fuck are you, man?' screamed the bloke who was searching me.

They weren't the biggest or hardest bunch, and it wouldn't have done my cover any harm if I'd tried to fight my way out, but the odds weren't great, and I decided to play passive. 'Sammy told me to come here for a ten bag,' I said.

'Ten bags! What do you mean ten bags? We don't do that shit!'

Then Sammy appeared from the doorway. 'OK, brudda,' he said. 'It's cool, we don't know who you are, that's all. Let him go.'

He handed me a ten bag of heroin. 'That's just a little present,' he said. 'Don't bother looking for me again unless you want bigger weights, yeah?'

I straightened my clothes up and Sammy shook my hand. 'No hard feelings, brudda. We just gotta be careful.'

Of course you have, you tosspot.

Sammy gave me his mobile number and I walked off down the street, my heart still pounding. It was the first time in a while that I had been patted down or manhandled, and it wasn't a pleasant feeling, at all. In fact, it had shaken me up quite badly. I'd never been a fan of carrying a smart phone, because it restricted my activities, but it would have been nice to have had one then.

At the day's debrief, Rick was flapping a bit. I wasn't exactly Mr Popular on the New Parks, and now I'd been fronted. This was quite unusual, so it got the health and safety nuts worried that the two might be connected, and that it might be ramped up next time. I was pretty sure they were not connected, and that I wasn't about to be stabbed, so we decided to crack on. I gave it a few days before calling Sammy after a teenth, a bigger quantity, to make it look natural.

On the morning of the deal I attached a digital tape recorder over the end of my mobile phone via a doughnut shaped microphone, and gave it the usual evidential spiel: 'The date is the 23rd July 2003 and the time is 12.30hrs. I'm a police officer within England and Wales and for the purpose of Operation Loud I will be known as Pete. I am about to dial the following number, 07XYZ 123456, and speak with a person I know as Sammy, with a view to purchasing Class A controlled drugs, namely heroin.'

I then dialled Sammy's mobile number and waited.

'Hello.'

'Sammy?'

'Yeah.'

'It's Pete, we met the other day with your mates down the alleyway.'

'What ya saying?'

'I just wondered if Tina was there?'

'Meet us at the cinema car park near the football ground,' he said.

Remembering my cock up with Kev, I made sure I'd hung up before I said, 'The time is now 12.32hrs and I'm turning the recorder off.'

I then sealed the tape and gave it, with the device, to Paddy. It wouldn't be opened up again unless it was needed in court as evidence in the future. I set off to meet Sammy, my smart phone safely tucked in my pocket. Once I arrived at the cinema I parked up and waited, until eventually the same Nissan Micra entered the car park and I saw that there were just two people in it, Sammy in the driving seat.

He parked up and I got out and walked over to them. I approached the front driver's door and said to Sammy, 'Hello, mate.'

'How ya doing, brudda?'

'Good, mate. You got a teenth for me?'

He spat a Clingfilmed package onto my palm. I paid him with my drug money, which, as always, had the serial numbers recorded in my pocket note book. When the dealer is eventually arrested and all his money seized, this can provide further evidence if some of the issued money is still in his possession. I jumped back in my car and drove back towards Beaumont Leys, and as I was driving through the heavy traffic I noticed that Sammy's Nissan was about three vehicles back from me and I suspected that I was being followed. I gave a running commentary into my smart phone, telling the team that I was going back to my flat for a few hours instead of returning to the covert premises.

I was followed by Sammy all the way. I parked up outside the block and went upstairs, where I made sure everything was in order in case he knocked and wanted to come in to check me out.

After a few minutes there was no sign of him, so I looked out of my kitchen window and saw him still parked at the entrance to the close.

Then after about five minutes Sammy drove off and I received a call from him a few minutes later. 'Pete, it's Sammy.'

'Hello, mate.'

'Is that gear I sold you OK?'

'I don't know mate. I haven't had any yet.'

'OK, brudda. I'll see ya later.'

He hung up. Had he skanked me? Maybe he was ringing to see if I'd tried smoking brick dust. I had to get the gear back to the covert premises straight away, so that if he had ripped me off, we could make contingency plans. I locked up the flat and legged it down to the van, then I turned my mobile phone off so that Sammy couldn't ring me until I was ready and drove back to the business park, putting in counter-surveillance measures all the way.

When we'd tested the substance I'd bought we found it to be heroin. But Sammy was clearly a slippery little eel, and was unsure about me. We'd have to handle him carefully.

After a couple of weeks he contacted me and said that he wanted to sell to me in my flat so that he could see that I did actually live there. I agreed, and we went through the charade of me giving him an address I knew he already had. Half an hour later, he pulled up and I buzzed him through the communal door. He got a bit of a surprise when he walked into my flat to be met by Lee, wearing nothing but a towel round his waist, which would be enough to scare anyone. Then I appeared from the kitchen with a roll up hanging from my lips, and wearing flip flops and a pair of shorts.

'Alright, mate?' I said. 'Do you fancy and coffee and a smoke with me and Lee?'

His eyes were goggling: he obviously thought he'd walked into some sort of gay smackhead love nest. 'Er… No thanks, Pete,' he spluttered. 'I've got to be off, actually.'

With that, he handed over the gear for my money before scampering back down to his car and roaring off in a cloud of dust.

* * *

WITH THIS, WE HAD enough to get Sammy out of the way but I wanted to get his brother, Baz. A week or so later, I made it my business to bump into Sammy, and asked if he knew anyone who could sort me out with a rock.

'Yeah, I think so, brudda,' he said. 'Me brethren can do it, but he only sells half teenths for £40.'

'That'll be enough.'

'I'll get Baz to text you when he's ready to sort you out.'

I went back to our hideout at the business park. While I waited for Baz to get in touch, I seized the opportunity to take the piss out of one of the girls in the office who we had given a shock to that morning. The cash box that contained all the drugs money and expenses was placed in the rafters above the false ceiling whenever we knocked off for the day. It was this girl's job each morning to retrieve the cash box and sort out what we needed for the days deployments. The evening before I was one of the last to leave after I'd written up my evidence, and as we were locking up I found a dead sparrow on the ground outside. I put the bird on top of the cash box so that the typist would put her hand on it when she was retrieving the box. Then I forgot all about it.

The next morning I was getting myself ready for deployment when a loud scream shattered the peace, and there was an almighty crash as the cash box flew across the room. I denied all knowledge, and was still protesting my innocence when I received a text from Baz: 'Meet me in town in 30 min.'

Fun over, I made my way to the meeting place and parked up on a side road near to the main Job Centre. After a short while, Baz rang me. 'Walk through the precinct and meet me in front of Woolworths,' he said.

I did as I was told, and a few minutes later I was approached by a fat Asian bloke with a goatee beard who I had seen with Sammy before. I looked at him. Was he one of the heavies who had grabbed me that day down the alley? He was. And, more to the point, he was Baz. He had a good look over his shoulder before slipping a rock wrapped in Clingfilm into my hand. I passed him the folded-up notes, and he said, 'Give me a ring anytime you need sorting. But make it in the afternoon because I don't get up till dinnertime.'

As it turned out, Baz was careless, and much easier to box off than his brother. But it still took a while because he was unpredictable – he'd agree to be in a certain place at a given time and just wouldn't turn up, or he'd switch his mobile phone off and disappear off the grid for a bit.

I persevered and booked a meeting with him in the centre of Leicester. I wore a covert body camera that had an on/off switch on a lead sewn into my jeans pocket. Baz was late as usual, and I paced impatiently up and down for a while. As I did so, I suddenly saw, to my horror, that I had a cable sticking out of the bottom of my jeans leg and trailing behind me for about three feet. Shit! I was desperately trying to pull it back up inside my jeans when I heard the tooting of a car horn. I looked up to see my man sitting in his car about 10 feet away on the side of the road. He was waving me over to him. Double shit!

I had to brass neck it, and just hope he wouldn't notice. I walked over and stood next to the car without crouching down, so that he had to look up at me and away from the ground. I smiled weakly and said. 'Hiya, Baz, how's it going?'

'Alright, Pete, I haven't seen you for a while.'

He held a rock of crack in his sweaty hand; I took it from him and handed over my drugs money. He pocketed the money and sat there waiting for me to either carry on the conversation or walk off. I obviously didn't want to walk away: I just wanted him to fuck off as soon as possible, before some helpful member of the public tapped me on the shoulder and pointed out I had a wire trailing from the bottom of my jeans. I leaned forward. 'Cheers, mate,' I said. 'I'll see you round. There's a gap just after this next car if you're quick.'

Baz grinned and nodded, and drove off into the flow of traffic, while I scurried off behind a wall to tuck myself in.

We now had enough to nail both brothers, and we were nearing strike day. When the lads put his doors in at dawn on the day in question, Sammy was stupid enough to have nine ounces of heroin tucked inside a sock in his bedside drawer – despite the fact that he was already on bail for drugs offences. What self-respecting drug dealer keeps gear at home?

Sammy and Baz's poor parents took it all very badly when they were nicked, according to Paddy, the technical officer on the job. This was an unusual situation: in most cases, drug dealers are from scummy families, going back generations, but these were decent people who had no idea what their boys were up to. Very sad.

***

AS THE OPERATION in Leicester drew to a close, we carried on scoring on the New Parks estate. I was still getting a bit of a hard time off crazy Cheryl, but she'd left it a bit late to keep me at arms' length. I'd bought from her a few times, so she was well and truly knackered (and ended up getting three-and-a-half years).

One day, I bumped into another junkie, a lad called with a stutter called Tyrone, and he asked if I was interested in buying weights. If so, an old dealer called Bertie was back on the scene and was selling teenths of heroin for £50.

Cheryl had been blabbing her concerns about me around the place for a few weeks now, and so we decided we would only proceed against Bertie in a strictly controlled way. We knew that he was living with a girl called Abigail and their young child in a big house that he owned, despite being unemployed. He spent most of his time in the pub, playing pool and dealing smack.

The next day I picked up the junkie and he made a call for me on my mobile phone. 'B-B-B-Bertie?' said the kid. 'It's T-T-T-T-yrone. I've g-g-g-g-got a m-m-mate called P-P-P-Pete who n-needs a s-s-score.'

I couldn't hear the other side of the conversation, but it was obvious that Bertie was giving Tyrone a hard time because of his stuttering. When he finally got a word in edgeways, Tyrone said, 'Nah, m-mate, P-Pete is s-sound. I've known him for y-y-y-years.'

Good lad. He probably thought he had. Most dealers and junkies don't even know they're lying.

This was good enough for Bertie, who told us to come to the boozer to meet him. Five minutes later, as I sat with Tyrone in the pub car park, Bertie waddled over to us, dressed in scruffy jeans and cardigan with his chins resting on his chest.

Bloody hell, I thought. *He isn't on the gear. He's fatter than I am!*

I just hoped he wasn't looking at me and thinking the same. Bertie leaned in through the front passenger door, Tyrone introduced us, and I handed over fifty sheets. In return, Bertie passed me a resealable bag with brown powder in. As simple as that. I dropped the junkie back off at his place and went straight to the business park so that we could test the heroin for strength. It was good stuff, so a few days later I called Bertie to repeat the scenario. The following day, as I pulled into the car park, I saw him sitting in the front passenger seat of a Ford Focus. In the driver's seat sat a blonde woman who I hadn't seen before, but whom I assumed was Abigail. I parked up and walked over to them. I was wearing a body camera, and wanted to get a good shot of both of them. As I approached I saw a young fair haired kid about two years old in the back. I asked for a teenth and gave the woman £50. Bertie then passed her a bag of heroin which she handed to me; I took it, got in the Astra and made my way back to base.

A day or two later, Bertie packed his bags and booked his family on a flight to Spain. Why? Well, he suspected I was an undercover cop, and fled to the Costa Del Crime to get out of the way. Unfortunately, he showed rather less resilience than Ronny Biggs; after a week of sun, sea, and sangria he got homesick, and came back home. Just in time for strike day, when we kicked his door down and confiscated all his property under the Proceeds of Crime Act. Life can be cruel.

A few months later, he pleaded guilty and was sentenced to five years. Abigail, who was also charged with supplying, didn't have the sense to plead, and instead went not out. After a three-day trial, at which I gave my evidence and was cross-examined behind the usual screen, she was found guilty. The video evidence was pivotal to the case, and in the new year the judge sentenced her to five-and-a-half years imprisonment – six months longer than Bertie. In my view, if she had pleaded guilty she would have got a suspended sentence. Crazy.

I'm not in the business of giving criminals advice, but I would just say this: don't put a UC in the witness box. Some judges really hate it – they appreciate the risks undercover cops take, and accord them the same respect as rape victims. They clear the court, put you behind a screen and all that impresses the jury no end. You're more likely to get convicted, and the judge will add a bit more sauce on top.

With that, the long Leicester operation was over. It had been exhaustive, and exhausting – but a major success. In the following months, 35 drug dealers were sentenced to several lifetimes inside. The local paper printed photographs and sentence details of them all on its front page, to name and shame them; it didn't mention that Kev the heroin dealer had crapped in his trousers when he was arrested, or that one of the dealers only got a suspended sentence because he was a police informant.

Within days, of course, the void was filled, and a new set of dealers were operating on the city's streets. This is the essential truth about the drugs trade; you can bust people right the way up the pyramid, you can give the law-abiding folks temporary respite, and you can shift it around geographically, but unless you can stem the supply at source, which is really a job for HM Customs, you will never stop it completely.

For me, it was back to Derbyshire, and a role as a plain clothes intelligence officer for a few months.

Chapter 11:

Murdering Yardie Scum

THIRTY-FIVE CONVICTIONS was a huge number – a landmark success for this type of work. A dozen would have been good. The downside was that I was getting weary, burned out, knackered. The longer you've been at it, the bigger the operations; the bigger the operations, the harder it is to infiltrate, and the more risks you have to take.

I took a decent amount of the annual leave I was storing up to recharge my batteries, and while I was away from work I reached the decision that it was time to pack it in: I knew it, Jazz knew it, Carmel – who was not far off giving birth, hopefully, to our third lad – certainly knew it. When I went back, I'd let them know. There had to be a nice job in some organised crime unit that I could move into.

I'd planned a weekend in London with some old mates from the Met and from my Army days – a giant piss-up, followed by the Remembrance Day parade at the Cenotaph. After that, I decided, I'd put my cards in.

But the UC life isn't like that. It's a bloody drug all of its own.

I was on a train heading back north, trying to ignore the throbbing in my head, which felt like it was full of crackhead bongo drummers, when my phone rang. It was Jazz. Reluctantly, I answered it.

'Pete?'

'Yep.'

'You alright, mate?'

'Nope.'

'Leicester job went OK in the end, didn't it? Nearly 40 arrests?'

'Yep.'

'Right… Anyway, Operation Stealth want you for a quick job. Heroin and crack… You'll be in and out in four weeks. You up for it?'

I stared out of the window. *I'm too old for this*, I thought. *Ten years undercover is enough for anyone.*

'Pete? You still there, mate?'

But I can't bloody give it up. Just one more job.

'Yep, I'm still here. Yeah, I suppose I'm up for it. When?'

'They want to start tomorrow.'

'Yeah. Alright, no problems.'

As I said at the start of the book, Op Stealth was Notts Police's version of the Met's Operation Trident, and had been set up to deal with an explosion of guns and drugs in the city. The murder of crack dealer Terrisia Jacobs in the crowded streets outside a nightclub was just the latest in a series of shootings – in all, 21 people were murdered in Nottingham in 2002, and many of the killings were gang-related. The local police were struggling to cope with these levels of crime, as the chief constable himself would publicly admit three years later.

I'd been called in as part of a major operation to begin taking out as many of the dealers as possible. It's a slow and painstaking process, and it won't stop drugs being available, but the more street-level dealers and smaller wholesalers you bust, the harder you make it for the big boys and, crucially, the more intelligence you can gather.

I'd barely recovered from my hangover when I met up the next morning with my liaison officer, Luko, a Derbyshire detective attached to the newly-formed EMSOU.

'You look like shit, mate,' he said, as he shook my hand at Notts Police HQ. 'Which is a good thing, obviously.'

We headed off to a briefing in the covert premises just outside Nottingham which was the base for Operation Stealth.

As we signed in, Luko leaned over the counter and winked at the civilian secretary. 'Christ,' he said. 'I'm going to rip my wife's knickers off when I get home tonight!'

'Oh?' said the woman, blinking at him.

'Yeah,' he said. 'They're bastard tight, and they're cutting off all the circulation at the top of my legs.'

Once through the barricades, I was introduced to Detective Inspector 'W' who ran Stealth, and a balding, wingnut-eared detective called Atto. Atto was a man after my own heart; he flew by the seat of his arse in a rollercoaster lifestyle that probably cost him his job prematurely. The walls were plastered with maps and mugshots, and there were thick files everywhere.

'You're aware that one Terrisia Jacobs, also known as Tina James, was shot dead in Nottingham in the early hours a few days ago, Pete,' said W. 'We're quite confident that the guy who did it is a well-known local crack dealer, which is where you come in. Atto will explain further.'

'We think we know who slotted Jacobs,' said Atto, naming the suspect. 'But we're having a bloody nightmare getting any evidence against the fucker and his mates. Loads of people there, but they were all looking the other way when it happened – you know the story. What we want you to do is score brown or white off as many of them as possible over the next few weeks. That way we can at least get them banged up for dealing.'

I nodded. Once these guys were off the streets and separated, it was likely to be much easier to get witnesses to come forward – or the various members of the killer's gang to start turning on each other.

'The shooter is part of a network of dealers who hold the monopoly in their area,' said Atto. 'The main guy is around 70 years old, would you believe. He lives in and deals from the 14th floor of this block of flats near Radford Road.' He showed me a selection of surveillance photos of the high rise. 'It's a right shithole. But don't underestimate the bastard – believe me, Pete, he's proper big time. His street name is Pops, and he's as busy as fuck. They're queuing halfway down the road to get served up. Our intelligence suggests that he sends around thirty grand a month back to Jamaica via Western Union. The other dealers are a mixture of male Yardies and Jamaican females who operate from a number of bedsits and crackhouses within a half-mile radius of Pops' place. The other key bloke goes by the street name of Blacks. He's in his twenties. But don't worry too much about him just yet. Start scoring off Pops, and let's see where that leads us.'

'Why did they slot her?' I said.

'We're not sure at the moment,' said Atto, 'but you know what these fuckers are like. She probably just bad-mouthed one of them, or trod on their toes somehow, which as we all know is never wise.'

'When do you want to deploy?' said W.

'No time like the present, I suppose,' I said. 'Normally I'd spend quite a while getting my face known about the place and building up a legend so that the dealers trust me. But if he's as busy as you say, he won't know one customer from the next. I don't need any kit for the first buy... I'm just testing the water. So I might as well start now.'

'Great,' said W. He read me the usual ACPO guidelines and I left with Luko. We headed through the grey, cold streets of Nottingham and out to the depressing estate where Pops was based. It was starting to drizzle, and people were hurrying to and fro with their hoods up. Why didn't I ever get sent to turn over the dealers somewhere nice?

Luko dropped me off half a mile from the plot. 'See what you can get your mitts on,' he said, 'and just give us a bell when you want picking up.'

I wandered through the estate to the main door of the flats, where three or four junkies were pressing on a buzzer trying to get in. I joined the queue to await developments, and others came along now and then. There were a lot of nervous looks, and people asking if anyone knew where Pops was – most of this lot were rattling, so I played along.

Suddenly, a voice behind us shouted, 'Are you people waiting for me?'

I turned and saw an elderly West Indian man limping towards us wearing a flat cap and a car coat, a Spar carrier bag-full of shopping in each hand. If you hadn't known what he was up to, you'd have had him down as somebody's kindly old granddad. He was certainly the least likely-looking drug dealer I've ever seen.

Everyone thronged around him at the entrance to the flat, and then as many as possible crammed into the lift alongside. There was no conversation between us, but Pops just kept chuckling away to himself. When the lift stopped we followed him to his front door and I noticed that he was acknowledging his neighbours in a cheery fashion as he passed them with the motley entourage following close behind. The only person who showed him any animosity was another West Indian man who looked like he was the janitor for the flats. He glared at us as we walked past, and shouted at Pops, 'You bring shame on us all! You'll be out of here one day!'

Pops just acknowledged him with a cheery wave, and said, 'We will all be out of here one day, my friend!'

He unlocked his door and disappeared inside with his shopping, and a few minutes later he reappeared and started dishing out wraps of heroin and rocks of crack like they were sweets to all and sundry. I bought one of each, and was on the phone to Luko asking to be picked up before he'd even had chance to get back to the covert premises.

Over the next few days, I scored repeatedly from Pops, eventually feeding in a covert camera so as to really bang in the nails on his coffin. He was surprisingly careless: in all, I bought from him on eight occasions, and each time his building was crawling with other smackheads and crackheads waiting to score. Imagine being a decent, law-abiding person living in that block.

The only fly in the ointment – and the real hero of this story – was the old black janitor who had challenged Pops the first time I met him. Although he was in his 60s himself, he did his best to keep the other residents safe, and spent half his life chasing junkies out of his building onto the concrete concourse outside. He was a total pain in the arse when I was trying to score, because he wouldn't leave you alone and take no for an answer, but he did his job fantastically well.

* * *

BY NOW, OPERATION STEALTH had made an arrest in connection with the murder of Terrisia Jacobs – though the arrested man later walked free from court after the prosecution offered no evidence – but there was no let-up in the war against the dealers. They were pleased that I'd managed to square Pops away, and wanted me to move in on the younger members of the gang.

We had a briefing one Tuesday evening. 'I mentioned that the second target is a Jamaican male known as Blacks,' said Detective Inspector W. 'He is a very violent and unpredictable individual with a raging crack habit of his own. He deals out of his own flat, which is on the 12th floor of this block, not far from Pops. There's dozens of lower level players, too, so maybe you could work your way down this lot while you're finding a way in to Blacks?'

He handed me a wish list of mobile phone numbers and, after the usual reading of the ACPO rules, I made my way out to the estate. Cold calls, whether to people's houses or mobiles, are rarely successful, but in certain busy inner city areas, where there's a massive turnover of users and dealers, the tactic sometimes works. I got myself into a filthy telephone kiosk and began dialling numbers.

For an hour or so there was the usual mixed bag of results – from dead number, to phone switched off, to 'Sorry mate, wrong number', to 'He's not here, ring back later.'

I eventually got down to someone known as 'Jay', and after half a dozen rings a voice with a heavy Jamaican accent answered.

'Yo.'

'Jay?'

'What ya sayin'?'

'One white and one brown?'

'Come down to Jack's in Lenton and ring me, yeah?'

I called the operational team to let them know of this development, and when I mentioned Jack's the Detective Sergeant said, 'Er, right… You OK with that?'

'Why shouldn't I be?'

'It's quite a scary place, that's all.'

'*Scary*? We're the fucking police, aren't we?' My bottle was being questioned – in my mind, at least – and I wasn't having that. 'No problem. Leave it with me. How do I find it?'

'Mate, it's right in the middle of this shithole estate, and it's literally like a bloody labyrinth. There's no street signs or anything, and if I try to give you directions you'll get lost and we'll never see you again. I'll get one of the lads to walk you past. You follow him at a reasonable distance, he'll indicate it to you and walk on by.'

Not long afterwards, a plain-clothed officer walked past me on the opposite side of the road, and I followed. He led me off the beaten track into a series of walkways and alleys, with groups of teenagers mooching around under lampposts and sitting on walls. As we approached, I could hear whistling noises as unseen lookouts signalled that strangers were in the area. We walked deeper and deeper into the estate – along deserted streets lined with burned-out cars and boarded-up houses. None of the street lights were working, and it was dark by now, but after a while I saw the officer casually lift up his right arm – the signal to indicate we were there. I saw an alleyway between two rows of maisonettes, with a couple of heavy-looking blokes wearing padded puffer jackets and hoodies standing by the entrance. They looked like some kind of security. I walked past them into the square, and tried to focus on my surroundings; it comprised a range of older Victorian houses and more modern 1970s-built maisonettes and flats. It seemed to be fed by just the one road in and out, and a number of rat runs. In one corner of the square was a pub, known locally as Jack's, which was brightly lit up and seemed to be very busy. There were a couple of bouncers standing outside and a phone box a few feet to one side.

Small groups of men stood around, huddled together in the ubiquitous padded jackets and jeans. I was the only white person in the area, as far as I could see.

I walked over to the telephone kiosk and dialled Jay's number. He answered after a couple of rings. 'It's Pete,' I said. 'I rang a bit ago, after one white and one brown?'

'Yeah, yeah,' he said. 'Just come into the pub.'

I hesitated. My bottle was being questioned again – only this time I was doing the questioning. 'Er... can you see me outside, mate?'

'Nah man. Just come inside.'

I hung up, walked over to the boozer, and peered through a window. It was packed to the gunwales with black men and women, with the odd bleached blonde thrown in. The blokes were all wearing Yardie street styles, and the women were dressed up to the nines in miniskirts, leather jackets and fur coats. There was a heavy beat coming from the place and clouds of smoke swirled around the ceiling. I thought about how this would go down. A white guy with a crew cut, a skinhead MA1 flight jacket and German para boots was going to stand out like a set of bulldogs' bollocks in there. A mad image flashed through my head – me walking up to the bar and ordering a Babycham, as the whole place fell silent. *Fuck that*, I thought to myself. These places *can* be turned over – but not like this, by one bloke, on spec.

I had a quick walk round the square and asked a couple of the groups standing around if they could sort me out with a rock. They didn't even reply but just stood there with thousand yards stares and said nothing until I walked off.

To add insult to injury, a young half-caste kid approached me as I was leaving with my tail between my legs. 'You scoring, mate?' he said.

'I'm after a rock,' I said. 'I was going to get one off Jay, but I don't fancy going in there, if you know what I mean?'

'No worries,' he said. 'Give me your twenty quid and I'll go in and get it.'

I handed him a £20 note, and he told me to wait by a bench in the middle of the square. I sat and watched as he walked towards the boozer… then straight past it, and then broke into a sprint and disappeared down an alleyway and off into the night with my dosh.

Humbled, I made my way out of the area and returned to Nottinghamshire Police Headquarters for a de-brief; it's fair to say that there were a few knowing looks and smiles from the operational team as I recalled the events of the night.

Another name on the list was 'Cane'. I came across him via a female dealer, from whom I ordered a 20 white (a £20 rock of crack) as a way of breaking the ice. To my surprise, she panicked a bit and started running round like a headless chicken. This made Cane cycle over to check me out and get in my face a bit. I repeated my order to him, and eventually he rode off. An hour or so later, a black BMW pulled up and the passenger called me over. 'Here you go, bwoy,' he said, proffering a bag. I handed him a twenty pound note, at which point he lost his composure completely and launched into a torrent of abuse before roaring off in a cloud of rubber and dust. It transpired that they thought I'd asked for 20 rocks, as opposed to a rock for 20 quid. Lancastrian Northern Monkey and Jamaican patois can break down in translation. What they thought I'd be doing with 20 rocks, I don't know. A lot of people took me for a bouncer at Rock City in Nottingham. Maybe they thought I'd be knocking the gear out to punters there.

About halfway through the operation, something happened which showed the potential for your backstory or legend to get you into trouble. During my TSG days, we had worked Sandringham Road in Stoke Newington on a regular basis, mostly targeting the crack dealers who sold their gear outside the Jerk Chicken take-away. The TSG would scream up in carriers from three different directions and 30 coppers would jump out and have dealers spread-eagled on the floor as we searched them.

Now, a boxer called Kirkland Laing lived in the area at the time. Kirkland, who had come down to the Smoke from Nottingham, was another classic case of the way drugs can fuck you up. He had been a hell of a fighter, possibly the most naturally gifted boxer from these shores. He trained at Canning Town with a number of world champions, and they couldn't lay a glove on him while sparring; famously, he beat the legendary Roberto Duran in 1982, in a tremendous bout that *Ring* magazine named its 'Upset of the Year'. But he loved a smoke, and because he spent half of the time stoned he lost fights he should have walked. He was a lovely lad, not a nasty bone in his body, and while we were searching these dealers he'd often be in the area. He'd wander over and have a laugh with the coppers, and generally defuse situations. He was genuinely good to have around. Over the years, I had worked him into my legend, blending it with stories told by the Rasta *Big Issue* man in Nottingham who also knew Laing from his time on 'the front line'. I'd got to the point where I was implying that Kirkland was a mate of mine, and that I had lived on Sandringham Road myself.

So, here I am, years later, standing in the doorway of a shop when a stocky West Indian bloke with a black woolly hat comes up to a bookies' window a few feet away from me and starts shadow-boxing. I stepped out to move away and he started ducking and weaving towards me, so I adopted the stance and played around with him for a minute or two. After a while, he stopped and introduced himself as 'Boxer'. He was a friendly sort of lad, and a raging crackhead, so we got on like a house on fire. Over the next few weeks, he introduced me to a number of faces in the area which helped things along very nicely. Everyone knew him so it was always useful to name drop him when being challenged.

Boxer wasn't a curious type, and wasn't interested in my past, so I didn't really mention my legend to him, which turned out to be quite fortunate.

One day, the Detective Sergeant on the operational team was driving through the plot with me hiding in the back of the car. 'Hey, Pete,' he said. 'Your mate Boxer's over there. By the way, do you know why they call him that?'

'No mate?'

'His best mate's that boxer Kirkland Laing… He was quite a promising fighter himself in his time.'

A cold shiver went down my back: all it would have taken was for me to blab my mouth about my chum Kirkland, and for this guy to ask me a few questions and get suspicious…

* * *

ANOTHER DEALER I CAME across then was Josie, an educated and intelligent woman whose number was also on the DI's list. Well-spoken, with a 2:1 degree in German and Russian, she should have been working as an interpreter at the UN, or in some big, international business set-up. She was in her mid-30s and would have been attractive, too, had she not looked 25 years older than she was. Her life had effectively been destroyed by heroin.

Some people think soft drugs inevitably lead onto hard drugs; I'm not one of them, but Josie was a prime example of how they can. She'd left university with the world at her feet – she had a good job, a wide social circle and great prospects. She enjoyed a night out, with the odd spliff and or occasional pill to make things go with a whirl. Then one day, some 'friend' offered her a smoke of a bit of brown powder from some tin foil. After the initial vomiting that comes with smoking heroin for the first time, Josie felt like she was wrapped up in a big, warm, sleeping bag – the feeling of contentment was beyond belief. She was soon hooked, and smoked the shit whenever she got chance.

Of course, your body becomes habituated to it, and you require larger and larger doses to achieve the same effect. Her habit grew and grew, to the point where she began stealing from friends and family to feed it. Close friends and relatives usually suffer massively when a loved one is on the gear; they often turn their backs on the junkie and eventually lose all contact with them – but only after years of lying and cheating. This had happened to Josie, too. As she was pulled further away from the straight world and drawn tighter into the web of the dealers and users, she decided to inject heroin for the first time. Initially, the rush of shooting up took her back to the early days of smoking, but before long she was injecting more and more just to be able to function and feel normal.

Desperate for cash, she started selling her body around Nottingham. It's not hard to imagine the horror she would have felt at how low she'd sunk – having unprotected sex in some bushes or an alleyway with a revolting stranger for twenty quid. Along with the obvious health risks, she was robbed and assaulted and arrested on numerous occasions, and had eventually teamed up with a number of other working girls to take their punters back to a ramshackle old terraced house that doubled as both brothel and crackhouse.

Which was where I met her, courtesy of one of the people on that list. The stink inside that place was indescribable. It was filthy and rotten from top to bottom, and I literally could not understand how anyone could want to go there to have sex with one of these lice-ridden, clap-soaked girls. The front downstairs living room was the boudoir – if you can call a stained mattress on a dirty nylon carpet littered with burnt tinfoil, discarded condoms and used syringes a boudoir. One of the women was picking this stuff up and putting it into a plastic bag; another was wiping down various surfaces with a sock which she was dipping into a plastic bowl of dirty water. Josie was yelling at some bloke to clear away his shit. He turned out to be her boyfriend – a likable bloke who once had me in fits telling me of his exploits for a Sunday league football team called 'Hardly Athletic', where he liked to eschew the half-time oranges in return for a quick fix in the bogs.

Josie scared the shit out of me from the word go. Despite her reduced and straitened circumstances, she was nobody's fool, and she treated me with huge suspicion. I think that, somewhere in the back of her mind, she knew I was a copper. Every time she opened her door to me, she'd invite me in and say, 'Welcome to my parlour, said the spider to the fly!' She also never missed an opportunity to roll a joint which I was expected to share with her, and I never enjoyed that. It wasn't the prospect of smoking cannabis that particularly bothered me – it was the massive boil that she had on her face which she continually picked at.

On one memorable occasion the door was answered by another woman dressed in high heels, mini skirt and waist length fur coat. 'Is Josie in?' I said.

'Yeah,' she said, holding the door open. I stepped inside, and saw that they were having a smoke together. 'I'm after a rock, ladies,' I said. 'Any chance?'

'We're out of gear at the minute,' said the girl in the fur coat. 'But if you hang on five minutes I'm off out to score.'

So I stood there twiddling my thumbs, waiting for them to finish binging on the last of their rocks, until she eventually stood up, staggered past me and told me to follow her. Perhaps naively, I assumed we'd be walking, but the next thing I knew we were standing at the door of a clapped-out Ford Escort and she was squinting and fumbling with the key. She got the door open and half-stumbled and fell into the driver's seat, before turning to look at me.

'Well?' she said. 'Get in then!'

This lass was completely off her face, so I must admit I hesitated.

'Get in the fucking car, love!' she yelled.

'Er... OK.'

I sat gingerly in the front passenger seat while this working girl madly revved the Escort, and then swerved out into the rush hour traffic like a maniac. I'm not a nervous passenger, by any means, but I was bricking myself and hanging on for dear life. She completely ignored red traffic lights – we could have been wiped out several times – and had people scattering in front of her as she ploughed on. It was with a feeling of deep relief that we pulled up outside a two-storey block of flats that had walkways along the front and a communal door leading to a stairwell. As we got out of the car, a couple of black women came out of the flats, spotted my friend and started screaming in her face. One came right up close, yelling, 'YOU FUCKING WHITE BITCH!'

A hate crime, if ever I saw one.

'FUCK YOU, SLAG!' replied my mate, at about 140 decibels. Then she lurched at the black bird, grabbed her hair and started swinging her round; the second black woman had now joined proceedings, and began wellying the fuck out of my girl. The whole thing was rapidly a blur of fingernails dug into faces, swinging fists full of hair, stabbing heels, and vile swearing. It went on for several minutes; there was no way that I was going to try and break them up, so I just stood to one side coughing politely and saying occasionally, 'Come on then, ladies... Let's give it a rest, eh? There's people watching!'

To no avail whatsoever. Eventually, I thought it best if I made myself scarce, so I slipped off quietly and left them to it.

Not long after, Josie was nicked for being concerned in the supply of crack cocaine to me, and eventually got two-and-a-half years. I like to think that may have saved her life.

***

AROUND THAT TIME, I finally managed to engineer a bump into Blacks, and asked him if he could sort me out with a rock. He was very suspicious of me right from the get-go – all decent level drug dealers are paranoid, and if they're smoking their own product they're even worse – but told me to wait outside my favourite KFC on the Radford Road. I made my way there and hung around for about half an hour until another Jamaican approached me, a lad who I recognised called 'Yankee', who I'd bought a bag of skunk off earlier in the operation.

'You looking to score off Blacks?' he said.

'Yes, mate,' I said.

He spat out a small Clingfilm package, and I gave him twenty quid in return. I then headed back to Nottinghamshire Police HQ where we unwrapped my exhibit and discovered that it was a pebble. It's not unusual to get ripped off when deployed buying – as it isn't if you're actually a user – and it had happened to me on quite a few occasions. As I said earlier, the key thing is how you handle it. I went straight back out onto the streets and hunted Yankee down. When I found him he was apologetic. 'Ah, man, I'm sorry 'bout that,' he said. 'Don't take it personal, man, yeah? Don't hold it against me.'

He was an amiable-enough lad, and I found it difficult to be annoyed with him. He was a raging crackhead himself, and he didn't have a pot to piss in.

'Oh fuck it,' I said. 'You owe me a rock next time you see me then, yeah?'

It was obvious that Blacks had skanked me, probably because he didn't trust me. He was an exceptionally violent individual, and it was agreed that I'd give him a wide berth for a bit before trying again. That opportunity came by chance one day, when I was loitering outside a Spar shop and bumped into a Scouse working girl I knew from another part of the city on another job.

She was only in her mid-20s, but she was another who was prematurely aged and mentally shot to pieces by her drug abuse. The first time I had met her, we'd been outside a dealer's house waiting to score. I was chit-chatting to her, both to pass the time of day and to glean bits and pieces of intelligence, when, completely unprompted, she said, 'Do you want to fuck me?'

Even street whores tend to be a little more subtle than that. I looked at her in surprise, and said, 'No, thanks love.'

'It's only a tenner,' she said.

'Nah, you're OK,' I said. 'It's nothing personal, it's not my thing.'

She didn't bat an eyelid, but just shrugged her shoulders and continued with the original conversation.

So there I was, hanging around outside the Spar, trying to blend in, when I saw the Scouser tottering over on her four-inch heels. I don't think she recognised me, but she clearly knew what I was after. Nottingham is so full of junkies that it's not hard to find them. 'Alright, love,' she said. 'You scoring?'

'I'm bloody struggling,' I said.

'You come with me,' she said. 'I know where there's some good rocks.'

I trotted after her, and we threaded our way through the alleyways and across the litter-strewn grass between various blocks, and into a lobby which stank of piss. The lift was out, obviously, so we began walking up the stairs. Before I knew it, we were standing, panting, outside Blacks' flat. There was nothing I could do about it.

Blacks answered the door and went ballistic when he saw me. 'What the fuck you doing bringing this batty bwoy piece of shit round here?' he yelled at the prostitute. 'I don' like this cunt, I don' trust him and I don' want him here!'

To give her her due, the Scouser was a game girl, and wasn't in the least cowed by this volatile Yardie lunatic, who would have had an assortment of bats, knives and – almost certainly – firearms – on the other side of his door. 'Fuck off you soft bastard,' she yelled back. 'D'yous think I'd fetch shit to your door? I've known this bloke for years and we've smoked gear together. He's fucking alright.'

Blacks didn't look convinced, but he sold us a rock each anyway. As we were leaving, the Scouser – bless her – said, 'Can he come back and score off yous again on his own, if I'm not around, like?'

He sucked his teeth and looked me up and down, but eventually nodded – just to get rid of us, I think.

It was been unpleasant and potentially dangerous, but I'd got another 'in' to Blacks. Over the next few weeks, I scored off him on several occasions, but he was never happy with me. He would always bollock me for some reason – whether it was knocking on his door too loudly, or wearing the wrong colour shirt. We discussed him at some length back at the office, the main issue being his ID, and whether or not to introduce cameras. I had made a number of clean buys, but the CPS were clear that we were going to struggle, evidentially, without some covert footage for identification purposes.

The feeling at the top of the op was that, given his propensity for violence and his aggressive attitude towards me, it was unsafe for me to wear a camera. He was likely to pat me down, and if he found it on me he was more than capable of knifing me – or, more likely, throwing me over his balcony and claiming I had fallen. Accidents like that happen all the time, don't they? But I took the Oscar Wilde approach: an idea that is not dangerous is unworthy of being called an idea at all. The job was reaching the end of its leash, financially. It was shit or bust time. I managed to convince them that I'd be OK.

I'm not saying I was particularly keen on this, or that I'm some sort of fearless adrenalin junkie. It just had to be done. We decided to meet to discuss the finer points \on the following Monday, and make the buy on the Friday. All over the preceding weekend, I tossed and turned and tried to come up with a plan on how not to get patted down. Somehow, I convinced myself that Jamaicans didn't like dogs, and that Scooby would give me some sort of cover. Not the greatest of plans, but it was all I had.

When I turned up for the briefing, I was horrified to discover that the only covert device available was one of those cumbersome, old-fashioned bag cameras – normally carried by female operatives who could get away with it.

'You want me to go in carrying this?' I said. 'It looks fucking mad!'

'It's the best we can do at the moment,' said the technical officer. 'The other equipment is either in for repair or in use elsewhere.'

'I think you should be carrying an open mike, Pete,' said Detective Inspector W. 'I know it's not policy, but that way the back-up lads will be able to keep tabs on you.'

It was against policy because it wasn't regarded as safe, health-and-safety wise, to have a permanent transmitter firing radio waves into your body. But needs must. Mind you, that back-up car would have to be parked a quarter of a mile away, because if they were seen on the estate the jungle drums and mobile phones would all get going, and all the dealers, Blacks included, would shut up shop. I did a quick mental calculation: a couple of minutes' drive to the door, then up the stairs for 12 storeys… they would be able to listen to me screaming for five or six minutes before they got to me.

'We'll send you in with a female UC,' said W. 'She'll stay in the lift and hold the doors open. That way, if it's coming on top, and you can get yourself out of the flat, at least you'll be able to get down in the lift.'

If it all sounds a bit seat-of-the-pants and back-of-a-fag-packet, that's because it was. That isn't a criticism, it's just the way these operations often go. There's no 100 per cent 'safe' way to turn over violent Yardie crackhead dealers.

Friday loomed large ahead of me all week, and rolled round all too quickly.

After the usual equipment check, reading of the ACPO regs and a last-minute intelligence briefing-cum-pep talk, I was dropped off with my partner – a new young UC girl called JJ – half a mile from Blacks' flat. We dragged our feet through the estate to the lobby, where we made for the lift and I pressed the button for the 12th floor. Thank God, it was working.

The whole place stank of urine; through the grimy, smeared windows, I could see similar blocks of high rise flats, mirror-images cesspits of vice climbing up into the black clouds. My bottle was intact, but only just. The stainless steel doors slid open, and we stepped into the lift. Scooby put his brakes on and flatly refused to walk any further; I had to drag him, shivering, inside, with his tail between his legs. He was more for image than back-up, but even so, a fat lot of good he was going to be. As the graffiti-scrawled lift ascended, I tried to focus. Next to me, JJ tapped her nails on the side of the lift and blew out, nervously. This was her first job in the department. She was usually a giddy character, full of enthusiasm and with an infectious laugh. That was all gone.

I looked down at the bag. It was basically a small rucksack with the battery and recorder in the main compartment and a lens in one of the straps, to allow me to film Blacks from three or four feet away. The rucksack was filled with dirty clothes to discourage him from searching it. Not a particularly scientific piece of kit – in fact, it was typically obsolete. The police have the worst computers, the crappiest cars, the cheapest clothing, so why would our cameras and microphones be any better?

As the lift climbed, so did my heart rate.

The doors pinged open on the 12th floor, and I dragged the shaking Scooby out into the drab-painted corridor. JJ stayed in the lift to hold the doors open and keep it on Blacks' level for a quick escape.

'Good luck,' she whispered.

I nodded, gritted my teeth and set off along to the flat. I was trying to look and feel like a crackhead, when I just felt like a knackered, scared old copper.

I knocked loudly on the door and waited. I could hear muffled drum and bass playing inside. After a few minutes, there was a shooting of bolts and the door was opened on a chain by Blacks. He stuck his head in the gap and looked at me. His eyes were yellow and bloodshot and had the usual crazed look about them. They were the only thing I recognised at first. Since I'd last seen him, he'd shaved the sides of his head and afro-d the rest of it skywards. He looked like a black Bart Simpson.

'What the fuck you want?' he said, aggressively.

'I'm just looking for some gear,' I said. 'I was just hoping…'

'I ain't got no gear,' he said. 'Fuck off.'

To be honest, that suited me just fine. 'Right,' I said, and turned away, being careful to shuffle and shamble as I walked.

Behind me, I heard the door swing open.

'Yo!' said Blacks. 'Where you fucking going? Get in, man, I might be able to help you out.'

Shit.

I sighed and dragged my shivering dog inside. The door was bolted behind me, and I knew straight away that I had fucked up. Big-time. The place was full of crack smoke and the stink of skunk, and through into the living room I could see 15 or so black guys, most with crack pipes stuck to their lips, all of them rocking back and forth to the beat of the shitty music. I recognised one or two of them. They were not big fans of the filth, to put it mildly. If I was discovered here I was in real, genuine danger.

Scooby wrapped himself around my leg and began whimpering. It was like he was looking to me for some sort of reassurance, which I wasn't best placed to give; I was using all my powers of concentration to stop myself shitting my pants.

'Smoke some of this shit with me, man,' said Blacks, holding up a crack pipe.

If the choice was between smoking a little class A drugs and having an involuntary free fall refresher lesson from the 12th floor, believe me, I would go for the crack every time. But I wasn't enthusiastic about the thought of getting off my face with Blacks and his posse, so I tried to talk my way out. 'Nah, man,' I said. 'I just want to score and fuck off, if that's alright with you?'

'What the fuck?' said Blacks, narrowing his eyes and staring at me. Hard. He was nobody's fool: there weren't many *bona fide* crackheads who would turn down a free hit, and I could see the cogs turning in his brain. Maybe I *wasn't* a *bona fide* crackhead? He shouted into the room next door. 'Man don't wanna smoke with me, innit? What the fuck?'

Guys in various stages of mental decomposition began drifting out of the living room and into the hallway. One or two of them clearly shared Blacks' suspicion. My gut churned a little harder. But, thank fuck, one of the dealers failed to grasp the delicacy of the situation. 'Here,' he said, holding out a bag full of rocks. 'Twenty notes.'

I took a rock in trembling fingers, and handed over twenty quid – in an assortment of fivers, pound coins and shrapnel. It's all about looking the part. I still didn't know how the fuck I was going to get out the place.

I looked at Blacks. Blacks looked at me, through the same narrowed eyes. Then there was a knock on the door, and someone unbolted it. A couple of scraggy junkies stood there, looking to score. Scooby seized his chance and made a bolt for freedom, closely followed by me and my bag. I legged it down the corridor, to a chorus of threats and jeers.

As I got to the lift, JJ had sensed the urgency of the situation and was frantically hitting the buttons to get the door to close.

'Stop pressing the fucking buttons,' I said. 'Just let the fucking thing close.'

And then they did, and the cables and motors started whirring, and we started descending to safety, with me and Scooby both shaking like shitting dogs.

The next day, Blacks and Pops' flats were raided. As the riot vans pulled up on the concourse below, windows on every floor opened and drugs of all kinds were flung out of them. It was raining gear.

Both of them were nicked and remanded in custody. Pops was eventually sentenced to five years, with a judge's recommendation that he be deported on completion of sentence. Unfortunately, Blacks was given bail by a magistrate who believed his lawyer's sob story, and disappeared into the night.

One day, maybe, I'd walk into another crackhouse somewhere, and find the psychotic lunatic sitting there, grinning at me. *Then* maybe I'd take that header off the 12th floor.

I really needed to have a think about this game.

Carmel had just given birth to our third son Daniel – a cause for much celebration, given her history of miscarriages. It was back to reality with a crash, and lots of sleep disturbance and dirty nappies. I didn't mind any of that, though: it forced me to look at my life in more perspective. Did I want another son to grow up hardly seeing his old man, and being embarrassed at the way I looked and smelled when he did?

No, I didn't. That was it – I'd had enough of this game.

Chapter 12:

One Last Job

I WAS LOUNGING on the sofa one Saturday morning, cradling baby Daniel in my arms, secretly waiting for the boozer to open, and mulling over all of this. I'd been off for a couple of weeks, and the stress of buying crack from armed Yardies in boarded up flats was just starting to ebb away.

Then Jazz rang me. 'Hello, Pete,' he said. 'How you enjoying retirement?'

'Fine, mate,' I said. 'I'm enjoying the rest. Don't even mind changing nappies.'

'Carmel and the kids OK?'

'Yes, they're fine, mate, ta.'

'New one doing alright?'

'Yep, got him with me now.'

'That's good, mate. How's Preston North End getting on these days?'

'What do you want, Jazz?'

'Nothing, mate. I'm just calling for a friendly chat.'

'Yeah, right. So… What is it you want, then?'

'Do you know where Northampton is?'

Five minutes later, I'd agreed to get back on the horse. This job was to be my biggest and most dangerous long-term infiltration.

Before 2004, if you'd asked me what Northampton was like I'd have said it was a quiet little market town an hour north of London. To an extent, that would have been correct: parts of the town are lovely, with lots of big Georgian stone-built houses, stunning old churches and a grand, Gothic Guildhall. The villages just outside have olde worlde names like Castle Ashby, Nether Heyford and Little Brington. The Althorp Estate, the childhood home of the late Princess Diana, is only five or six miles away.

But that's far from the whole picture.

There was a really unpleasant sub-culture in the place at that time. It was a hotbed of drugs and prostitution, and gang-related violence was rife. An industrial estate in the centre of the town operated as a red light area between 7pm and 7am. Known to locals as 'The Jungle', there were automatic ANPR cameras set up to record vehicles entering and leaving the estate, and the keeper of any vehicle which entered more than a given number of times between seven and seven would receive a letter advising him of the fact. But marked police vehicle patrols were a rarity, and it seemed to me that the area was *de facto* controlled by pimps and drug dealers, with only a token police presence.

While the prostitution world was timetabled, roughly, from dusk to dawn, the drug market ran 24 hours a day and seven days a week around the tower blocks and housing estates of this ostensibly quaint little market town. The main players were a few local dealers, who sold via sellers of the *Big Issue*, a smattering of Jamaican Yardies, and a notoriously vicious gang from Birmingham called the Burger Bar Boys. There was a never-ending turf war going on, but the Burgers were basically in charge. They had stabbed, beaten up and generally scared off most of their rivals, taking over much of the town's heroin and crack cocaine market in the process.

This particular gang had sprung up in the 1980s. Racial attacks in the Handsworth area of Brum reached an epidemic as white and Asian thugs frequently attacked black people. The Handsworth riots ensued, and out of the ashes a group of young West Indian kids formed the Burger Bar Boys, named after a fast-food joint on the city's Soho Road, as a type of community defence group. Their reasoning was that the police had proved incapable of defending them, so they'd defend themselves.

Unfortunately, black gangster rap music arrived from America at around the same time, and it all formed a toxic cocktail with the loss of police control, mass unemployment, and the breakdown of the traditional, disciplined West Indian family, and the values that had long gone with it. Like many others, the disaffected Burger Bar

Boys turned to their heroes across the pond for role models. Gangs, guns, and gear became the way out for lots of inner city teenagers and young men, and this led to a horrific increase in black-on-black murders.

By the late 1990s, the Burger Bar Boys had evolved into a terrifying gang that controlled the sub-culture in big areas of Birmingham. Their rivalry and turf wars with The Johnson Crew – named after the Johnson Café on Heathfield Road – had led to a series of increasingly vicious stabbings, torturings, and shootings, including dozens of tit-for-tat murders. Among these were the brutal killing of a leading member of the Johnson Crew, Chris Clarke, who was kicked, punched and stabbed to death by a 20-strong gang of Burger Bar Boys in 2000. His death was avenged with the brutal execution of one Yohanne Martin, a Burger who was shot six times as he sat in a Mercedes SLK in West Bromwich two years later. The Burgers – led by Yohanne Martin's brother, Nathan – in turn sought revenge, which led to the most notorious gangland murder in Britain in recent years.

In January 2003, four members of the Burgers staged a drive-by shooting at a New Year party at a hair salon in a part of Birmingham the Johnsons considered to be theirs. At the party were a large number of the Johnson Crew, including those believed to have been involved in planning or carrying out the Yohanne Martin job. The gunmen sprayed the party with dozens of rounds from a Mac-10 machine pistol and two handguns, but only succeeded in killing two innocent teenage girls, Letisha Shakespeare and Charlene Ellis.

This shocked the nation, and the public outcry led West Midlands Police to set up its own Gang Crime Unit to target both gangs, who were making small fortunes running Birmingham's crack and heroin markets. They quickly identified and arrested the shooters – who were all later jailed for 30-odd years – and applied a general and very welcome pressure to the remaining hoodlums.

Of course, people like this don't give up their lives of birds and bling easily. Brum was too hot, but all that meant was they had to look for fresh markets elsewhere. The Burger Bar Boys headed east along the M6 for the not-very-bright lights of Northampton.

It made sense. They already had contacts in the town – the Ford Mondeo car from which the shots which killed Letisha and Charlene were fired was bought from an unsuspecting car dealer there – and they found a ready market. It was run, up to that point, by local toughs who were quite unprepared for the savagery and violence of the big city thugs. The Burgers opened for business daily at about ten in the morning, and continued into the early hours, driving around Northampton in throw-away cars, four up, armed and stacked up to the gunwales with heroin and crack. The unarmed local police were pretty much powerless to stop them: health and safety hysteria, combined with no little common sense, meant uniformed officers couldn't conduct effective stop-and-searches on the Burgers. They never stopped for police, anyway. On the few occasions someone did try to give them a tug, they would drive off at speed, utterly uncaring as to the possibility of killing pedestrians or themselves. Invariably, they'd get away, and as soon as they'd left plod behind they would screech to a halt, get out of the 'work' vehicle and just walk away, abandoning it, drugs and all.

A big factor that made the Burgers difficult to deal with was that, unusually among even hardened criminals, they really didn't give a toss: each member expected to be either dead or serving a substantial prison sentence by the time he reached his mid-20s. They lived for the moment. The usual rules of society meant nothing. Informants were more scared of them than they were of us, and the normal channels of law enforcement were useless. So it was left to our team to give it our best shot.

Jazz set up covert premises in an office complex on the Althorp estate, and a team of about 15 officers and support staff were installed. I was pleased when I was paired up with Shabby again. He always kept me upbeat, and was a first-rate UC. A third undercover, a Londoner called Daz, worked mostly alone.

The criminals we were targeting were a step up from the spaced-out wasters of Leicester and Derby, both in terms of their scale and organisation, and their propensity for violence. They would be armed, and among their ranks were genuine psychopaths – men who would not hesitate to use lethal force against us if they suspected that we were Old Bill. Because of this, we needed a crack back-up squad. We were placed under the protection of a very professional group from the force's firearms unit. They were ultra-fit and 100 per cent efficient, though not averse to having a laugh. One of the back-up lads drove a Ford Galaxy with blacked out windows, which he used to pick us up and ferry us around Northampton. He used to complain about the smell of sweat when he picked us up: that was unavoidable, due to the nature and pressure of the work, and the need for us to look and stink like junkies. One evening, I tied my lucky underpants to his headrest, as you do. Nothing was said about it, but in the early hours of the following morning, as I was heading home in my own car, I noticed a pungent smell developing. By the time I reached the M1 I was gagging, so I pulled over to the hard shoulder and searched the car. I found a dead pheasant under my seat – and not one from Waitrose. The damned thing must have croaked weeks ago. I dumped it on the side of the road and carried on my way, but it took days to get rid of the stink.

***

WE DIDN'T HAVE THE luxury of an insider on the local housing authority so I had to sort my own flat out, which I did through a bent letting company. Using my pseudonym with no official identity documents, I managed to get a pokey bedsit room in a house that smelled of boiled cabbage and was full of eastern Europeans. The bloke who ran the agency was a sleazy bastard who had previously been convicted of renting his properties out to prostitutes, and secretly videoing them and their clients in action, and selling the tapes via sex shops and the internet. I checked my room over thoroughly when I first moved in – not that I was planning to do anything dodgier than hiding out there and ringing the operational team from time to time. I think the landlord suspected that I wasn't 100 per cent kosher: one day he rang me to ask if he could go into my room and change a broken window latch, which was odd, given that most of the window panes were cracked and the communal toilet wouldn't flush.

I was a little surprised, and unhappy, to be given the same Astra van that I had used in Leicester the previous year. They had put a new set of fake 'ghost' plates on it, but it wasn't ideal. Worse, whoever had provided the vehicle had – in a fit of stupidity, or incompetence, or both – hidden the old registration plates and tax disc under the front seat. This was to have implications later on.

The liaison officer was a kid called Caddy who was switched on, and had done a bit of buying himself in the past. All in all, it was a good team who were well up to the job in hand.

The drugs market in the town revolved around three main groups. There were the daytime, town centre dealers who sold their heroin and crack via the *Big Issue* sellers. Then the Jamaicans, who tended to work the red light area. Finally, the Burger Bar Boys operated from cars.

Although the Burgers were the main team we were after, it was clear from the outset of the operation that we would be working long days and nights and actively targeting every market.

As always, I spent the first few weeks of the job acclimatising myself to the area and getting my face and vehicle seen by the drug fraternity. You don't want to be a stranger.

I must be honest: it was a frightening and intimidating place. The estate had working girls standing every 10 yards or so, and groups of pimps and dealers at certain vantage points protecting their territory. Violence and aggression simmered just below the surface; the very first night I walked through the area, I saw a pimp slapping a working girl around. As he sent her sprawling across the pavement, he glared threateningly at me as if to challenge me to say something. Thuggery was an accepted part of life in The Jungle, not least because few of the people who frequented the area were prepared to talk to the police. Obviously, any serious offences – a stabbing, say, or a rape – would have brought a rapid and no doubt effective response, but in day-to-day terms I'd say that the area policed itself via the pimps.

The first briefing ahead of deployment was a communal affair held in one of the rooms within the office complex. It seemed incongruous to be talking about crack-smoking pimps, gun-toting gangsters and smackhead whores within spitting distance of where Lady Di had ridden her pony as a young girl. The walls of the office were adorned with aerial photographs of Northampton highlighting 'drugs hotspots', but photographs of suspects were discouraged, because – thanks to the dictates of human rights law, and the suffocating police culture of political correctness – we had to be seen to be targeting areas and problems, not individuals.

The SIO started proceedings by going through the usual admin points regarding overtime forms etc, and then the Intelligence Officer informed us of any overnight developments in the area. This was followed by Caddy, the team Detective Sergeant, and EMSOU liaison officer, informing us all as to our jobs for the day.

'Shabby, can you deploy to the Racecourse area and put in a call to the target Lewy who needs boxing off, please. Pete, can you pay particular attention to the red light area and tower blocks surrounding The Jungle from around 7pm onwards.'

'No probs,' I said. 'Can I have some extra expenses to stock up my food in my bedsit? I'm running a bit low.'

'Are your Latvian house mates pilfering your stocks, mate?'

'Do I look like a bloke who would horde cabbage and beetroot?'

Caddy chuckled. 'Getting back to the point, Pete, can you try getting into Edwin? He hangs around the distribution warehouse, which is strangely ironic. If he's not there, he'll probably be down behind the wall there with his crack pipe.'

Whenever Edwin was preparing his pipe for smoking, he would crouch over it, brow creased in concentration, singing *By The Rivers Of Babylon* under his breath.

'He's quite an approachable bloke, and a good target to cut your teeth on in the area. As well as the gear, he's got around six regular girls grafting for him and his mate BJ, and they also tax individual prostitutes who wander onto their patch. Do take care if BJ is with him, though.'

'What's the problem with BJ?'

The Intelligence Officer spoke up. 'BJ's the enforcer of the pair, and is a nasty individual. Known to be very violent.'

'Any descriptions?'

'Yeah, they're both black blokes, aged around 35. Edwin usually wears a three-quarter length leather jacket, thinks he's Shaft, and BJ's usually got a New York Yankees baseball cap on.'

The briefing was wrapped up, and the buyers went off to be individually briefed, to draw their drug money and props, and sign the various required forms and declarations before deployment. Then I headed out in my Astra on my first scoring visit to The Jungle. The first port of call was the working girls themselves. Because the area was so busy and potentially lucrative, women travelled from as far afield as Birmingham and London to work there. They were mostly smackheads or crack addicts, of course – I can only remember one girl, called Jeannie, who wasn't on the gear. She came from Wolverhampton every night, and had a young family; they thought that she was working in a hotel, but the money she could earn on the game was so good that she obviously considered it worth the risks.

Those who used could point me in Edwin's direction, if I played my cards right. Prostitutes tend not to be particularly chatty with strangers, unless the conversation involves blow jobs or money, and asking too many questions can quickly spook them. They are simply there to do their job, usually with pimps watching them. The conversation – at first, anyway – is usually limited to you responding to, 'Are you after business, darling?'

But, if you tread carefully and get your face known, they gradually let you have titbits. The knack is to share a fag with them and allow the conversation to develop naturally. By now, the Astra van was reasonably well-known in the area, and I'd made sure I'd been seen out and about. I could chance my arm by stopping for a chat. I pulled up at the first girl I saw near to the distribution centre – a skinny blonde in a micro skirt and pink top.

She sashayed over to the van and leaned in. 'You after business, love?'

'No thanks, sweetheart,' I said. 'Have you seen Edwin?'

She hadn't, and neither had the next couple of women I spoke to over the next couple of hours. But finally, I pulled up next to a black woman who was walking her beat and, after going through the whole rigmarole of convincing her that I really didn't want to shag her, I really did just want to see Edwin for some crack, she eventually jumped into the van. With one eye in my mirror – I was asking for a tug for kerb-crawling here – I set off.

'Drive around till I find me mate,' she said.

A minute or so later, we pulled up next to an emaciated white girl with bleached blonde hair. She jumped in and sat on the black lass's knee as she told me to drive to a telephone kiosk. The black girl demanded some change and then disappeared into the telephone kiosk while her mate sat twiddling chewing gum round her finger and trying to interest me in a quick gobble.

Soon enough, the black girl friend returned. This time she sat on the blonde's knee, and told me to drive to the basement car park of a block of flats.

'He's on his way out,' she said, as I parked up. 'You'd better get your money ready.'

Almost immediately, a Rastafarian on a mountain bike pulled up next to the car and spat a lump of crack onto the upturned hand of my passenger. She handed him my cash, and they had a short conversation in thick Jamaican patois. I must confess I didn't understand a word of it, but I got the gist: they weren't my biggest fans. From time to time, they would look at me, shake their heads, and suck their teeth. Eventually, the Rasta – who I never saw again, he was one of many walk-on, walk-off dealers in my life at the time – cleared off on his bike and the girls took me to a secluded car park, shrouded in darkness, where they produced crack pipes from their handbags.

It was 2am. I remember looking out of the window and thinking about Carmel and the boys. They were probably tucked up safely in bed, back at home, where my real life was. And here was I: sitting alone in a battered old Astra, in the early hours of the morning, in a town ravaged by a violent turf war, with two skanky, smelly prostitutes puffing away on crack pipes, smoking my drugs. At least there was no danger of them asking me to smoke some, and wondering why I was refusing. They wanted it all for themselves.

One of them took a big drag, and then inhaled crack smoke all over me. 'This is fucking good gear,' she said.

I thought I ought to make some sort of a fuss about it, for appearances' sake. 'Right,' I said, 'you've had fucking enough of it now. There'll be none left for me. Gizzit here.'

Reluctantly, the black girl handed a bit of rock to me – the smallest exhibit in history, which I dropped in the bottom of my fag packet for safe keeping.

'Oh, giz one,' said the blonde, on spotting the packet, so I handed over a couple of fags which they sparked up, before insisting that I drop them off back on their beats. As I drove away they both shouted at me to come back anytime I wanted a rock. Thanks very much, ladies.

* * *

NOT LONG AFTERWARDS, still during the early days of the operation, I decided to walk through the estate on foot one evening, looking for Edwin. I thought I saw him standing in his usual place, alongside a stocky, bald-headed white bloke who I had seen hanging around the red light area a couple of times. I walked over, and only realised my mistake when I came face to face with the violent BJ. I'd been told to avoid this nutter if at all possible, but I couldn't very well turn on my heel and walk away.

'Is Edwin about?' I said.

BJ narrowed his eyes and looked at me. 'Why do you want to see Edwin?'

'I'm just after a couple of rocks.'

BJ held my gaze for a few moments: it was like he was boring into my head. Then he looked at the white bloke. 'You got any gear?'

'Nah, I'm after scoring myself.'

BJ took out his phone and said, 'I'll give Errol a bell.'

He walked away talking into his mobile phone and the white bloke turned to me. 'Where you from, mate?'

'I've just moved into town. I'm renting a place a mile or so away.'

'I'm a lorry driver,' he said. 'I park up near the railway station every night to help look after the girls. My name's Scotty, by the way.'

A pimping trucker, then.

'Pete,' I said, and shook his hand.

'I've been on the crack for about a year now,' he said. 'Sometimes we score off a Yardie from up near the Racecourse. Just a word to the wise, if we go there later be on your fucking toes because he's a right nasty bastard, and if he doesn't know you he could flip.'

Just what I wanted to hear. I was considering making my excuses, when BJ returned. 'Errol's gonna be in his usual place in about half an hour. I'll go and get me car.'

He walked off, and soon returned in an old style BMW. The lorry driver walked over to a small wall and reached behind it. He pulled out a large, chrome tube, which was obviously quite heavy by the way he was carrying it. 'I always take this,' he said. 'Just in case.'

Splendid.

Scotty got into the front passenger seat, tucking the metal bar down beside his seat and BJ motioned for me to get in the back. I didn't have a smart phone on me: it being early days, I couldn't be sure I wouldn't be searched, or robbed. This meant I had no way of alerting the back-up team to the fact that I was going off plot. The team were wearing body armour and cruising around four-up in a new vehicle: they would have stuck out like a bulldog's bollocks, and made all the residents jumpy. That would have made my job practically impossible, so, as usual, the team had to sit off out of the area and respond as best they could if they worked out that I needed help — not ideal but better than nothing.

Off I went with two violent pimps to God knows where to meet a violent Yardie in order to buy crack cocaine. I kept my mouth shut and tried to keep a low profile while we drove along. With good reason. BJ broke the uncomfortable silence by saying, 'Edwin's never mentioned dealing to you before.'

I shifted uncomfortably in my seat. 'It's only been a couple of times.'

'Yeah? I'm sure he'd have said something.'

He pulled over next to a rough-looking boozer and dialled a number on his mobile phone. Someone answered. BJ said, 'I've got that guy with me. We're outside now.'

A minute or so later, Edwin walked out of the pub and over to us. I was fucking nervous, and seriously considered getting out of the car, so I'd have a bit more of a chance of fighting my way out of whatever this situation developed into. But something made me stay put.

Edwin leaned in through the front driver's door and looked back at me. He had a puzzled look on his face at first, but then that lifted and he seemed to recognise me. 'You're the white van man, right?' he said.

'Yes, mate.'

Edwin turned to BJ. 'Yeah,' he said. 'That's him.'

'You ever had a smoke with him?' said BJ. 'Ever seen him smoke?'

'Nah,' said Edwin.

'OK, man,' said BJ.

They bumped fists; Edwin walked back into the boozer and we drove off.

These were serious people, and I knew I was in a dangerous position. At the very least, I expected that we'd soon be having a smoke together. After driving round and round for a while, BJ eventually pulled up next to an alleyway in a quiet residential street. We sat there in silence for a while. Eventually, a black bloke in a long leather jacket appeared from the alleyway.

'Here he is,' said BJ. 'Christ, I fucking hate this bloke.'

Then he turned to me. 'Give me your money and stay in the car. I won't introduce you because if he don't like you he'll just fucking shoot you, man. Simple as that.'

That seemed reasonable. I handed over forty quid for two rocks. He got out of the car and stepped up the alleyway to do the deal. The pimping lorry driver watched him go, and then looked back at me. 'Stay and have a smoke one night,' he said. 'Then everything'll be alright. There's a lot of shit going off at the minute, so everyone's a bit paranoid, that's all.'

After a few minutes, BJ came back to the car, muttering about the bloke he'd just been dealing with. He slammed the door and handed out the crack to me and the lorry driver. As he began driving back to the red light area, the trucker pulled out a crack pipe. He lit up a fag, unwrapped one of his rocks and then flicked some ash on the pipe's gauze – to help prevent bits of crumbling crack from falling through the gauze into the pipe while he was smoking it – before placing a bit of the rock on top. He passed the fag to BJ and stuck the crack pipe to his mouth, using his fag lighter to burn the rock. He took a deep lung full of smoke, held it in for about five seconds, and then let it out in a white cloud. His head arched back and he let out a low moan. 'Oh, mama, mama, mama…'

Good gear, then.

I was trying to work out how I could get away without doing the same thing, while maintaining some sort of credibility, when – thankfully – we pulled up on their patch and a group of five or so working girls surrounded the car. I took advantage of the distraction to leap out, and thanked the two of them before beating a hasty retreat.

Things continued in this vein for the next few weeks, as I gradually got myself better known in The Jungle. It was what you might call a target-rich environment. Some guys were so stupid or blasé that they virtually nicked themselves; others were a bit sharper, and never got tugged. One of the latter was a Yardie called Benji. He was a Jamaican who sold through a network of white junkie runners who operated around the churchyard just near the railway station. You called Benji on his mobile to put in your order, he would tell you to wait on a grassed area by the church, and then he'd send one of his lads out to you. This was all very safe for him, as he never had to physically exchange the drugs. In fact, the local police didn't have any firm idea of who he was, despite the fact that he was wanted for the attempted murder of a rival white dealer in a turf war over part of the drug scene in the red light area. Benji had stabbed the guy, who had been lucky to survive.

Because he was wanted for the attempt murder, we were always trying to lure him out into the open. I was tasked to keep on buying off him, upping the amount of drugs I wanted to buy, but I never had any physical contact with him. He earned an absolute fortune from us; every time we got one runner boxed off another would pop up.

One day he wouldn't answer his mobile, and it came to light that one of his runners had literally done a runner with lots of his drugs. This bloke had apparently legged it to Nottingham and the word around Northampton was that Benji had paid someone to kill him. I was waiting to score off one of his other gofers shortly after this incident, when a car pulled up and an overweight white bloke wearing a jumper over a white-collared shirt leaned out.

'You waiting to score off Benji?' he said.

I looked at him. *Yeah, right.* I could smell a fellow copper a mile off.

'Fuck off,' I said. 'I don't talk to the pigs.'

We embarked on a ridiculous scenario, of me denying I was after drugs, and him trying to convince me that he wasn't a policeman. This went on for some time until he got Benji on the line to vouch for him.

My nose had been wrong.

This fat guy became Benji's main runner, and I soon managed to catch him on video dealing to me in my car. Shortly after that, he was sitting in the Astra passing the time of day after sorting me out, when we got onto the subject of the missing drugs. 'I'm going up to Nottingham every day, looking for the kid who nicked Benji's stash,' he said.

'What are you going to do when you find him?'

'Put a bullet in his head.'

Fair enough.

A few days later, his car was involved in a head-on crash and Fat Bloke had to be taken to hospital. His car had a silent PNC marker on it so that the back-up team would always know when it was being checked out by police without the police knowing the vehicle was of interest to them. The back-up team learned of the collision, and took the opportunity to search the car. In the glove compartment they found a large amount of heroin and crack, which wasn't particularly surprising. But under the front passenger seat they found a loaded handgun. Imagine Fatty's surprise when he regained consciousness to be greeted by a couple of armed police officers stood at the end of his bed. He eventually pleaded guilty, and the judge gave him seven years.

* * *

MOST OF THE town centre day time dealing revolved around a group of about ten *Big Issue* sellers who squatted in a derelict hospital nearby, and plied their trade in the main shopping precinct. These were a sickly-looking bunch, led by a skinny white kid who always wore a red leather biker jacket. We knew him as 'Red Leather Jacket' on de-briefs, and 'mate' to his face. (It's not a hard-and-fast rule, but in briefings you rarely use suspects' names – and UCs are never told their real names by the operational team. Dealers don't often use their real names on the street, so if a buyer uses the real name alarm bells will ring inside the heads of all but the densest. This was especially the case with the Burgers, where we almost always used descriptive names for the suspects.)

The Jacket didn't look like he had long left on this mortal coil, and had the most chewed set of finger nails I have ever seen – they looked like sticks of celery that somebody had hit with a lump hammer. But, despite this apparent handicap, he was remarkably quick at unwrapping heroin covered in Clingfilm. If that was an Olympic sport, he'd have been a medal contender. This crew was supplied by a group of jocks from Corby – a town 20-odd miles northeast of Northampton largely populated by Scottish steelworkers and their descendants – who delivered to them a couple of times a day. They had a smart little system going. If you approached one and he didn't have any gear, he would direct you down to another shop doorway where his mate would sort you out. But if that failed, and the boys had sold all their copies of the *Big Issue*, they'd take call out a bearded, grey-haired Jamaican called Toots. Toots was a big player in the local scene, and was considered untouchable by the operational team. That was, until Daz bumped into him one summer evening outside the Afro Caribbean Club. During warm summer nights, the reinforced steel doors of the club were left open, and the drinkers would spill out onto the grassed area around the building. Daz was walking past one evening when he saw a couple of junkies walking through an underpass near the club. He tagged along, they stopped outside the club and joined a queue, and he stood behind them. Toots walked out of the club and assumed that Daz was with the other two. They in turn assumed that Toots knew Daz, and so an exchange took place. Cleverly, Daz also used the opportunity to sell Toots a 'stolen' mobile phone, so that he would remember him.

On the next briefing, the intelligence officer told us that a team of dealers from Corby were muscling in on the town centre scene, and had set up shop in another graveyard near to the shopping precinct. So I went over there and spent all morning waiting for something to happen. Something did happen, but it wasn't exactly what I had expected or hoped for. As I sat puffing away on a fag, I heard a bit of a disturbance near the church. I pricked up my ears – this might relieve the boredom of mooching around. I could see a pair of traffic wardens walking through the graveyard, and they were copping a lot of filthy abuse from a group of blokes in their early twenties. One of them, in particular, was directing the most mind-numbingly sick bile towards the female warden. No-one likes traffic wardens, but even his mates looked a bit uncomfortable. Working on the principle that two wrongs sometimes make a right, I walked up behind the yob and stubbed my fag out on the back of his neck.

I don't know what possessed me to do it – it was a really stupid thing to do – but I was pleasantly surprised by his reaction. He shrieked and jumped in the air and then turned round with a look of shock on his face. I smiled, and then began walking off in the direction of the town centre.

I also don't know why I thought I was going to get away with this misguided act of chivalry. The yob and his mates began jogging after me, while he called the police on his mobile. I could see the CCTV cameras swinging round and following me as I walked along and I could hear police sirens approaching. The group kept their distance – clearly, there was a fair chance that anyone who would stub a fag out on another man's neck on behalf of a traffic warden was some kind of psychopath. Every time I stopped and turned they stopped and kept well back, like some weird game of Grandmother's Footsteps.

'He stabbed me!' the bloke with the burn on his neck was shouting. 'That bastard stabbed me!'

This was attracting a lot of attention from passers-by, so I decided that my best course of action was to stay close to the traffic wardens and hope they told the police about the behaviour of the yobs. Eventually, several cars turned up, and a load of plod ran over. 'Stand here, please,' one of them ordered me. 'Put your hands on the bonnet of our car.'

I did as I was told, mentally flogging myself for getting into this mess. A policewoman took my bogus details and then got her hands in my pockets. As she searched me, she said, 'What's your version of events, then?'

'I was just walking past these lads having a fag,' I said. 'That one there was shouting abuse at some traffic wardens, and he jumped back and bumped into me. My fag caught the back of his neck. The whole thing was an accident.'

She looked sceptical, but I could see the traffic wardens talking to some other bobbies and pointing at the group of yobs. 'I'll be a witness for you if you need one,' I shouted over, helpfully. 'I heard it all.'

By now, the woman bobby was running some checks on me over her radio; as she did so, another copper wandered over. 'The guy with the burn is saying it had to have been done on purpose,' he said, half to me, half to the female officer. 'But the traffic wardens are making counter allegations against him, so he's decided he doesn't want us to take any further action. So you'd better get on your bike before we change our minds.'

Very reasonable: I legged it back to base, cursing myself and my stupidity all the way and still wondering what the fuck had come over me. The guy was a dickhead, but you don't burn dickheads, especially if you're a police officer – not least because it's a criminal offence. I'd been on the brink of chucking my job away, all because of some gobby twat.

As I write this, some years later, I still don't know exactly what possessed me. Let's put it down to the stress of the job. I had been doing this kind of work for years, and I had been mixing with shit, day in and day out. As the saying goes, 'You mix with shit, you become shit.' At least, I think that's a saying.

My behaviour off duty was becoming more erratic, too. At times, we three undercover buyers would be out doing three or four deals a day, in some extremely dangerous circumstances. This cycle went on for months on end, 12 to 14 hours a day, six days a week. At the same time – though whether it was a symptom or a cause I'm not sure – I was drinking far too much. I would usually finish work at about midnight. Then I'd drive home, an hour away. When I got there, I'd usually have a shower and then I'd sit and watch early morning telly, allowing the stress and shit of the day to ebb away while I drank a few cans of beer to help me sleep. I'd eventually go to bed around 4am, only to be back up a few hours later when the kids got up. Then I'd set off again at around 8.30am to get to the Althorp Estate for a 10am briefing. It was shit – for me, for Carmel and the kids.

I saw myself ageing in the mirror, and others saw it, too. There are very few full-time buyers; most have day jobs as detectives or intelligence officers. Obviously, good buyers – and I flatter myself that I was one – are in demand and usually away grafting. But throughout my years as a UC, I still nominally had a job as a bog-standard PC back in Derbyshire, and I had to appear there from time to time. On one occasion, I had to whiz up from Northampton to go back to my home nick to sign some statements. I let myself in and was wandering through a corridor when I bumped into a female copper I knew well. She immediately challenged me. 'Excuse me. This area is off-limits to members of the public. It's for police officers only. Who are you?'

'It's me, Sharon,' I said. 'Pete. Pete Ashton. I work here.'

'Christ!' she said, her face softening into one of concern. 'I'm sorry, Pete. I didn't recognise you. Have you been ill?'

Meeting my inspector wasn't much more uplifting. He took one look at me, and said, 'Bloody hell, Pete. You look like shit, mate!'

I had always attended those compulsory counselling sessions with a force welfare officer after each job, but I never really took them seriously; it always seemed to me that they just allowed the bosses at EMSOU to tick a box. But shortly after that appearance at the nick, they slotted another counselling session in. It was only halfway through this particular job. Presumably it was due to the heightened danger, which was obviously showing in my appearance.

But that was for later. Now, I said my goodbyes to the crew at my nick and returned to the gutter.

* * *

THE WEST SIDE of Northampton has a sprawling mass of housing estates, full to the brim with white, right-wing, working class people with a strong mix of Scottish descendants. Halfway through this operation, I was asked to test the water there and see if I could get a foothold in the heroin scene. Once again, I was under no illusion that my task was going to be difficult, but at least my white skin wouldn't jar in this BNP stronghold.

My first job was to find a pet junkie. The back of my van was full of supposedly dodgy power tools and other bits and pieces, and I had my usual batch of flyers to dish out round the estate. I found a group of kids who were interested in buying my snide Burberry polo shirts, but no matter how much I intimated that I was after heroin none of them took the bait. The pressure to expedite the job necessitated quick decision-making and some corner-cutting, and there was always a fine line between making progress and screwing up a chance to take out a player. I'd been scratching the surface for a couple of weeks when someone suggested I should hang around a particular local boozer one night when England were playing a qualifier for the European Championships. I parked up outside a row of shops next to the pub and saw a few familiar faces drinking in the beer garden. As I sat there wondering how to move things forward, I noticed a bloke coming out of a nearby betting shop. As he walked past the van, I called him over and handed him a flyer. 'Here you go, mate,' I said. 'I also buy mountain bikes, so if you can get hold of any give me a ring.'

He walked off in the direction of the boozer without saying a word, but was still clutching my flyer. It wasn't long before I was getting quite a bit of attention from the blokes in the beer garden. They walked into the middle of the road and started staring at me. Then my mobile rang, and when I answered it whoever was on the other end was making siren noises. I heard a shout of, 'Evening, officer!'

I was new in this area, and they were guessing. But I was still pissing up a waterfall, so I decided not to waste any more time. I drove off into the estate, and my luck changed immediately when I spotted a kid, nervously pacing up and down by a junction, obviously waiting to score. I pulled up next to him and leaned out of the window. 'Hello, mate,' I said. 'Do you know anyone who might want to buy some power tools?'

'I might,' he said.

I grinned, got out and went to the back, and opened up my Aladdin's Cave of goodies.

His eyes widened. 'Where the fuck did you get that lot from?'

'You know how it is,' I said. 'I buy bits and bobs at car boot sales, pick up stuff here and there. I'm always buying as well as selling, so if you come across anything you think I might be interested in…'

'Do you pay?' he said.

'Obviously, yeah.' I handed him a flyer. 'Are you scoring?' I said, casually.

'Yeah, mate,' he said, hopping from foot to foot and looking up and down the road. 'I'm waiting for my man now but he's late – as fucking usual.'

'You can use my phone to ring him if you like,' I said, ever the helpful soul.

'That'd be great, ta,' he said, taking the mobile.

He dialled his man. Another number stored.

'It's Dan,' he said. 'Where are you? You said you'd be here half an hour ago… Two minutes? Right, OK.'

'You reckon I can get some gear meself, like?' I said, taking the phone back.

'I'm sure he'll sort you out if I ask him,' he said. 'I'll just pretend we know each other. His name's Declan. He's a bit of a gyppo, but his gear's good.'

As he spoke, a white bloke in his mid-twenties, and wearing a Celtic shirt, walked up. Dan perked up immediately. 'Alright, Dec? My mate's got a load of power tools if you want any.'

Declan eyed me suspiciously as I opened the back of my van. Not without reason: as I did so, I used my key fob to activate the video camera hidden in the back of my headrest.

Dec gave the tools a cursory going over, turned to Dan and said, 'Here's your stuff.'

Dan, keen to help me, said, 'Can you sort my mate with an Arthur?'

I stepped forward and handed Dec a twenty pound note, a tenner and a fiver. I think he was caught off guard: to my delight and surprise, he handed me a small Clingfilm package containing brown powder.

'Can he come through you direct?' said Dan.

'How long have you known him?'

'About 10 minutes,' said Dan, forgetting his original story.

Dec looked like he was about to faint.

'You twat!' he said, before pulling the front of his shirt up over his face and bolting off into the nearby bushes.

I looked quizzically at my new mate. 'What was all that about? He didn't seem too pleased.'

Dan shrugged, philosophically. 'Fuck him,' he said. 'It won't be the first kicking that I've ever had off him.'

I jumped in my van and disappeared, leaving Dan to contemplate his uncertain future.

Dec was due to fly out to Ibiza on holiday the following day. He was either too busy packing his sun block, or didn't particularly like the bloke who was running his business while he was away, because he forgot to mention to him that he had dealt to me, and that he had his suspicions. So when I rang him the following day asking for the same again, a voice said, 'It's not Dec, it's Chris. I'm looking after things while Dec's away. Come to the community centre next to the doctor's and call me when you get there.'

That is what I call service. Clearly the business was in good hands. I made my way to the community centre, parked up and rang Chris again. Five minutes later he appeared, a white bloke in his early 40s with a crew cut and heavily tattooed arms. I switched on my steering column camera and opened my passenger door to try to bring him into shot. He bent down near to the front passenger seat and said, 'Hello, mate, what you after?'

'Can you do me a half teenth?'

Chris dropped the gear onto the front passenger seat and I passed him the money. 'Give me a call any time,' he said. 'I'll either meet you round here or at the Windmill pub just up the road.'

When I returned to base, I looked at the video with the intelligence officer.

'Chris is very well-connected on the estate,' he said. 'He's only just come out of prison for trafficking.'

Ooh, unlucky.

I might have looked like shit to people in the normal world, but on the drug scene I was a picture of health – nowhere near skinny and pale enough to be getting through half a teenth in a day. If I went back too soon, even a lummox like Chris was going to get suspicious. So I decided to steer clear of him for a day or two and go back to the centre of town.

* * *

THE FOLLOWING AFTERNOON, I was wandering through the high rise flats dotted around the edge of the red light area when I heard a woman shouting, 'Oi, geezer!'

I looked around and recognised a prostitute who I'd spoken to a few times when she was working her beat. She was staggering up the main road with a bloke, waving like mad in my direction. As I walked over, I could see that the bloke was completely off his face: he was happily hoovering heroin smoke off a piece of tin foil, in broad daylight, in the middle of a busy street. People were walking past looking in disgust at us, but the two of them were oblivious.

'This is Jasper,' said the girl, by way of an introduction to her friend. He looked an attractive character, with prison tear tattoos coming down his cheek, and teeth stained brown thanks to decades of smoking gear. 'You got anything on you?' she said.

'I'm trying to score myself,' I said. 'But I'm struggling.'

She turned to her mate and said, 'Jasper, give Paul a ring.'

'I've no fucking money, so unless your mate here wants to give us a smoke there's no point.'

'I don't mind giving you a line each as long as you can get me a score,' I said.

Technically, I suppose this meant that I would be supplying controlled drugs, but these two were going to get heroin whether I was there or not, and undercover officers are allowed to join an existing conspiracy – just not to create one. Jasper certainly wasn't thinking of legal niceties. He was on his mobile phone in a flash calling his dealer and motioning me to hand over some cash. He hung up and said, 'You wait here with her while I go and meet him, yeah?'

So we waited. And waited. The girl kept assuring me that Jasper was a diamond geezer and would soon be back with the gear, but I could see she was thinking what I was thinking. As it happened, we were both wrong – or partly wrong. When Jasper did eventually reappear he was in a worse state than when he'd left, so he'd obviously had a crafty smoke before returning. But he hadn't had it all, and handed over a tatty little bag of smack. There's always a tension for UCs in situations like this. On the one hand, you need to act like a police officer. On the other hand, you need to act like a junkie. The problem with that is, junkies are unpredictable, to say the least, and it's not always easy to know which way to go. In this situation, would a real addict go mental about the theft of his drugs? If I didn't, how would that look? Should I still make good my promise to let them have a line each? If I didn't, I knew Jasper and the girl would accuse me of stiffing them – and that Jasper would deny touching any of the gear earlier. The bottom line was, I needed to keep them onside, so I gave them a bit of the heroin each. Then, as a quid pro quo, I said, 'Any chance you could introduce me to Paul? So as I can score off him meself?'

They both jumped back in horror. 'Not a fucking chance,' said the girl. 'These are serious bastards. Have you never heard of the Burger Bar Boys?'

'I don't think so,' I said.

'These are big, bad bastards,' said Jasper. 'I mean, they move kilos of smack a week, and if they don't like you you're a fucking dead man.'

Clearly, I'd have to find another way in. But at least I had a name. Paul.

By the way, I saw Jasper a few weeks later. I was on my way to score in the Racecourse area, when a top-of-the-range Mercedes – fifty or sixty grand's-worth of motor – screamed up next to me. To my surprise, Jasper leaned out of the driver's window. 'Alright, geezer?' he said, with a cheery grin.

I was even more shocked that he'd recognised me than with the fact that he was driving such a vehicle. 'Where d'you nick that from?' I said.

I think I offended him. 'Nicked?' he said. 'Fuck off! It's my new job. I deliver them for people.'

I must have raised my eyebrows, because he dug around in the glove-box and came out with some paperwork. 'Here's me fucking delivery note, you cheeky bastard!' he said, with a grin.

I shook my head. Who the hell would trust a lowlife like him, with tear-shaped prison tattoos on his face, to deliver cars like this to their customers?

Then, in a cloud of burnt rubber and exhaust fumes, he was gone.

* * *

THE NEXT EVENING, enough time having elapsed for me to have gone through the gear I'd bought from him, I rang Chris. He told me to be outside the Windmill in 20 minutes. It was on a main road through the estate and beside a row of shops, but these places are like rabbit warrens and it took me a while to find it. There was a car park to the rear, and I parked as near to the back door as possible. There was no lighting, and as soon as I turned the engine off everything was black. I called Chris again to tell him I was there, and waited for my eyes to become accustomed to the darkness. Before long, I could vaguely make out bushes and trees surrounding the car park, and could see that there were about a dozen other vehicles parked up.

I gave my headlights a double flash, and a figure emerged from the bushes, hurried over to the Astra and climbed into the front passenger seat. As I squinted at him through the darkness, I realised I had never seen him before in my life. He was heavy-built with a big mop of hair and wearing one of those crappy padded lumberjack shirts. As soon as he sat down he began to babble. 'Look, mate, I'm on my arse... I've tried to get the money, but she says she needs it to feed the kids. I've been looking for Cookie all week, but he's obviously fucked off. I've tried ringing you all day and left messages on your answer phone. I know you're pissed off with me, and I wouldn't blame you if you gave me a shoeing, but all I'm asking for is a couple more days to get the money.' He hesitated briefly, looked at me, then carried on jabbering away. 'And I was wondering if you could let me have a few more grammes, which I fucking *promise*, mate, I will pay you back for.'

Eventually I managed to get a word in. 'I think you've got the wrong bloke.'

He looked at me for a few seconds. Then the penny dropped, and he said, 'Mark?'

'No, Pete.'

'Oh fuck!'

He leapt out of the van and ran back into the bushes.

A few minutes later, someone pulled into the car park in a blaze of headlights. A group of lads got out and walked past me, and I recognised Chris opening my front passenger door. He knelt down beside the door and I turned the interior light on to get a better picture on the video camera.

'You after the usual?' he said.

'Yes, mate, if that's OK. Plus, er, I don't suppose you've got any rocks on you?'

'I don't, no, I only do the smack. But my lad does crack, and my brother does the speed and pills and weed and that. If you wait here, Pete, I'll get my lad out to you.'

He walked off into the boozer, and I dropped the heroin exhibit into my fag packet. A few moments later, to my disappointment, Chris himself came back. He leaned in and dropped a rock on the front passenger seat, saying, 'He's too fucking lazy to come himself... Kids, eh?'

I'd have liked to have nabbed the son, as well, but there you go.

I gave it another couple of days before calling Chris again, and I had to ring a few times before he finally answered. When he did, he didn't seem his normal chirpy self. 'I've got no white,' he said, 'and my lad isn't around so I can only help you with the brown. Come to the front of the Windmill in quarter of an hour.'

I pulled up on the main road outside the boozer and waited for Chris. There was no sign of him, but there was a fat woman in pink leggings and a white top pacing up and down and studying all the cars as they drove past. After a while, she walked over to me and said, 'You Pete?'

'Yeah.'

'Chris told me to give you this.'

She handed me a Clingfilm wrap containing brown powder, and I gave her the money.

'Why did he send you?' I said.

'Fucking ask him,' she said, and turned on her pudgy heel.

OK. That didn't sound promising. I headed back to the covert office with my exhibit, wondering if I was blown. As I arrived, my phone rang.

It was Chris. 'Pete, I need you to come and meet me?'

'Er... why?'

'Some mates of mine reckon that you're a copper.'

'I'm no copper, Chris,' I said. 'Fuck me, do I look like one?'

'You just can't tell, Pete. They're crafty cunts, some of them. Anyway, I'm not going to deal to you anymore until I see you smoking a bit of heroin, so come to the back of the Windmill. I'll give you some gear for nothing and you can sit and have a toot with me. That way we can sort things out.'

'I'm away on a buying trip around the car boots over the next few days,' I said. 'I'll give you a bell when I get back.'

'You fucking do that.'

Bollocks.

The intelligence officer and I pieced together what had happened. Apparently, Chris had met up with the other dealers on the estate to collect some gear and hand over the last week's takings to the main supplier. The conversation had turned to the dodgy bloke in the white Astra van who was driving around the estate, buying and selling power tools and trying to score heroin. The more switched-on lags strongly suspected that I was a cop, and couldn't understand how anyone would be stupid enough to fall for that old trick. That left Chris in quite a predicament. If I was a cop, it was only a matter of time before he would get nicked and banged up. Given that he'd only just got out, he'd be looking at a decent stretch. And he knew what the other scumbags on the estate knew – that people who are looking at lengthy prison sentences tend to grass. It's as simple as that. That made Chris a security risk, and about as popular as anthrax.

This was why Chris had sent his wife out to deal to me. The SIO and I mulled things over. We had Chris and a couple of smaller dealers from the estate, but it looked like the chances of getting anywhere else were slim, to say the least. Given that my cover was still intact in the red light area and the surrounding tower blocks, maybe I should leave the estate alone and concentrate on those parts of town?

Any doubt that this was the correct course of action evaporated when Declan returned from Ibiza and Chris mentioned his little dilemma. Declan hit the roof. That evening, Dan the junkie was playing on his computer in his bedsit when he answered a knock on his front door. He was met by a group of blokes wearing ski masks and wielding baseball bats who knocked him unconscious, smashed up his computer, and – just for good measure – stabbed him in his arms and legs.

The following day I received a phone call from a withheld number. When I answered, a voice said, 'Stay away from the fucking estate or you'll get the same as that grassing bastard Dan.'

I stayed away from the estate.

Chapter 13:

Big Fish, Small Pool

THERE WERE A FEW CHARACTERS who we assumed would be untouchable – at least, given the remit and budget of our operation.

One of these was a guy named Zak, a Jamaican with collar-length dreadlocks and a beard, who worked the red light district riding a mountain bike. He was thought to be responsible for bringing the Burger Bar Boys into Northampton in the first place, as he was a blood relative of one of their main faces. I had only ever caught fleeting glimpses of him as he pedalled through his territory. Until one night.

I was standing on the fringes of the red light district with a group of junkies and prostitutes who were waiting to be served up. I had been on the scene for long enough now, and nobody batted an eyelid whenever I appeared. We were waiting for Zak. He'd been called by one of the girls, much to the approval of the rest of the crowd as his gear was known to be banging. Apart from one lad who stuttered, 'Er... I'm out of here... I owe him money.'

Five minutes turned into 20, as the group bobbed up and down, scanning the horizon for the dreadlocked pusher. Eventually, he appeared, casually cycling along without a care in the world, as if he was peddling along the beach at Montego Bay, or at least Skeggy. He pulled up by us and was immediately surrounded by his customers. Far from being untouchable, scoring off Zak proved to be easy. I just joined on the end of the queue and waited my turn to be served. I got to him, he smiled at me and said, 'Hey, big fella, what ya sayin'?'

'One white.'

He spat a rock out of his mouth – he must have had dozens stuffed into his cheeks.

'Can I have your mobile number?' I said.

'Sure, man. Get it off one of the girls.'

With that, he rode off into the darkness, and I headed off back to Althorp to give the team the good news.

I soon found out that you were wasting your time if you tried ringing Zak before seven. His clientele consisted almost exclusively of the sex workers and the related flotsam and jetsam, and he kept to their hours. One night as I was waiting for him, I was approached by another bloke, a skinny little bastard who turned out to be his cousin, Carlton. Carlton I knew about from briefings: although he was a little squirt, in terms of the trade he was a big hitter who brought drugs up in weight from London. He also had a little side-line as a street robber, working with his brother, Dee, to stalk victims in the underpasses on the periphery of the red light district. Dee, an athletic bloke with dreadlocks down to the small of his back, was the muscle, and a particularly naughty lad to boot. He had just done five-and-a-half years in prison for selling a handgun to an undercover policeman. So Carlton coming over to speak to me was something of a result. 'I seen you hanging around a bit,' he said.

He went on to explain how had spotted me weeks earlier, and couldn't work out my connection to the area. He'd been in two minds whether I was a new pimp to the area, or a copper, and he eventually asked a couple of the girls who I was. They told him that I was a crackhead who sold dodgy power tools. Now he viewed me as a potential customer. 'You don't wanna score off Zak,' he said. 'In fact, man, you should come with me now, down by the Racecourse. I can call my man out. He does bigger and better rocks.'

This wasn't an attractive proposition. It was around midnight, and the Racecourse – a large open space that hosted hundreds of public executions in the 1700s and 1800s – has no street lighting. Heading off there with a known robber who knew I had money on me didn't exactly flick my switch. Against that, I was 16 stone and six-foot and a bit, and Carlton was an emaciated, seven-stone crackhead. The chances of him successfully robbing me, even if he was tooled up, were slim – unless Dee showed up. I decided to tag along.

We set off at a spurt, only stopping *en route* to ring the dealer. I offered him my mobile phone but he was having none of it, and popped into a telephone kiosk. When he came out, he said, 'When I'm scoring you need to stay well hidden, yeah, 'cos this man we're going to meet, he's the top man in the area and he don't like strangers.'

It took us around 15 minutes to get to the Racecourse and when we got to the public toilets there Carlton asked me for my money. I handed it over, convinced that was the last I'd see of it, and he set off towards the shops and bars on the main road.

That night, I later discovered, there were a couple of members of the operational team parked on the main road at the time. (Some members of the team were seconded from the force drug squad, and they had a tendency, if not otherwise engaged, to go for a swan round the plot to see what was happening. The locals were used to seeing them, and they never caused a stir.) The detectives were very happy with what they saw. Carlton walked across the road and stopped in the doorway of a Caribbean restaurant. Then a Rasta wearing a bright red kaftan joined him, and they hugged like long-lost brothers. The bloke in the kaftan was a National Crime Squad target, suspected of importing hundreds of kilos of cocaine into the country each year. The pair chatted for a few minutes, before the exchange took place, and Carlton trotted back across the road to join me. The reason he'd been so keen to help me score was that he knew he would get a lick of the rock before he handed it over. So the next port of call was the gents', where he broke my rock in half and handed me the smaller piece.

'You going to stay for a smoke?' he said.

'No,' I said. 'My mate's waiting for me at our flat and he'll go fucking mad if I smoke all the gear.'

At the debrief back at the covert office that night I had to stay out of the way. I hadn't been told the restaurant owner's name by Carlton, and it was better I didn't know it. The last thing that I or anyone else wanted was me inadvertently letting slip this major suspect's name when my arse was twitching the next time I was stumbling across the Racecourse with Carlton during the wee small hours. But the focus of the operation quickly shifted from Zak to Carlton and Mr Big.

My brief for the following night was to hang around the red light area until I bumped into Carlton, and then to engineer another trip to the Caribbean Restaurant in order to score. It was doubtful that the owner would deal directly to me, but the operational team were hoping that they would be able to link him to the deals via DNA on the Clingfilm wrapped around the crack cocaine.

When I arrived for the afternoon brief I noticed that I had the four meanest lads from the back-up team covering me that night. Pinned up on the wall of the briefing room was a large head and shoulders photograph of Carlton's brother, Dee.

'There was an attempted wages snatch earlier today,' said the intelligence officer. 'The suspects strongly resemble Carlton and Dee. Intelligence indicates that Dee has been bingeing on crack for days and is basically capable of anything.'

The SIO said, 'Pete, the back-up team will be as close as possible at all times, and we want you to take a smart phone into the red light area with you. Given the state that Dee is in, his general reputation for violence, and his likely unpredictability based on his crack use, we need to know where you are at all times. Keep your eyes peeled, and if the pair of them are together you need to be on your guard.'

So it was with some trepidation that I made my way in at about 10pm. I kicked around, avoiding the likes of Edwin and BJ who were already boxed off, but scored off Zak because it would have looked odd if I hadn't bought when he rode up to me, smiling from ear to ear. I nipped off and met the back-up team behind Toys R Us, where I placed the drugs in an exhibit bag so as to avoid cross-contamination with other purchases later in the evening. The team were in a Ford Galaxy people carrier with tinted windows: it pulled up next to me and I jumped into the back, safely concealed from any onlookers by the darkened glass. One of the lads handed me an exhibit bag and I placed the gear inside, sealed the bag and signed and dated the exhibit label. I then handed the bag back to the cop. 'By fuck,' he said. 'You've been busy lately, Pete.'

'I know, mate. I'm knackered'

'You staying for a quick beer after we finish?'

'Yeah, no problems, mate. If God spares me!'

'You'll be OK, mate. What's the worst that can happen?'

I didn't want to think about the worst that could happen, but it tickled the rest of the sick bastards, who all hooted with laughter.

'Go on,' said one of them. 'Fuck off, you stink like a polecat.'

Sighing, I climbed out of the vehicle and lit a fag, whilst the back-up team opened the windows to let some fresh air in. After a few pulls on the cigarette, I headed slowly back to The Jungle. As I walked up the hill, my legs felt like lead. I was dreading the next few hours. Part of me hoped I hadn't missed my date with Carlton and Dee; a significant additional part of me was quietly praying that they had both stepped out in front of a bus.

I walked past the ladies of the night and onto the main route through the estate. Almost immediately, I bumped into Carlton. He was chatting to a couple of guys, and when he caught my eye he made his excuses to them before ushering me to a secluded spot. 'You after scoring, Pete?' he said.

'Yeah, mate,' I said. 'Just a twenty pound rock, if that's OK?'

'No problem,' he said. 'Let's go up the Racecourse.'

We set off walking, but it was soon apparent that he was taking me by a different route. I felt my apprehension levels rising, and as we walked underneath the legs at the base of a high-rise block, and a figure stepped out of the shadows, they went through the roof. It was Dee. My stomach boiling with apprehension, I made sure I stood back a good six feet as they got their heads together, talking in low voices. Eventually, Carlton looked back at me. He didn't introduce me to his brother, but just indicated that I should follow them, and said, 'Come on then. Chop, chop!'

They set off at quite a fast pace, and I followed, reluctantly. This had moved on leaps and bounds, and I now seriously feared for my safety. If they robbed me, there were no ifs and buts about it: I was going to hand over all my money and just hope the back-up team got to me before things got any worse. The problem was, I didn't know if they realised that Dee was with us. I wasn't carrying a smartphone; I seem to recall that it was in case they robbed me, and EMSOU lost an expensive bit of kit. But as we jogged across the main road, I saw the back-up team Galaxy cruise past us, which gave me some comfort.

The two brothers led me down through a series of subways and underpasses. These were dark, smelly and very lonely at the best of times, but now it was like going down into Hades. They didn't talk to me, just walked on with purpose, about 10 feet apart. I hung back, and it turned into a bit of a dance routine, with me trying to keep them in front of me where I could keep eyes-on, without making it look too obvious. I was worried that if they got behind me then they would jump me and roll me for my money. They were known to use knives and had stabbed victims in previous robberies. This all kept me very much on my toes: I was constantly looking for escape routes and potential weapons that I could defend myself with as we made our way through the labyrinth of tunnels.

We eventually left the subways, but my relief was short-lived. We walked up a side street and into the Racecourse park. This meant that, if things went tits up, the back-up lads would be at least 400 yards away across a series of football pitches and cricket fields.

Once we got to the public toilets, Carlton said, 'Giz the money and stay here and wait.'

They went directly to the restaurant, met the owner, and scored in the side street that runs alongside it, and then they walked away in the opposite direction and disappeared into the night. The back-up team was watching them from a car park a little further up the road. But the first I knew was when I got a phone call from the liaison officer who told me that I had been stood up. I suppose being skanked was better than being robbed, but in a strange way it still pissed me off. Anyway, that was the last I saw of them, because they were nicked the next day as they attempted to rob a bookies', and remanded in custody. At least I didn't have to react to the skank.

I believe they each ended up with five or six years inside for being concerned in the supply of controlled drugs and armed robbery. I never found out what happened to the Mr Big who Carlton had met. The fragmented and secretive nature of my work meant that once my role as a buyer was over I moved on and lost contact with the area –

even with many of the cops I'd worked so closely with. All I do know is that I was never called to give evidence against him.

* * *

SO WE'D HAD SOME results in the first few months of the operation, but we hadn't made much headway with the Burgers. I felt a bit of a failure, though really it was simple enough: people didn't know or trust us enough to introduce us to them.

Unbeknown to me and Shabby, however, the Burgers had noticed us. One morning I was walking through the town centre when I bumped into a beggar called Mick who I'd befriended. He was a decent bloke in his late 40s, who had once owned a smallholding up north. His marriage had broken up, he had lost the farm and had ended up homeless where he had got into the brown. Rather than turn to crime, he would sit with his dog in the shopping precinct and beg. A group of office girls had taken pity on him; being nice, wholesome young ladies, they were convinced that he was begging to feed himself and his dog, so they used to give generously, much to his delight. Obviously, 90 per cent of what he was given went into the foil and got smoked; the other 10 per cent went on dog food, and he ate out of the bins.

'You scoring, Mick?' I said.

'I'm a bit skint,' he said, rubbing his dog's ears, a sad grin on his face.

'I'll chip in,' I said. 'We could share half a teenth?'

He brightened up immediately, and we made our way to his bedsit where he scrabbled around in a drawer for his dealer's mobile number, which was written on a scrap of paper. He made his call, and a short time later a car pulled up directly outside his flat. I recognised it straight away as a Burger vehicle: suddenly, things had become very interesting.

'Wait here, Pete,' said Mick.

He went out into the street to score. I looked out of the window, and saw that he was leaning in and talking to someone in the vehicle, and gesticulating towards the flat. As I watched, one of the occupants got out. I quickly sat down on the only seat in the room and tried to look nonchalant. The door opened and in they walked.

'Pete, this is Paul,' said Mick. 'He wanted to meet you.'

Paul was a black lad in his early 20s. He was dressed in flashy designer clothes, in strong contrast to the Worzel-Gummidge-meets-Steptoe look that Mick and I had gone for. He had an air of arrogance and aggression, and he eyed me suspiciously. In a strong Birmingham accent, he asked me the usual questions to check my drug habit. He didn't seem particularly interested in my answers.

'Where you from?'

'I'm from Stockport, but I live here now. Up near the football ground.'

'How do you take your gear?'

'I toot.'

'Who do you normally score off?'

'From the *Big Issue* sellers in the precinct, or I call Benji.'

He ruminated on this for a few moments. Then he said, 'Yeah, I seen you around. From now on, you score off me, nobody else, you get me?'

'Suits me, mate,' I said.

'I'm not your fucking mate.'

'OK, no problems.'

'And next time you score from me, I want to come to your flat so I can check you out, yeah?'

'Yeah, sure.'

'You can get my number from this guy,' he said, nodding in the direction of Mick the beggar.

With that, he was gone.

Wow. What a massive buzz. This had been a risky and dangerous introduction, but I was in now – I was in, and doing my job. The adrenalin coursing through my veins battered away all thoughts of quitting. I felt up for it, focused. I made my way back to my flat, just in case Paul was watching me, or had someone doing it for him.

I knew that this latest development would get the liaison officer flapping. It wasn't ideal for the Burgers to know where I was supposed to be living, in case they dropped by unannounced to check me out. As usual, although I'd rented the flat I never actually lived there, because that would mean my protection team, in this case Northampton's firearms unit, would have to be on duty 24 hours a day to cover me. Instead, we varied the times during day and night that I was deployed, and seen out and about, to create the illusion that I lived in the area.

At the debrief in the meeting room, there was an odd, excited atmosphere. I sensed more than a hint of trepidation. We had potentially got into the Burgers, but we might just have opened Pandora's Box. I sat there nursing a brew, my t-shirt stuck to my back with sweat that was rapidly cooling; the lads on the backup team sat next to me, trying not to breathe in my BO. The SIO entered the room, a worried frown on his face He called for a bit of hush and asked me for a detailed account of the deployment. As I spoke, the Intelligence Officer scribbled notes for his intel logs.

As I wrapped up, I couldn't help noticing that although the SIO seemed happy that we'd got a toehold into the Burgers, something was bothering him. 'Just let me clarify,' he said. 'Paul is insisting on meeting you next time at your flat?'

'Yep, that's right, boss.'

'Why do you think he wants to do that?'

'I suppose he just wants to check me out and have a look round. I don't see there being any real problems. After all, he came to Mick's house today to sort us out and he's a regular customer.'

'Will your bedsit stand up to his scrutiny?' he said. 'I'm not being funny, but does it look authentic? Because if this fucker gets wind of you being Old Bill, anything could happen.'

It's nice to know they're concerned, but if he thought I hadn't thought of that... 'Yeah,' I said. 'No problems, boss, it looks the part… Half a bowl of soggy cornflakes on the side, a few old pizza boxes, burnt tinfoil, bedclothes and dirty socks all over the gaff, that sort of thing. I've got to have it looking right in case the landlord pops in, apart from anything else.'

'Good,' he said, scratching his chin. 'Right, we'll stand down for the day, now. Caddy, we need to chat about maybe getting someone from West Midlands on board as soon as possible to help with identifying these bastards. And after that, I need a pint.'

A member of the West Midlands' gun crime unit was hastily drafted over to assist in the identification of the Burgers – it turned out that Paul was a big fish in their smelly little pond – and rest days were cancelled for the foreseeable future to give us a clear run. The next day I made my way to my flat and called Paul around noon. He answered after a couple of rings. 'Yeah?'

'Paul?'

'Who the fuck is this?'

'It's Pete. I met you yesterday? You told me to…'

'Shut the fuck up! Don't fucking use my name! What do you fucking want?'

'Can you do me one white and one brown?'

'Come to the Racecourse and ring me when you get there.'

Well, that was a less than amicable exchange. Clearly, pleasantries were not the order of the day. On the upside, he had obviously changed his mind about visiting. And I'd made all that effort to make my bedsit look right! Oh well, better do as he says. I called the protection team. 'We're switching locations to the Racecourse,' I said.

'OK, mate,' came the reply. 'Watch yourself.'

Fifteen minutes later, I parked up the Astra and walked over to a playground on the edge of the park. There was a road leading up to the park, with bollards at the end to prevent cars driving onto the grass. I lit up a cigarette, and waited. A car horn sounded, and I looked over to the bollards. A car was flashing its headlights at me. I walked slowly over, and as I got closer I could see three black kids inside. The driver's window was wound down, and Paul's ugly mug appeared. 'Get in the back,' he said.

I climbed in and sat next to a lad in his late teens. Almost before I'd shut the door, the car reversed sharply and at speed and then three-point turned, and we were gone. We drove round the block before anyone spoke. Eventually, the bloke in the front passenger seat leaned back and said, 'Who told you to use my mate's name when you called?'

'No-one, mate… I didn't think…'

'That's fucking right, white boy, you didn't fucking think. The cops listen to our calls, and you said our name. You do that again, and I swear they'll find you in a ditch.'

I felt very alone just at that moment, and acutely conscious of how vulnerable I was. I had no smart phone on me – though that turned out to be a very good thing indeed – and the back-up could have had only the vaguest idea of my whereabouts. The car pulled over into a small car park in a row of terraced streets.

The kid sitting next to me said, 'Lean back, man.'

Then he swiftly ran his hands over my body, searching for a recorder.

After he had finished patting me down, he said, 'Nothing.'

'What did you say you was after?' said Paul.

'One white and one brown. Please.'

The front seat passenger produced two large paper bags, the sort corner shops sell sweets in. I could see that one was full of rocks, and that the other contained different-sized deals of heroin.

The atmosphere in the car was horrible. I could feel the breath of the bloke who had searched me on the side of my face, and sensed his eyes burning into me. I was actually scared. The guy in the front seat handed me a rock and a bag of heroin, and I passed back the money.

'Get out of the fucking car,' he said.

I was only too happy to oblige. I climbed out and they screeched off out of sight. I breathed a heavy sigh of relief and made my way back for a debrief. Back at base the fact that I was patted down caused quite a bit of concern. So the SIO decided that we would use no covert recording equipment or smart phones until the Burgers were a bit happier with me. We gave it until around 9pm, to give me time to have got through the white and brown I'd bought earlier that day, especially as my cover story was that I was sharing it with Shabby. Then I put another call into Paul, and asked him for the same again. He told me to make my way to a terraced street near the Racecourse and call him again. About half an hour later I arrived and called him. 'Hello… er, I'm here now.'

'So come to the fucking car, then!'

Absolutely no idea of customer service.

'I've walked up the street once and I can't see you.'

'How fucking difficult can it be? Just come to the car or I swear to fuck, man, I'm going to drive off!'

There was a bit of street lighting but it was close to midnight, and visibility was poor. I honestly couldn't see the fucking vehicle, so I did another circuit. As I was passing a brand new VW Golf, I noticed its engine was running. I looked in and saw a bloke in the driver's seat. He was hunched up, and had a baseball cap pulled down low over his eyes. The front passenger window wound down and he said, 'Get fucking in, will you?'

I'd found the car, then.

The interior reeked of polished leather: this was a nice motor, not the type of throwaway vehicle that the Burgers normally drove around in.

Paul was alone and his usual charming self. 'What do you want?'

'Just one white and one brown, mate.'

'I'm not your fucking mate, so don't call me that.'

We made the exchange, and Paul said his usual goodbyes. As the car drove away I memorised the number on the registration plate and later reported it to the intelligence officer. She checked it out on the PNC, and then double-checked the number with me. 'Sir,' she said, addressing the SIO. 'There's an outstanding PNC report on that vehicle. If it's found, it needs to be recovered and preserved for forensics.'

Apparently, a girl had been walking home through Birmingham a couple of nights earlier, and the Golf had pulled up beside her. The driver had offered her a lift, and she climbed in. There were three other men in the car at the time, and they gang-raped her before dumping her, sobbing, at the roadside.

The SIO had to make a call as to whether to report our contact with the car, and who had been driving it, or to protect our operation, and me. He decided to circulate the number to local officers. A couple of days later, a local mobile patrol saw the vehicle and tried to stop it. A short chase followed before they found the car abandoned in a side street. So it was recovered without any suspicion falling on my shoulders.

* * *

OVER THE NEXT WEEK or so, I scored off the Burgers once or twice a day, and although their manners didn't improve there was no repeat of the patting down. So we decided that I should introduce Shabby to them; once they were happy with him, we could then start wearing covert body cameras to try to get some of them identified.

We managed to get Shabby in without a hitch. We decided against anything elaborate; he just started turning up with me whenever I was scoring, and the Burgers didn't bat an eyelid. By now, he'd shown his face around town for weeks, especially in the red light area, so he was obviously a face they thought they knew and could trust.

Once he was properly known to them, it was decided that Shabby and I should go our separate ways and score off them individually while both wearing body cameras. This was a risky strategy, because if either of us was alone when a car load of Burgers turned up they were more likely to order him into the car. The thought of being in a vehicle with these people and them finding a camera on me did nothing to help me sleep well at night. The best I could hope for was a serious kicking; at worst, I could easily be driven out of town to somewhere nice and remote and topped. I didn't really fancy filming my own demise.

The Burgers often frequented a pool bar in Northampton called Q Ball. One night, Shabby was out trying to score off them without a camera. He was told to go to the toilets in the bar. He did so, and called them again once he was in the bogs. About 10 minutes later, a group of young blacks entered the toilets. Shabby recognised one of them: a couple of weeks earlier, he had been arrested on a fail-to-appear warrant and had been held in custody at Northampton police station before being placed back before the courts. He had already sold to us a few times, and was almost in the bag; but when the operational team heard that he was in custody they had volunteered to process him in order to have a good look at him. He had been charged with failing to appear, so he had to have his fingerprints and photographs taken, and the team used this as an opportunity to chat him up.

As they were fingerprinting him, they had a read of his previous convictions – these are attached to the fingerprints form – and one of them commented on his conviction for attempted murder, when he had shot a rival in the chest and got a substantial custodial sentence. I was later told that he replied, 'I'm not proud of that. I really let my mum down. Having to visit me in prison all those years nearly killed her. But I'm keeping out of trouble these days.'

The big fibber.

So, having bought from this lad before, Shabby assumed that he would recognise him and that the deal would go without a hitch. He said, 'Hello mate.'

The Burgers ignored him, and opened all the cubicle doors as if searching for somebody. Then the attempt-murderer said, 'What you doing here?'

'I'm waiting to score, mate, I rang you about half an hour ago and you told me to come here and wait.'

'Who the fuck are you?'

'I'm Shabby. You sorted me out a few times.'

One of the others grabbed Shabby by his collar and dragged him into one of the cubicles and pinned him up against the wall.

One of the Burgers patted him down while another screamed into his face, 'Don't ever fucking come into here looking for us! Who are you?'

'I'm Shabby, Pete's mate'

'Who the fuck's Pete?'

'He's been scoring off you for ages.'

'Never fucking heard of him. I think you're a copper.'

They found Shabby's mobile phone and began flicking through the dialled numbers to see how many times he had called their number recently. Eventually they found that he had called them out a few times and seemed to relax a bit.

'What did you say you wanted?' said the attempt-murderer.

'I'm after one white and one brown,' croaked Shabby.

The bloke handed Shabby back his mobile phone, and they served him. He was then released and he bolted for the outside world. The Burgers obviously didn't like punters appearing at their club and so we decided to give the place a wide berth.

* * *

THE PATTERN CONTINUED over the next few days – both of us making buys now and then, just keeping our faces in, keeping the momentum going. We'd started wearing body cams, and were getting lots of good clean buys on video. Although the Burgers were the main targets, the place was awash with drugs; you lifted one stone, and they all scurried to the next. The nature of undercover work is that you are constantly looking at new targets, so a few of these other dealers were roped in, too. Shabby in particular was moved off the plot, assisted by a new female buyer given a walk-on role, to get into a pub where a decent level smack dealer worked.

But the following Friday lunch time, we were awaiting the arrival of the Burgers. They turned up, the deal went to plan, and off they drove. Unfortunately, a marked patrol car was waiting round the corner, and the officers attempted to stop their vehicle. The Burgers floored it and screamed off at 100mph, and the inevitable chase caused chaos throughout Northampton, until the scum shook off the cops and abandoned their car in a side street. The police always have to be mindful of killing random innocents in the pursuit of the dregs of humanity, but it is galling when these people behave like this and then get to walk off into the sun.

Of course, this development was a potential nightmare for us – there was a very good chance that the Burgers would be blaming me and Shabby for fitting them up. I had reported back to the SIO as soon as we heard the cop car start after our boys, and we were quickly recalled to Althorp to draw up a plan. After much thrashing out of the various options, it was decided that the best thing to do was to carry on with the operation as though nothing had happened, and attempt to score off them later that day. This, after all, would be precisely what they didn't expect if they thought we were grasses – grasses would be avoiding them like the black death, whereas bog standard punters wouldn't give a monkeys about what had happened, probably wouldn't even know, would just want their fix.

We just had to hope that we were right about that – and I wouldn't wear the camera in case I got grabbed and patted down.

Unfortunately, Shabby had to go home to sort some personal business out, so for that day it was left up to me to bite the bullet. I spent a few hours mulling over the unpleasant possibilities that awaited me, with fingernails gnawed to the flesh, a gurgling stomach, and, no doubt, very high blood pressure. Eventually, at about 9pm I called the Burger's number.

It went straight to answer phone. I tried again, and again, and again. Obviously, the mobile was switched off.

A report came back to the team via a silent PNC marker that the other known Northampton-based Burger vehicle had recently been seen in Brum. They must have nipped back home to pick up a fresh stash. I waited for a bit, and around 11pm I called the number again. This time I got through.

'Yeah?'

'Hello, it's Pete. Can I have one white and one brown?'

Pause.

'OK, meet us at the Q Ball.'

I felt slightly faint. The fucking *Q Ball*. I really didn't want to get cornered in that shithole. I rang the liaison officer to update him, hoping that he'd tell me not to go there alone, to bin it for the night, and make my way home.

But he listened and tutted, then said, 'Well, what do you want to do?'

'I'm not bothered either way,' I lied. 'I'll do whatever the SIO thinks best.'

A few minutes later the SIO called me. 'It's up to you, Pete,' he said. 'Do whatever *you* think's best.'

Shit. We were getting closer to a result, but then I was potentially heading for a showdown.

Oh fuck it! In for a penny, in for a pound.

But first I was going to have a McDonalds, just in case it was my last chance.

I didn't really fancy my Big Mac; in fact, I felt quite sick as I tried to force it down. The protection team were all on standby near the Q Ball but that was of minimal reassurance. I tested my smart phone. 'Caddy, are you receiving me?'

The phone began buzzing in my jeans pocket to signal that Caddy was picking up my transmissions back at the covert premises. I slipped an empty Stella bottle into my jacket pocket – it was the best I could do, but I wasn't going to go down without a fight if it all kicked off – and walked into the Q Ball, and through to the toilets.

I called the Burgers and told them I was in the bogs. They never seemed to be in a hurry, and the usual half an hour slipped by, extremely slowly. I was looking for any excuse to walk out of there – surely I could just say they hadn't shown up? – but something, pride probably, kept me hanging around.

Then a couple of them walked in. I'd scored off them a few times already, but they glared at me and walked over to the cubicles and kicked the doors back to make sure no one was hiding behind them. The taller of the two said, 'Why do you never call us out to where you fucking live?'

I hadn't been expecting that – they set the ground rules, not me. 'I just ring you and you tell me where to go,' I said. I could feel my hands shaking with adrenalin. 'You told me to meet you here. You can come to my place anytime.'

Lots of teeth-sucking, hard stares at me and glances between the pair of them. Eventually, the tall guy said, 'What do you want?'

'One brown, one white,' I said. 'Please.'

The other one spat a wrap and a rock onto the toilet floor. I handed over my money and as they left I scrabbled around on the urine-splashed tiles for my gear before breathing a sigh of relief and bolting for the street outside, and relative safety.

Outside, I sat on some steps, shaking. I had been living on my wits for years, now, and I felt absolutely knackered. These bastards had been playing mind games with me again; once more, I vowed to pack in the buying after this one last job.

I knew I was burnt out. Once you start feeling fear – real fear – it's over. Apart from the odd brief triumph, I no longer enjoyed the work, and I was getting no buzz from it. Part of getting in-role is feeling right, and checking yourself out in shop windows as you walk along. You see yourself staring back – a dirty and unshaven and unkempt and haggard version of you – and you think, 'Yes, I look the fucking part. *I'd* nick me.' I was no longer looking in shop windows, because I didn't think I looked the part anymore. I looked like what I was – a greying, old copper, with the start of a mid-life spread, aggravated by the amount of beer I was drinking. I had to shave my head close because the grey was becoming more noticeable.

I got up, dropped the Stella bottle in a bin and walked away from the Q Ball, back to the Astra. I never wanted to talk to junkies or dealers about drugs again. As soon as the debrief at Althorp was over, I had a quick beer with the lads, trying to hide how shit I felt, jumped into my hire car, and drove home for the weekend.

* * *

THE FOLLOWING MONDAY, I started work in the afternoon, went to Althorp to plan the final weeks of the operation, before setting off in my Astra around the red light area with Daz, the lone undercover from London. We were looking for my old friend Edwin to box him off. I'd driven through a couple of times and had stopped at some traffic lights when a police motorcyclist pulled up next to me. The rider knocked on my side window and told me to pull over on the other side of the lights.

Daz called the back-up team to tell them we were being stopped, and possibly arrested. I turned the engine off and we were immediately surrounded by police officers. It became clear that we had driven into a pre-planned operation, targeting the red light area, about which our operational team had known nothing.

'Get out of the car please, sir,' said the motorcyclist.

I did as instructed, but as I stood up my crack pipe fell out of the door panel onto the tarmac.

The cop's eyes immediately lit up. So I was off to Northampton nick for a drugs search, which I knew would involve stripping naked and touching my toes in front of two male coppers. I sighed as I sat in the back of a police car watching them going over the Astra with a fine tooth comb. One cop was checking me, Daz, and the vehicle out on the PNC while another began searching the vehicle. Then I saw the searching officer stand up holding a set of number plates and a tax disc.

As Daz was dumped next to me in the back of the car, he said, 'I've been nicked on suspicion of theft of the vehicle.'

Soon enough, I was arrested for the same thing.

The numbers stencilled on the Astra's windows didn't match the number on the registration plate, so they assumed it had been pinched and false plates had been stuck on it. Not an unreasonable assumption – but what really confused them was that the numbers on the tax disc and registration plates found underneath the driver's seat *did* match the numbers on the windscreen. Moreover, the number on the plates displayed on the vehicle PNC'd to the same PO Box as the plates found under the seat! They knew *something* was wrong, but they couldn't quite work out what – unsurprisingly.

It dawned on me that someone at EMSOU had done the van cheap and quick. They hadn't bothered to check for window stencilling, or thought to remove the old number plates and tax disc: instead, they'd stuffed them under the driver's seat and forgot about them. Bloody brilliant. I didn't know whether to laugh or cry.

This was the second time in a year that I'd been arrested. I took some comfort that, for all my concern that I no longer looked like a junkie or criminal, I was managing to convince plod easily enough.

Back at the nick, the coppers' bewilderment moved to a higher level when they found the wires for the covert camera sewn into my jacket. When two members of the operational team, who were also Drug Squad officers, arrived the traffic cops asked why a crackhead car thief would have wires sewn into his clothing. The lads told them it was for a new type of scanning equipment that let criminals listen to encrypted police radios. Good thinking. So we were banged up in our cells and sat on the lovely blue plastic mattresses to await developments.

While I compared this cell to my last one, the Drug Squad boys were telling the traffic officers that we were targets of theirs and part of an ongoing operation. They asked if they could take over the job and interview us themselves. The traffic cops readily agreed and gratefully handed all the paperwork over to the team. They were happy to get rid of this headache, but still congratulated themselves on a good arrest. They had known as soon as they stopped us that we were bad men!

The operational team 'interviewed' us, gave us false bail dates, returned our car and kicked us out onto the street. As we signed for our Astra back, the traffic boys were setting out on to the streets after mopping up their paperwork, and looked shocked to see us being released. As we disappeared they started a shouting match with the Drug Squad lads, accusing them of doing a half-cocked job and letting us go so soon. Luckily for them, the duty inspector heard the commotion and split everyone up, otherwise I suspect our boys may have had a little sport with them.

* * *

BY NOW, WE HAD built up a really good picture of the Burger's activities in Northampton. We knew there were between six and eight main faces working the town, and between eight and a dozen lower level dealers.

There was always a Burger car in the area, but they worked a shift system and the cars and faces varied throughout the day.

The operational team eventually managed to put most of the names to faces, and one by one we boxed them off with clean buys on camera. In each case, we'd gradually reduce our contact as we tried to get into the next name on the sheet. This caused some problems. One summer evening, as I strolled through the red light area, a familiar car pulled up next to me and Paul stuck his head out of the driver's window.

'Hello, Pete. Where have you been?'

'Er...'

'Jump in the car, I want a chat.'

I looked inside and saw there were three of them in it; one of them looked particularly mean, and about the size of a gorilla. I didn't really fancy getting in for a cosy chat with these characters so I tried to buy some time.

'I haven't got any money,' I said.

He was unimpressed. 'Get in the fucking car.'

The gorilla climbed out of the front passenger seat, walked around the car and opened the back door. It would have been rude to decline this invitation, so I reluctantly climbed in, and sat next to a sneering little bastard who I had never seen before. Paul drove off, waiting a few moments before speaking. 'Is our gear shit, Pete?'

'No mate, it's banging.'

'Really?'

'Yeah.'

'Have we offended you, then?'

'No.'

'So why've we become strangers?'

'I'm trying to get off the gear and I've had nothing for a couple of days.'

The three men laughed out loud and the gorilla slapped the dash board with his hand which made me nearly jump out of my skin.

Paul said, 'Do you think you can buy off us one day and then stop? Just like that?'

'Well…'

'The thing is, Pete, we account for all our users. When you don't score off us every day, that fucks up our figures, which fucks us off, and that's not really fair, is it?'

He stopped the car, turned to the bloke sat next to me, and said, 'Serve him up one white and one brown.'

'I've got no fucking money,' I said.

'That's OK,' he said. 'You can pay us for today's gear when you score off us again tomorrow. Now, Pete, get out of the fucking car, and call us tomorrow when you're ready to score.'

I jumped out of the car and watched it disappear into the night. If I'd been a proper junkie, this situation would have caused me quite a panic. I would have had to raise enough money not only for the gear I was being ordered to buy tomorrow, but for that which I'd just been forced to take tonight. But that wouldn't concern the dealer. If I was unable to get enough money together then the dealer would lay it on again, which would treble my debt. Once I owed him a considerable amount of money, the violence and colossal interest rates would start, and I would have to do something massive to relieve the debt. This is how drugs and crime are inextricably linked.

I wasn't in that position, thank goodness, but it wasn't exactly straightforward for me, either. I could easily have just signed for more drugs money. But it would have looked suspicious to the Burgers if I was on my arse one day, and rolling in dosh the next. So I decided to try paying for one white and one brown with a laptop computer from the stash of goodies the operational team had liberated from the police property store, and enough money for the rest of the drugs in pound coins and old coppers. The SIO delayed sending me out me until around the same time as the previous day's transaction, in the hope that Paul would be dishing out. When I called him I received the usual curt instructions, although I couldn't be sure it was Paul. I made my way to the usual street next to the Racecourse and waited for 20 minutes or so until he appeared with another bloke who I didn't recognise.

'What do you want?' he said.

'One white and one brown.'

The passenger rummaged around under his seat and then handed me a rock and a wrap. I gave Paul thirty quid.

His face dropped. 'What the fuck's this? Do you think I'm a charity? Where's my fucking money for the gear I gave you yesterday, Pete?'

'I haven't got the cash,' I said, 'but I've got this.'

I showed him the laptop which he snatched off me and studied under the interior light. 'I want cash,' he said. 'Why've you brought me this?'

'I can't get the cash, but that's worth a lot more than thirty quid.'

Paul looked unimpressed again, but handed the laptop to his mate and said, 'I tell you what. I'll show this computer to a man I know, and if he says it's worth the money you owe me then we'll call it quits. If he says it's worth shit then you still owe me. Now fuck off.'

* * *

STRIKE DAY WAS NOW only a week off, but it was too risky to avoid Paul in case he took offence and hadn't accepted the laptop as payment. So I set off again the next day with enough money to pay him off if required. I worked the morning and afternoon markets around the town centre and peripheral streets of the red light area, scoring off a couple of kids who sold me underweight bags of heavily-cut heroin. They were known to the operational team as a pain in the arse, so we decided they could just have a charge each for supplying once; that would hopefully get them off the streets for six months or so.

Around 11 o'clock that night, I called Paul and he told me to go to the railway station car park and ring him again. This time I was in the Astra, and had no intention of getting out of it and into Paul's motor. So I positioned myself next to a wall so that they would pull up next to my window. And I made sure the smart phone was working. I'd been there for about 20 minutes when Paul pulled up next to me. There was a bloke in the front passenger seat and it looked like there were two girls in the back, so I assumed I was their last call of the night.

The other bloke said, 'What do you want?'

'One white and one brown.'

'What about the money you owe us for the gear we laid on you the other day?'

'I thought that I paid for that with the laptop?'

Paul shook his head. 'The thing is, we were stopped by the police the other night so before they saw it we had to throw it out of the car in case it was nicked. Sorry about that Pete, but you still owe me.'

I handed them over the money and the passenger smirked as he dropped the gear on the floor by my car. Their car slammed into reverse and they shot off into the night as I picked my drugs up, happy that my work was done.

* * *

THE STRIKE DAY WENT to plan, and most of the dealers were arrested in a joint effort between Northamptonshire and West Midlands police.

My good mate Paul had a special operation all to himself. We had a number of addresses for him in the West Mids, but couldn't be certain where he would be when the doors went in. So we decided to do a buy-and-bust on him, to avoid him hearing about all the arrests on the jungle drums and doing a runner.

The back-up firearms team was ready to do a forced stop on a team of dealers who were probably going to be armed. The plan was for me and Shabby to go out together in the covert vehicle and put a call into Paul.

The surveillance team was split into five high-performance unmarked cars and one motor cycle, and would follow us from a fixed point and turn up when we were scoring. Using the smart phone, we would give the make, registration number and direction of Paul's car and update the liaison officer as to how many other Burgers were in the car. He in turn would pass this onto the firearms units.

Hopefully, the surveillance team could stay with the Burgers long enough to follow them to a safe area with no schools or large numbers of civilians and they could then call the firearms lads in for the strike.

Shabby called Paul and got his answer phone. So we tried every 10 minutes for the next hour, until we eventually got through. We were told to go to a small car park behind a dodgy designer clothes outlet in a part of Northampton that we weren't familiar with. Half an hour later, we called Paul to tell him we were there. There were a few more cars parked up with junkie types in, so we assumed it was going to be a mass drop of gear which would hopefully buy us more time.

Shabby and I sat waiting in the Astra, not saying much. We were both pretty fucking nervous at this point. We needed to nail Paul, and that largely hinged on him actually being in the Burger car. If he wasn't, he would vanish as soon as he heard about all the arrests – probably out of the country.

Suddenly, here they were. *Was Paul in the car?* Yes, he fucking was, he was at the wheel.

Shabby jumped out of our vehicle and walked as nonchalantly as he could over to the Burgers. I kept up a running commentary as I saw him lean in through the passenger window to make the buy.

'OK, standby, standby. Blue Ford Escort, index ABC123, onto plot containing four IC/3 [black] males. I can confirm Paul is the front seat passenger. Shabby is approaching front passenger window... Vehicle is parked nose into car park... All occupants remaining in vehicle... Shabby speaking to Paul... Items being passed... Shabby walking away from subject vehicle back to me and subject vehicle manoeuvring... Shabby is walking back to my vehicle... Subject vehicle moving towards the main road, left-hand indicator... Held at junction... Standby, standby. Vehicle exiting car park left onto Sagar Road and out of my view.'

As I said that, Shabby opened the door and got in next to me. We watched the Escort head off and turned to each other grinning, and almost whooping with delight.

'Yes, you bastard!' yelled Shabby. 'That's him fucked!'

After 30 seconds or so, we exited the car park, and did our best to follow the surveillance team at a reasonable distance. I was hoping we'd get to see the Burgers dying in a hail of bullets – or at least watch Paul crap himself at having a loaded MP5 submachine gun stuck up his nose. Yes, I'd have given my right arm to see how the nasty little Brummy fucker liked them apples. Sadly, we lost them in the busy traffic and had to make do with picking up as much of the drama as we could over the phone as we made our way back to the covert premises to sort our evidence out.

The Burgers were known for their relatively sophisticated counter-surveillance techniques, and their paranoia, and following them was no small job. The surveillance team skilfully slotted in behind Paul and his team in the busy early evening traffic. A motorcyclist was used to keep in touch with the suspect car and follow it through traffic lights should the remainder of the team, in several cars, get blocked. The team commander had a direct link to the firearms unit – carrying those nice, Gucci MP5s, Glock pistols and wearing black jumpsuits and checked baseball caps – who were following a bit further behind in four armoured Range Rovers.

The Burgers drove straight to the red light area and the motorcyclist followed them into the estate, reporting that they had parked up on a side street and were dishing out gear to working girls. There were only three roads that the Burgers could use to leave the estate, so the team split up and one car watched each point of entry while the firearms team backed well off and parked in a quiet residential area nearby. Eventually, the Burgers left the estate and set off through Northampton town centre towards the Racecourse. As they drove along Wellingborough Road, they were approaching a semi-rural area. Fewer people about, a good place to strike.

The gunships began moving in, overtaking long lines of vehicles as they bunched up, and made ground on the suspect vehicle, while still keeping out of sight of the Burgers. As Paul entered the tree-lined avenues that lead up to the Racecourse, the surveillance team boss handed the follow over to the firearms unit.

Paul entered a slight right hand bend, and suddenly saw a big black Range Rover over taking him with blacked out windows. He gave them a blast of his car horn and shouted, 'Wankers!'

Then he saw another Range Rover overtaking him, and yet another one screaming up his arse end. He instantly knew that he was being busted and shouted at his mates to start ditching the drugs.

As the windows were hastily wound down, the Range Rover immediately in front of them slammed on its brakes. There was nowhere for Paul to go, other than across the nearside pavement. He was boxed in on three sides, so he pulled his car over, mounted the pavement and accelerated. But the speed in which he hit the kerb caused his front tyre to burst. He managed to swerve round the vehicle in front and was edging his way back onto the road when the fourth Range Rover rammed him into a nearby wall.

All four Range Rovers pulled up, blocking him in, and eight heavily-armed men in black surrounded the Burger's car with weapons levelled at them screaming, 'Armed police – hands up!'

At that, most people would shit themselves and do as they were told. Not the Burgers. To be fair to them, they came out fighting, throwing themselves at the firearms team with fists flailing. Up against a rattling junkie, or even a lone undercover copper backed against the wall in the bogs in a shithouse snooker club, they could put the fear of God into you; but this was a bit different, and they were clubbed to the ground before they knew what was happening. Face down on the road, breathing in tarmac, the screaming and spitting Burgers were handcuffed and placed in separate marked police cars, while search teams retrieved the drugs from the road and searched the vehicle.

They found a replica firearm converted to fire 9mm rounds under the rear passenger seat.

* * *

WE ENDED UP hanging around the Althorp estate for a few weeks after the job finished in order to complete statements, attend ID parades, and tidy up all the usual domestic chores that these jobs produce. Towards the end, we jumped on a train down to London for an end-of-job piss-up with everyone involved. As we were waiting on the platform one of the lads produced a frozen bottle of vodka from his bag, which started things off nicely; when we arrived in the smoke we hit the bars around King's Cross before ending up in some lap-dancing club. The rest is pretty vague.

Some months later, the Burgers appeared in court – with armed cops ringing the precinct – and pleaded guilty to a variety of serious drugs and firearms offences. With the case that Shabby, Daz and I had helped put together, they didn't have much option. It meant that – as usually happened – I didn't get to give evidence, which was a shame: I would very much have enjoyed looking at Paul and his mates in the dock.

They all got big, big sentences – not that anyone bothered to inform me. I'd finally done it and jacked in the undercover life, and only found out about the result via one of the liaison officers from Northants with whom I'd stayed in touch. He'd seen the bosses at EMSOU a day or two after sentencing, amid all the back-patting, and asked them if they'd told me and Shabby about the results.

They gave him a puzzled look, and one of them asked the question.

'Why would they care?'

Epilogue

ONCE YOU'VE LEFT, they say, you should never go back.

Wise words. If only I had listened.

'We have heard and read evidence concerning your antecedents and character. Your service of 18 years as a police officer is exemplary in a number of respects. We are now dealing with this matter. After a full hearing you have been found by the panel to have been dishonest in relation to elements of the charge put before you. The panel appreciates it has to act fairly towards you but it is also mindful of its accountability to the public generally, especially where sanctions are imposed. These are serious breaches. So far as honesty and integrity are concerned, the code clearly states that "it is of paramount importance that the public has faith in the honesty and integrity of police officers". Your actions in relation to these charges fell below the level of honesty and integrity demanded by the public of its police officers, and, further, you failed in the performance of your duty.

'We therefore come to the conclusion that the correct and appropriate penalty to impose is that you be required to resign as a police officer of the Derbyshire Constabulary. Such resignation to take effect forthwith. This concludes the panel's judgement.'

The insipid little bastard then looked at me for the first time in four days and asked if I had any comment to make. I kept my dignity intact and said nothing.

He quickly broke eye contact, stood up and led the panel in shuffling from the room. I was taken through a side door whilst the gathered ranks from the professional standards unit gathered in the corner patted each other on the back, shook hands, and congratulated themselves on a job well done.

I was then taken to an adjoining room where the execution was to take place. A short time later I was made to sign my application for resignation and my warrant card was confiscated by an Inspector with whom I'd had a run in a few years earlier. I thought that I detected a slight smile on his face.

I was then escorted from the premises and kicked out into the car park of the Catalyst centre in Derby by a very embarrassed Federation representative.

I made my way to my car and sat behind the steering wheel in a state of shock. Eighteen years thrown down the drain; 18 years of honest graft, where I had put my balls on the chopping block and taken risks, time and time again, in situations that would give most people nightmares.

How had it come to this?

After the Burgers, I'd gone to London for a Level One course aimed at infiltrating animal rights nutcases, and while there I had finally decided I'd had enough. So I'd hung up my undercover boots for a more sedate life, and to await the fruits of my labour i.e. a fat commutation, and a decent pension to see out my days.

I spent six or seven months of paper shuffling as a Regional Intelligence Officer attached to NCIS. It was boring to the point of distraction, but it was do-able. If I'd had any sense, I'd have got my head down, done my nine-to-fives, and counted the days until I could retire to spend my last couple of decades collecting old ska records, tinkering with a nice little Vespa and enjoying the odd lager-fuelled Saturday night out with the lads…

Unfortunately, I've never had any sense.

For reasons that now escape me, I approached a mate at EMSOU and pulled in a favour so I could go back to UC work. Thanks to this outstanding piece of wisdom, I found myself re-deployed onto an ongoing undercover operation targeting heroin dealers in Stoke-on-Trent. The job was run on a shoestring, and I was less than welcome from the word go – the other two UCs saw me as a prima donna and washed out has-been (a friend in the Staffordshire Special Operations Unit passed this on to me). Maybe they were right.

Anyway, after my first deployment I had to leave the area in an unmarked vehicle I'd been issued. I hadn't yet familiarised myself with the locale, and after a wrong turn or two I found myself driving through the operational plot. This is a no-no, for obvious reasons, so I put my foot down and got out of there as quickly as possible, chucking in a few counter-surveillance manoeuvres along the way.

The problem was that – unbeknown to me – I had activated a speed camera on the way out.

Some eight weeks later, at the conclusion of the drugs operation, I was approached by the SIO and the Detective Sergeant from the operational team and questioned about the speeding offence. The best thing to do, in hindsight, would have been to have admitted the offence – while stressing that I had no knowledge of it – and to have made a full disclosure of my reasons for exceeding the speed limit. I might have ended up with points on my licence, but I doubt it would have gone any further than that.

Unfortunately, I was a stubborn and fairly stupid bastard from the old school, where we took a confrontational attitude to such matters. You kept your mouth shut and said nothing when asked about an offence, until at the very least you had a Police Federation representative with you to help you out (yeah, right). This still seems entirely fair to me: if a copper nicks a suspect, the suspect is perfectly within his rights to make no comment to any questions, and what is sauce for the goose should be sauce for the gander. But a new set of police discipline regulations had been brought in a few years earlier. These lowered the burden of proof from 'beyond reasonable doubt' to 'on the balance of probabilities' and, crucially, also made it the duty of any police officer under investigation to be open and honest with the investigating officers. Not being a student of police discipline regulations, this had passed me by. Consequently, over the following few weeks, I walked into ambush after ambush, and dug myself deeper into trouble – looking for all the world as though I had something to hide, which I genuinely didn't.

I was eventually placed on restricted duties, until a four-day misconduct hearing at which the above travesty of justice took place. As well as being required to resign, I lost my pension until the age of 60. If I make 60, I'll be surprised, but you never know.

The lesson I took out of this – belatedly – is that no matter how good you are at your job (and I actually was quite good) and how hard you work (very), if you go through life sticking two fingers up at the bosses and flying by the seat of your pants eventually you will cock up. That's when all the people you have pissed off over the years will come for you and your pension (especially your pension) with all guns blazing.

It's a hard old lesson, too.